THE
VANISHING
India's
Wildlife Crisis

PRERNA
SINGH
BINDRA

'An engaging, informative, must-read chronicle of the
desperate scenarios we have allowed to unfold'
Pradip Krishen

PENGUIN
VIKING

VIKING

USA | Canada | UK | Ireland | Australia
New Zealand | India | South Africa | China

Viking is part of the Penguin Random House group of companies
whose addresses can be found at global.penguinrandomhouse.com

Published by Penguin Random House India Pvt. Ltd
7th Floor, Infinity Tower C, DLF Cyber City,
Gurgaon 122 002, Haryana, India

First published in Viking by Penguin Random House India 2017

ISBN 9780670088874

Typeset in Bembo Std by Manipal Digital Systems, Manipal
Printed at Thomson Press India Ltd, New Delhi

www.penguin.co.in

For Ma,
For any, and all, good in me.
For Ashok Kumar,
For making my world, wild.
For all earth heroes,
Who died unsung, protecting the wild.
For India's wild denizens,
This is for you.

One of the penalties of an ecological education is that one lives alone in a world of wounds. Much of the damage inflicted on land is quite invisible to laymen. An ecologist must either harden his shell and make believe that the consequences of science are none of his business, or he must be the doctor who sees the marks of death in a community that believes itself well and does not want to be told otherwise.

—Aldo Leopold, *A Sand County Almanac*

He sees the planet as his fief
Where every hair or drop or leaf
Or seed or blade or grain of sand
Is destined for his mouth or hand.

—Vikram Seth, 'The Elephant and the Tragopan',
Beastly Tales from Here and There

Pavan paani dharati aakas ghar mandar har bani
(Air, water, earth and sky are God's home and temple)

—*Guru Granth Sahebji*

Contents

Contents

Prologue

My penchant for vanishing into the wilderness goes a long way back. I would have been about eight when I failed to alight from the school bus at St Ann's Convent, Jamnagar (Gujarat), causing the city police to swing into action (more so as my father was the superintendent of the district). It was my mother—they do know their children—who eventually found me, well camouflaged behind the bougainvillea, in the riotous backyard of our bungalow. Her tears of relief and pent-up anger were met with an indignant, 'But the peahen has laid eggs, I am waiting for the chicks to come out.' Was maths, I implied, more important than this momentous event? Apparently it was, though I still maintain it wasn't . . . but let's reserve that debate for later.

This was in the late 1970s, the golden period of India's wildlife that saw the establishment of a strong legal and policy framework to protect forests and wildlife

At that young age, all this 'larger picture' stuff was beyond my understanding. My relationship with nature was personal. As an introverted child, I sought the solicitude of nature, and the unobtrusive company of books and animals. A favourite spot was a cranny in a ficus tree, that offered a secluded vantage point to observe the critters around: a resident spotted owlet, squirrels—who scurried about boldly, cheeks bulging with food—a mongoose family that burrowed somewhere in the shrubbery, the occasional langur visitors swooping in on the jamun[1] tree . . . My horizons expanded as I grew older, and I explored the small ponds, wetlands and woods in the neighbourhood, with the occasional trip to the nearby Gir National Park.

My affinity with animals was indulged, encouraged even, especially by my mother, but it was considered separate from the conventional life I was expected to charter—score well in school, get a degree, hold a job, marry and settle down as 'good' Indian girls do.

I went with the flow, postgraduating in management in the early 1990s. It was an exciting time to be embarking on a managerial career. India had shed its socialist leanings, opened its markets, accelerating the economy, drawing in new investments and diverse industries. My career got a head start at a top management institute in Ahmedabad, but my heart was elsewhere.

I was increasingly disturbed by the rapid transformation of my immediate environment. High-rise apartments and shopping complexes came up where the peafowl nested, the neighbourhood woods—and the city's lungs—were shaved to make way for an electric power station, and the limpid pools we dunked in to escape the summer heat had reduced to smelly drains, frothing with toxic fumes. We daren't dip a toe in. A chunk of the Narayan Sarovar Sanctuary (Gujarat), where I saw my first wolves was cut up to accommodate a cement plant.

I was watching my world disintegrate around me.

It was a microcosm of the rapid transformation of the country's landscape. What perplexed me was the silence that surrounded this obliteration of green spaces, the stripping of forests and the deteriorating environment, almost as if it wasn't occurring, or was taking place in a parallel world.

It was this kinship with nature, and its rapid retreat, that deeply influenced me. It started me on my tryst with wildlife, and I write about it here. It's a personal story, and I have penned it with the conviction that 'backyard extinctions' are something most of us would relate to, were we to reflect on nature around us.

At the time, I took a decision—against all sage advice—to ditch a potentially lucrative career, and move to the newsroom. I had no supporting academic qualifications or background, only an idealistic notion, and determination—to highlight, and mainstream, ecological and wildlife issues.

So began my journey into the wilds, which eventually became my life's purpose: exploring the remotest of India's forests, and striving to protect them. As I travelled I realized anew how remarkably blessed our country is with natural wealth—India ranks amongst the top countries of the world in biodiversity. It has evergreen forests, grasslands, deserts, mountains, mangroves, seas, wetlands and marshlands—diverse ecosystems that harbour a rich variety of wildlife. I met with rare wild animals, and people who observed, studied and protected them.

I encountered India's only ape, the hoolock gibbon, in the evergreen jungles of the North-east; I met and fell in love with the tiger in the dry forests of Ranthambhore; glimpsed a fishing cat in Howrah, a predator symbolic of wetlands and marshlands; was enchanted by a flamboyance of flamingos in Kutch; went in search (and failed to find) the elusive ghost of the mountains, the snow leopard, in the upper reaches of the Himalayas; and swam with a green sea turtle off the coast of the Andaman islands.

This is the most exciting, rewarding part of conservation work. Being in the field and meeting with wildlife makes all the battles, and the struggles, worthwhile.

The encounters were a revelation, opening my mind beyond the narrow scope of what we consider 'animals'—whom we usually judge, and measure, by the yardstick of man. It suits us to slot them as automatons. Likely, because this makes it easier for us to use, and abuse, them—as beasts of burden, tools of entertainment, or kill them for flesh and trophy.

Meeting the animals taught me different. Over the years, I learnt animals have their own social structures, and kinships, possess language, feel empathy and have thought processes. As scientists are discovering, the animal mind is a 'place of richness, joy, thought and even nuance'.[2] Elephants mourn the loss of their own and use signature calls that serve as 'names'. In popular perception, leopards are largely maligned as bloodthirsty predators on the prowl eyeing human victims. On the contrary, this big cat is secretive, and shy, with an instinct to avoid humans.

I simply had to share this, to break myths, expand our limited perception of 'beasts', and lure people into their mysterious, magical world. I have woven the nature of animals into *The Vanishing*.

I was also faced with the harsh reality of how imperilled India's wildlife is—poaching is ruthlessly exterminating animals, and habitat destruction and fragmentation is wiping out wildlife. It took a heartbreaking encounter with an orphan elephant in North Bengal to comprehend the repercussions of slicing a forest into pieces. The calf would have been about two years old, and one of its feet was shackled by chains as he shuffled after the other domesticated elephants employed by the forest department for patrolling the jungles—and carting tourists. Unlike some of its older compatriots, this one was born wild. His mother and one or two other members of the herd had been crushed in a train accident. The railway line links Siliguri to Alipurduar (West Bengal) through sanctuaries, forests and paths frequently used by the elephants. This little baby was found bellowing next to his dead mother, sucking bewilderedly at her lifeless teats.

He was a victim of mindless, unplanned, non-inclusive development, which does not factor in ecological considerations or consequences. In my mind, that little elephant calf became the face of what destruction of forests does to wildlife. This railway line has caused havoc to the resident elephant populations, with over forty of the animals crushed by trains in the past decade. Along with other development activities such as roads, it has destructed forests pushing the distraught animals into the rapidly expanded urban areas that now engulf their jungles. This is increasing the confrontation between humans and elephants. Such human–wildlife conflict finds space in the book, though I deconstruct this struggle to present wild animals living in peace with people. Conflict is *man-made*: a product of not just the large-scale annihilation of habitats, but also of our conduct—or should I say misconduct—around wildlife.

As I evolved into a conservationist, the nature of my forays changed, took on another dimension. The underpinned purpose now was to assess, understand and try and resolve problems and threats that afflicted forests and wildlife. I ventured into sanctuaries under siege to understand how conservation plays out in habitats ridden with insurgency and conflict. I travelled to forests in the heart of India, where coal mining and expanding highways were splintering one of the world's finest tiger habitats; I wandered along India's coasts to find remote beaches and turtle nesting sites obliterated by ports and tourism infrastructure. I visited reserves burdened with insipid, disinterested management. You will find some of these stories woven into the narrative of this book.

Problems in the field, albeit crucial, are only one part of the conservation matrix. The other action is in the corridors of power, where policies, regulations, laws governing the environment are made and unmade. I had an opportunity to observe this closely and be a part of the decision-making process as a member of various government committees, particularly the standing committee of the National Board for Wildlife (NBWL). The standing committee regulates diversion of land from our sanctuaries and parks for projects—mostly tagged as 'development'. Almost all such projects carry an ecological cost, yet most sail through committees and boards which have a mandate to conserve.

I was appalled at how a body constituted to be an independent watchdog, and regulator for wildlife protection legitimizes the process of its destruction, kowtowing to the government's agenda of development at all costs. Till I became part of it, I was woefully unaware of the committee's role or import in the country's wildlife conservation scenario, which is what compelled me to write an insider's account of it.

My tenure also reiterated the gravity of the wildlife crisis.

Before I move forward, it must be said that the phenomenon is global: Our planet is in the midst of the Sixth Great Extinction of plants and animals. As a natural phenomenon, extinction occurs at a background rate of one to five species per year; what we are losing now is between 1,000 to 10,000 species a year. It's the worst spate of die-offs since the giant meteorite that hit earth some 65 million years ago wiping out the dinosaurs, and over half the planet's species. Unlike the previous mass extinctions caused by such asteroid strikes and volcanic eruptions, the demon meteor this time is us—*Homo sapiens*. Our impact has game-changed the planet— altered and destroyed natural habitats, changed the climate, rapidly making the earth inhospitable. This massive impact of humans on the planet has placed us in that phase of history commonly referred to as the Anthropocene.

The statistics are frightening, numbing and real. Global populations of fish, birds, mammals, amphibians and reptiles have declined by an astounding 58 per cent in the four decades spanning 1970 to 2012.[3] One in five species faces extinction. A tenth of the world's wilderness has been destroyed since the 1990s,[4] and we are in real danger of losing it all by 2050. What it signifies is that there will be no untouched wilderness, no beautiful vistas—the expanse of the sea, the magnificence of mountains, the dense mystery of a rainforest—for your grandchildren, and their children, to see, experience, marvel at, commune with. We would have destroyed or trashed them all.

If it all sounds remote and 'out there', I would suggest you look into your backyard. Try and remember when you last saw a bee, or a hive, in your surrounds. I know of a time when beehives hung heavy from trees in the gardens of our colony. The trees have long vanished, and so have the bees. The decline is catastrophic, global, caused primarily by extensive use of pesticides and herbicides. The Sixth Extinction is here—and it's emptying our neighbourhood, and forests. A number of wild animals are at death's door—

like the hangul, a species of red deer, of which fewer than 200 survive in the 141-sq km Dachigam National Park in Kashmir. We can give them a future, but only if we call the crisis, and place its conservation as a priority. A sheep-breeding farm flourishes—illegally—occupying prime hangul habitat inside its only sanctuary, Dachigam. A state that prioritizes sheep (a species that could just as easily breed anywhere else) over critically endangered wildlife *within* a protected zone, leaves little scope for its revival.

The Vanishing chronicles a few such species living on the edge—telling their histories, what is pushing them to the brink of extinction, the possible solutions on which their survival rests, and why their loss should worry us all.

I find a seeming indifference to this wave of vanishings that we are witnessing, but the loss of a species is more than a statistic, a name on the list of the dead. Its extermination alters the planet, irreversibly, taking with it the ecological role it played, and the plants, insects and microorganisms whose survival is linked to it. Humans are not disassociated with extinction—we are connected to and dependent on other species. As pollinators, bees are a fundamental part of food production. Along with other animal pollinators like butterflies, beetles, bats, they are believed to service one-third of crop plants from apples to almonds to coffee. Collectively animal pollination has been calculated to have an annual output worth between \$235 bn and \$577 bn.[5] Without such pollinators, our diet would be deprived of nutrients, besides being pretty boring. And that which is killing the bees—pesticides—is slow poison for us as well.

Extinction matters.

The near-extinction of vultures has meant the loss of an efficient garbage–carcass disposal system and a vital health-care service, which I discuss in the book.

It is not 'only' about the animals, the annihilation of forests cuts at the root of our survival. About 75 per cent of the world's accessible fresh water we use—be it for domestic purpose or agriculture—comes from forests.[6] Forests are river watersheds. Chipping away at Dachigam will not just mean the end of a species of deer, it will shrivel up Kashmir's capital, Srinagar. Dachigam was protected by the erstwhile royals of Kashmir primarily to safeguard the catchment of the Dagwan river which pours its waters into Dal Lake, providing pure drinking water to Srinagar.

Saving the forest is crucial for the economy too—India's forests serve as a carbon sink tank, neutralizing over 11 per cent of India's total greenhouse gas emissions. If we were to put a monetary value, this 'ecosystem service' would amount to Rs 6,00,000 crores.[7]

Yet, we continue to clear—at a conservative estimate—no less than 135 hectares of forests a day,[8] diverting it for various projects such as highways, mines and cement factories.

And we pitch their protection, and that of a healthy environment, against development.

It is these issues and ideas that this book dwells and expands on, with the colossal loss of wild habitats at its core. As you will read in *The Vanishing* even the last, and tiny, refuges of the wild—Protected Areas—are not really 'protected'; they are being siphoned off to appease our insatiable demand for finite natural resources.

This book does not mean to undermine other threats. Its intent is not to ignore the struggle to protect a park with no funds, caused by long-drawn delays, and a skeletal manpower. Or to brush aside the corruption that has seeped into the behemoth bureaucracy which is the guardian of India's largest 'unexploited' land bank—20 per cent of forests in India. Nor is it shying away from the fact that poaching is a key cause of extinction. The relentless, horrifying slaughter of wild animals is emptying our forests.

One main reason I chose to focus on habitat destruction is that it burns the planet. Deforestation is a key—and often ignored—driver of climate change, which is transforming the earth in rapid, epic, horrific ways. It's heating the planet, melting glaciers, warming the seas, causing extreme weather conditions, droughts, storms, driving extinctions; as Naomi Klein's book title puts it: *This*[9]

Changes Everything. We now have to conceive a future where our planet will be inhospitable.

Forests, and other wildlife habitats like mangroves, wetlands, grasslands, buffer the damage. Biodiversity strengthens ecosystems that store and sequester carbon. For instance, mangroves have the potential to store about 2.5 times as much CO_2 as humans produce globally each year! Globally, at 25 to 30 per cent[10]—deforestation is responsible for more emissions than the transport sector, the traditional culprit of climate change.

Simply put, if we lose the forests, we lose the fight against climate change.

Yet, rules, regulations, policies and laws that protect wildlife and forests are being diluted to accommodate industry, infrastructure, and what is deemed as 'development'.

The Vanishing makes a case that far from being a 'hurdle', nature is the bedrock on which the country's development, and the welfare of its people, rests.

It briefly studies the schizophrenic nature of the Indian economy—which is growing in leaps and bounds, but leaving behind a large chunk of its citizens in penury and distress—and a devastated environment.

The ecological holocaust has engulfed our forests, rivers, deserts, mountains, seas. It threatens to obliterate even the most celebrated of species—the tiger. While their populations have stabilized, even increased in the past few years, tigers face mounting threats as their reserves and corridors are disembowelled and fragmented. Read the real tiger story that takes you beyond the numbers.

The tiger is the collateral damage of what we call progress. Rather, unbridled progress.

The conservation *vs* development debate has polarized society: if you are not with development—in the way it is currently defined, then you are against the nation. If you defend a forest, or would rather have tigers than a wider road, then you are anti-national. There is little attempt to factor in ecological considerations in the development agenda, or balance both imperatives. More than anything else, it is this dangerous notion that conservation or a clean environment is not for the national good that compelled me to highlight the wildlife crisis.

The idea of India embraces not only the diversity of its cultures and people, but also of its flora and fauna. India's culture, land, people are grounded in its ecology. A country's geography is defined by its natural features. The seas shape India's 7,500-km coastline, the Himalayas provide a natural barrier to its northern and northeastern borders, and rivers are the veins that pulse across this vast land. Rivers are embedded in Indian culture and spirituality. We worship rivers—they are intrinsic to our religious rituals, so much so that even as we leave the earth our ashes are immersed in them to gain salvation. Each river has its own entity, personality, legend.

The Ganga is the holiest of them all. When the Goddess Ganga descended on the earth, it was astride the gharial but our rapacity has rendered this ancient crocodilian species extinct in the river.

The Gandak that flows in the north is said be produced off the sweat of Lord Vishnu, while the river Tapi spread across Madhya Pradesh, Maharashtra and Gujarat is the daughter of Surya, the sun god. While most of our rivers are female, the Brahmaputra is male, the son of Lord Brahma, the mighty creator. Narmada is the lone 'virgin' among our rivers; hence the plan to link it to the 'married' river Kshipra has been scorned by the seers—it goes against the scriptures. This is part of India's hubristic project to interlink its major rivers, altering their contours and course; ruining their ecology.

How does one reconcile playing god with rivers, when we revere them as gods?

Equally, excessive development is eroding our shorelines, and we are blasting and tunnelling the mighty Himalayas that have risen in our defence and nurture us, with the rivers that flow from its glaciers.

This ecocide is redefining India, irrevocably altering its geography, its physical entity, striking at its ecological and economic security. When we ravage nature, we are despoiling our culture, threatening our future.

When we war with wildlife, it is a war against ourselves.

What I am trying to say here, through *The Vanishing*, is that we are part of the problem. We are culpable not just by our complicity, but also by our avaricious lifestyles that are trashing the planet, consuming natural resources at a level that will leave a hollowed earth for our children.

We—and that includes me, and you, the reader—are central to the wildlife crisis. We rise in patriotic fervour—and rightly so—when our nation faces external threats. Then why this silence, if not acquiescence, to the threat from within? We are our own colonizers, enriching ourselves, impoverishing future generations. But then . . . the enemy within is always the hardest to overcome.

There is one last thing I want to leave you with before you embark on this book. As you may have gathered by now, the subject is bleak. A crisis has the tendency to be so, and the book does not shy away from it. I mince no words to describe the enormity of it, or the task, to retain, and restore, our fractured landscape, and preserve wildlife. The crisis is enormous and urgent, but it need not be overwhelming.

There is hope. There is time . . . even though the clock is ticking away.

The act of writing the book itself signatures hope—it is a rallying call: only if we call the crisis, will we act to resolve it. Most of the stories I write carry this message and offer potential solutions. The chapter, 'To Save a Tiger', is not just the way forward for the national animal, but largely speaks for all wildlife. In my travels to document the crisis, I met with people engaging in resolving it. Researchers, officers and conservationists who have devoted their lives to understand and preserve wildlife, communities whose lives are linked with nature, and who are its stewards. And most of all watchers, trackers, forest guards, rangers—who are on the frontlines of wildlife protection. Few of us know they exist, much less the role they play or the hardships they endure—working out of remote outposts with the bare minimal of facilities and in the harshest of conditions. Most I met have developed a rare empathy for the animals in their trust. The risks they face are extraordinary. Many have been felled by poachers, or met a grisly death by sand and timber mafia. They are the unsung green army—putting their lives on the line to protect our wildlife, forests and ecosystems that are vital to our survival.

You will meet the elephant trackers who form the 'Athgarh Conflict Mitigation Squad', and read of the enduring bonds they share with the animals in their charge. *The Vanishing* documents, if briefly, those engaged in reversing the tide, and securing a future for wildlife. They give me hope.

Their numbers, and strength, need to grow. We need to empower them, honour them. Be one among them.

If we are part of the problem, we are also the solution.

Fall of the Wild

Do animals have funds or votes—
Or anything but vocal throats
Will you help me get reelected?
You are speechless? Just as I expected.

—Vikram Seth, 'The Elephant and the Tragopan',
Beastly Tales from Here and There

India: A Global Conservation Leader

In two decades of roaming India's forests I have had the most amazing natural history moments—a royal Bengal tiger stalking its prey, a mating pair of greater one-horned rhinos, rambunctious wolf packs at play, a young elephant calf curiously peeking out from a protective pillar of legs that formed her herd.

Such moments are special, etched in memory and heart. My most prized encounter, though, is of a rather nondescript nature: a chunky little bird that sat bunched into a ball, with its disproportionately strong talons—to catch prey double its size—hooked on to the branch of a naked tree in the Melghat Tiger Reserve in Central India. It lifted its drab greyish-brown crown and I found myself looking into the startled yellow eyes of the forest owlet, a bird believed to have been extinct for over a century—

it was last seen in the wild in 1884—till it was found 113 years later, again nonchalantly perched on one such tree in 1997.[1] This was unique—I was meeting a creature once believed *extinct*. And I thought, we know so little about what we have . . . and we value it even less.

This was well over a decade ago but the wonder of it stays with me as though it had occurred just yesterday. In the grim world of wildlife conservation, this tiny forest owlet was a beacon of hope. India's increasingly battered forests still harbour secrets—and species we thought had vanished, or did not even know existed. In the rich forests of the Western Ghats and India's North-east, both biodiversity hotspots, scientists have discovered no less than 100 new species of frogs over the past fifteen years, at a time when amphibians globally are undergoing die-offs.

This miracle of discoveries when the natural world is so imperilled is a remarkable legacy of India's strict protectionist laws—considered among the best in the world—and policy that govern its forests and wildlife, as well as a deep cultural connect with nature. India is looked upon as a global leader in conservation having pioneered initiatives to protect tigers and other rare species. India is also the custodian of species that are extinct—or found only in very low numbers elsewhere. One among these is the Gangetic dolphin—over 80 per cent of the global population inhabit the Ganga–Meghna–Brahmaputra river basin.

Wild predators like tigers and leopards, and megafauna such as elephants and bears, continue to thrive among a human population of 1.3 billion—about 17 per cent of the world population—all contained in just over 2 per cent of the global land mass. India's people are remarkably accepting of predators in their midst. It's more usual to hear of horrifying incidents of a tiger lynched by a mob, or of a leopard set aflame by villagers, but this is not the entire story. This is stuff that makes news. What goes largely unheard are the everyday stories of people and predators living as tolerant neighbours across the country. A study[2] in the agricultural landscape of Western Maharashtra found ten large carnivores—leopards and hyenas—per 100 sq km sharing this space with about 30,000 people! Equally under-reported is the active support of people in protecting potentially dangerous beasts. One of the most moving stories I have come across is of a tigress who had given birth in the sugar cane fields in the Amariya village close to Pilibhit Tiger Reserve in Uttar Pradesh. The villagers were understandably nervous. The forest department, along with World Wildlife Fund (WWF)-India, stepped up their vigil, monitoring the movement of the tiger family 24x7. They enrolled the support of the villagers, appealing to them to stay calm, explained how best confrontation could be avoided, and told them that the tigress had sought refuge in their village when she was at her most vulnerable—like a married daughter who traditionally seeks the comfort of her maternal family at the time of giving birth. This struck a chord with the villagers (besides the fact that the presence of predators kept wild boar that raided their fields away!), and the tigress and her cubs stayed safe, till they dispersed as near-adults some twenty months later.

Contrast this to countries that still shoot predators as policy, or market hunting as a sport. In India, culling as a policy, or shooting a tiger or an elephant for a few thousand rupees is nothing short of blasphemy. It is such ethics and compassion that have kept much of India's wildlife alive.

India has retained species wiped out from most parts of the earth, despite its burgeoning population and consequent pressures, even as the Western world and much of South East Asia have lost a lot of their megafauna. For instance, the Asiatic lion historically ranged in most of South West Asia, stretching from Eastern Europe through to Persia and Sindh and onwards to India; which is its only sanctuary now. The bulk of the greater one-horned rhinos, that once roamed along the Indus, Ganges and Brahmaputra river basins, from Pakistan to Bangladesh, are currently found in Kaziranga in Assam. India also has the maximum number of tigers and Asiatic elephants in the world.

However, the tide has turned. India's wildlife is on a slippery slope. If we revisit the happy stories I initially narrated, there is an ominous footnote to them all. The forest owlet is a fortunate bird, not only because it came back from the dead, but because its main stronghold is the highly protected Melghat Tiger Reserve. But even here, in the sanctum sanctorum of the reserve, there are plans to slice off 160 hectares of forest to expand an existing railway line.[3] And its scattered population elsewhere is severely threatened by degradation and encroachment, prompting its classification as 'critically endangered'. Equally threatened are most of the new frog species: 'They could be dying out even before they are found,' says S.D. Biju, the main force behind these discoveries. Biju fears that the rapid habitat depletion could lead to a near-annihilation of India's amphibian populations—including species yet undiscovered by science.[4] The Gangetic dolphin has dwindled to a mere 2,000, struggling for survival as their universe—free-flowing, crystal-clear rivers—is choked by a multitude of dams and barrages, and sullied by filth.

The status of these species is pretty much representative of the Indian wildlife scenario. Today, India's spectacular wildlife wealth is more imperilled than ever. Hunting and illegal trade of wildlife derivatives are decimating populations of most wild creatures— leopards and otters for their pelts, star tortoise for the pet market, owls that are sacrificed for black magic rituals, and so on. The market is driving many species to extinction. Like the pangolin, an elusive, nocturnal animal also called the 'scaly anteater', which is being trapped, snared, killed by the thousands to meet a demand for its meat and scales for international markets in the Far East and South East Asia.

The other killer is the loss and destruction of habitat. Wild havens are shrinking, fragmenting, pushing even India's emblematic species to the brink—the great Indian bustard, one of the world's heaviest flying birds; the hangul, a species of deer confined to a tiny sanctuary in Kashmir; the sangai or brow-antlered deer, which clings to survival in its unique habitat, the Keibul Lamjao, in Manipur, the only floating national park in the world; the Indian wolf vanishing along with the grassland and scrub forest it inhabits.

The root cause of this tragic decline of the wilds is the erosion of will to conserve them. Over time, the narrative of India's conservation story has shifted gears from where it set the standard in global conservation efforts to where the dominant discourse views environment, and the laws that conserve it, as hindering India's rapid economic growth.

How Did this Come to Be?

It is not a coincidence that Britain's Industrial Revolution in the late 1700s started less than twenty years after the conquest of east India. Britain's modern industry and the consequent prosperity, was built on the back of its colonies. India provided capital from the revenue collected by the East India Company, cheap raw material and a captive market for the finished products. By the end of the nineteenth century, India was Britain's biggest cash cow—and the world's biggest purchaser of British goods and exports.[5]

Such depredations for over 200 years impoverished India. When the Company landed on Indian shores, it was the 'sone ki chidiya'—the golden bird—with nearly a quarter share in the world's produce, mainly exporting spices, cotton and iron weapons. At the time of Independence, India's share had reduced to about 2 per cent of the world economy.

The colonial rule also marked the beginning of the systematic and extensive plunder of India's immense natural wealth. Thousands of square miles of forests were destroyed for timber, and land mined for coal, for Britain's maritime expansion, shipping industry, and to build and maintain the Indian railways. Contrary to what is believed—that the railways were for the benefit of the subcontinent—its purpose was to be beneficial 'to the commerce, government and military control of the country'. It served British industry, transporting extracted resources such as coal, iron ore and so on to ports from where they would be shipped home for use in their own factories[6] at India's expense. India's natural resources were being stripped to enrich its colonizers. The colonial rule also imposed on the country a vision of nature that viewed beasts as vermin, a scourge to be eliminated, a perspective that was new to the Indian ethos, and led to a 'veritable war against errant species'.[7]

Bounties were set in British-ruled territories in the subcontinent on beasts deemed dangerous and poisonous—tigers, leopards, wolves, cheetahs, snakes, to name a few. Most predators had been wiped off the British Isles already, and a similar war was declared in its colonies. This wasn't some small undertaking, the off-take was huge—for example, some 2 lakh wolves and 1.5 lakh leopards were annihilated in the forty years between 1875 and 1915.[8]

The British pursued big-game hunting too, a sport indulged in with equal fervour by Indian royalty.

Post-independence, India largely retained this utilitarian view of the forest and the exploitation continued.

India's priorities were dictated by the issues that confronted it at the time: settling refugees displaced by the Partition—which created Pakistan—poverty, inequity and a rapidly growing population. India's food situation was tight; it was reeling under famines, the most recent being the terrible famine of Bengal in 1943, in which an estimated 3 million people died. Food security was imperative, and expanding agriculture ate into India's forest cover. Swathes of prime forests were cleared to settle Partition refugees in the finest of forests in the Terai (mainly present-day Uttar Pradesh and Uttarakhand) and other regions.

As a young nation, India had to find its place in the world. Its vision was to be self-sufficient, which resulted in a push to build infrastructure—roads, large dams, power plants—and expand the productive base of the economy. The result: extensive deforestation and submergence of huge tracts of forest.

Wildlife was on the decline. The year India gained independence, 1947, saw the extinction of the Asiatic cheetah. The last record is of three males—brothers—shot in Koriya in present-day Chhattisgarh, incidentally by Maharaja Ramanuj Pratap Singh Deo, infamous for shooting over 1,100 tigers! The Javan rhino, once found in the jungles of north-east India had disappeared in the early part of the century, as had the pink-headed duck, an inhabitant of the wetlands, last recorded in Darbhanga in Bihar in 1935.

By the 1950s, pioneering conservationists E.P. Gee, M. Krishnan, Sálim Ali, Zafar Futehally, Anne Wright and others had started raising concerns regarding the destruction of the country's natural heritage.

Hunting was rampant. Wild animals were a sitting target for anyone with a gun (freely available) and pursued relentlessly in vehicles in hitherto inaccessible jungles. Tigers were a prized trophy—with big-game hunting safaris organized for 'dollar' tourists. Many shikar companies 'guaranteed' a tiger trophy. Conservationist and historian Mahesh Rangarajan writes about the Lucknow-based Carlton Company which 'promised a client a tiger every fortnight'.[9]

Tiger, leopard, snow leopard, fox skins were haute couture. The craze for leopard skin coats is said to have triggered when Jacqueline Kennedy draped one for an official engagement with her husband, US President John F. Kennedy in 1962. Jacqueline was a style icon and it became instant fashion, resulting in the slaughter of lakhs of leopards, including in India.

In 1969, the first great Indian bustard survey was conducted, which indicated only 1,260 birds; three years later, an all-India tiger census counted about 1,800 tigers, a sharp decline from the guesstimate of about 40,000 at the turn of the nineteenth century. It wasn't only about numbers. M. Krishnan, a naturalist and key figure in wildlife conservation from the 1950s until his death in 1996, believed that a reliable way to assess the decline of a species would be to look at places where 'until recently, even common animals have become locally extinct or quite rare'. Krishnan cited the example of the blackbuck: 'exclusively Indian, arrestingly beautiful and the fastest long distance runner on earth',[10] which was once a fairly common animal of the Indian plains but now survived only in small, isolated pockets. Other creatures were also on the retreat: tigers, wolves, fox, floricans, bustards, chinkaras, sloth bears, had vanished from large parts of their ranges, and were now confined to isolated patches.

The future looked bleak for India's wildlife, and when Indira Gandhi took over the country's leadership in 1966, she inherited a crisis. Her response was strident—she took quick, strong action, giving wildlife a much-needed reprieve. Tiger hunting was banned in 1970. Over the next decade, a legal framework for protecting the environment was established through the enactment of the Wildlife (Protection) Act, 1972, the Forest (Conservation) Act, 1980, the Water (Prevention and Control of Pollution) Act, 1974 and the Air (Prevention and Control of Pollution) Act, 1981. In 1973, Project Tiger was initiated—the biggest conservation initiative of the time, globally, to save a species.

Another historical move was the 42nd Amendment of the Constitution, which came into force in January 1977. Posterity will, perhaps, perceive this amendment as one of the most controversial revisions of the Indian Constitution, with its attempt to curtail the powers of the judiciary and curb the democratic rights of ordinary citizens. But an often overlooked fact is that it placed 'Forests and Wildlife' on the concurrent list—meaning, it gave both the central and state governments jurisdiction over environment, with the former prevailing in case of any difference. One spur was the fact that states usually have a shortsighted vision of their natural assets, and forests were easily sacrificed for immediate economic gains.

It was now the fundamental duty of both the state and the citizens to preserve the environment.

This was a strong signal, shifting perceptions of nature from a purely utilitarian and commercial viewpoint to one that valued it as national heritage, whose preservation was a national goal and the task of every citizen.

The seventies and eighties also saw major environment conflicts over large dams on the river Narmada which centred on issues of rehabilitation and social justice. Further south in Kerala, there was a massive grass-roots people's movement to save the Silent Valley, a pristine rainforest and its unique fauna from a hydroelectric project.

The legacy was carried forward—if not with the same fervour—by the next prime minister, Rajiv Gandhi, who came into power in 1984 following his mother's assassination. One of his first moves as prime minister was to create a department of forest and wildlife, and then in 1986 he established the ministry of environment and forests (MoEF). He strengthened the legal framework by enacting the Environment (Protection) Act, 1986 and the Coastal Regulation Zone (CRZ) in 1991, in response to the drastic land use changes with tourism infrastructure, industry and ports rapidly coming up along the coast. Industrial-scale fishing was taking over the seas, edging out traditional fishing communities. The CRZ was promulgated with a view to protect the fragile ecology of India's 7,500-km coastline, which supports no less than 30 per cent of the country's population.

This protectionist legal framework, wasn't, as is usually alleged, the result of a personal passion, or whim, of an authoritarian leader. India's environment laws were a response to the demand of the times: the Environment (Protection) Act, 1986 was enacted following the Bhopal gas tragedy in 1984—the world's worst industrial disaster. The Wildlife (Protection) Act, 1972 was drafted to stem the alarming decline in wildlife and remains a key legal instrument for its conservation. By the late 1970s, forests were being destroyed on a massive scale for agriculture, industry and infrastructure—by some estimates over 1 lakh hectares annually between 1951 and 1976,[11] serving as an impetus for the Forest (Conservation) Act in 1980. The act strictly regulated commercial activities in forests, and mandated approval from the Union government for diverting it for any non-forest activity or afforestation (recognizing that planted trees are *not* replacements for natural, old-growth forests). Despite the fact that the act has been circumvented and abused, it considerably slowed the process of destruction of forests to 38,000 hectares annually[12] in the years following its enactment.

❧

The 1990s—the decade of changes—saw a dramatic transformation in India's political and economic climate, which had significant consequences for conservation. Political support for the environment was fast eroding. The Union–state relationship was also changing. From a strong central government, power began to tilt towards states. Power at the Centre was increasingly factional. Wildlife conservation, which, over the past two decades was driven from the top, now had no strong champions.

After Indira Gandhi and her son Rajiv's stints, no government felt the compelling necessity to take an active interest in wildlife conservation. The Indian Board of Wildlife,[13] an apex advisory body, with the prime minister as chair, did not even bother to meet for eight years between 1989 and 1997. And when it did meet in 1997, the then prime minister H.D. Deve Gowda is said to have dozed through the meeting![14] Incidentally, he wasn't the only one. When the board met the following year, Prime Minister I.K. Gujral took the opportunity to catch up on his sleep as well!

The 1990s saw sanctuaries being dismembered to make way for industry and infrastructure. Himachal Pradesh denotified the Darlaghat Sanctuary for a cement factory, and expunged the verdant Jiwanal Valley in its Great Himalayan National Park to accommodate a hydel project.[15] The valley was a stronghold for the western tragopan—a beautiful, brilliantly plumed pheasant—and other rare wildlife. Some cuts felt particularly brutal. I had visited the Narayan Sarovar Sanctuary in Gujarat as a child, and had spent time in its arid landscape, surprisingly flush with wildlife. It was here that I saw my first wolf, and recall the excitement of watching my dog's wild ancestors! The sanctuary was disembowelled and a power station now occupies the lair of the wolf. No less than 40 per cent of Narayan Sarovar was denotified to make way for mining for limestone, lignite and bauxite.

Till 2000, states could slice—and write off—Protected Areas, till a 2002 order by the Supreme Court mandated that all such projects be placed before the standing committee of the National Board for Wildlife.

The loss of political support ran parallel with the economic reforms that began in the early 1990s, under the regime of Prime Minister Narasimha Rao, and largely driven by his finance minister, Manmohan Singh. The economy was in fourth gear, and the general climate of deregulation saw the loosening of the environment safeguards painstakingly built over the past two decades. Laws were also manipulated, circumvented, bypassed—with quiescent, if not active, political and bureaucratic support.

At the heart of the narrative that pitched growth targets against environment protection are three regulatory procedures. One is Environment Clearance, which largely depends on the Environmental Impact Assessment (EIA). The EIA appraises the ecological feasibility and impact of a project, and also involves—at least on paper—a public consultative process. Projects which involve diversion of land from Protected Areas, and in its immediate zone of influence (Eco-Sensitive Zones)[16] require wildlife clearance from the National Board for Wildlife's (NBWL) standing committee.

Clearance under the Forest (Conservation) Act is mandatory for projects that require forest land for any non-forest use—be it real estate or a mine or a factory—and is widely considered a 'nuisance', an obstacle to the opening up of huge tracts of forest lands.

Officially, India has about 20 per cent of land under forest cover, and this is pretty much the only land now available: the rest has been swallowed by our teeming millions and the endless demand for building industry, infrastructure, expanding agriculture and urbanization. Forests are up for grabs, for a pittance, with user agencies (project proponents who seek forest land) required to pay peanuts (as compared to sky-high market rates) as 'compensation' for forest lands destroyed.

Using forest land was also considered less 'messy', a project proponent confided. Unlike agriculture or private land, it does not require land acquisition, a necessarily fraught, sensitive process. *Everyone* wants a slice of the forest. One Union environment minister told me about the flood of requests—from the corporate sector, state chief ministers and Cabinet colleagues—to do away with the Forest (Conservation) Act. This was about five years ago, but there was nothing new in this—over time many states have asked for the Act to be scrapped, or diluted to allow greater powers of diverting forests to states.

A government-appointed committee in 2002 identified these 'cumbersome environment and forest clearance procedures as the single cause of delaying investment'.[17] So, to facilitate investment and growth, the government generously snipped at environment regulations in what it packaged as the 'reforms' process. The EIA was diluted in 2006 to make it easier for industries and other projects to get approvals.[18] The CRZ was tweaked as well—there have been no less than twenty-four changes since its original notification in 1991—each to allow and accommodate construction in eco-fragile areas just 500 m from the sea.[19]

Rarely was an industry or project turned down for possible environmental impact. Between 2006 and 2008, all 1,086 industrial and thermal power projects—known to be heavily polluting and a key contributor to global warming—that sought clearance were approved by the environment ministry.[20] The portfolio then was held by A. Raja, from the regional party Dravida Munnetra Kazhagam (DMK) from 2004–7. Interestingly, his next stint was minister for communication and information technology, and he was to become embroiled in a multi-billion rupee telecom scam—'the 2G scam'—considered the largest political corruption case in modern Indian history. His role as environment minister, and the over 2,000 clearances he gave in these two years were to come under the scanner as well.[21]

It was evident that it wasn't *environment* considerations that dictated clearances.

Indeed, due diligence was a rare animal in the process of giving approvals, projects were rubber-stamped on the basis of incomplete, often misleading information. And these were projects that could obliterate and swallow, poison and pollute land, forest, field, river, mountain, meadow, valley, sea, sky.

The collapse of environmental governance is best illustrated with the example of the 3,000 MW Dibang Multipurpose Project in Arunachal Pradesh. As one of the world's largest and highest dams—its capacity is more than double of the controversial Sardar Sarovar dam on the Narmada—it demanded careful scrutiny. Besides, its ecological impacts are humongous—the Dibang project will divert and drown about 4,500 hectares of rich evergreen forests, with red pandas, tigers, bears, clouded leopards, hoolock gibbons, elephants, and fell over 3.2 lakh trees.

The EIA for the project, however, showcases how this crucial safeguard can be reduced to a sham. The EIA was shoddy. It listed different tiger species (the world has only one) and unearthed two king cobra species (again, there is just the one) and discovered birds previously unknown, like the brown pied hornbill (there's no such bird). Flycatchers were 'flying catchers', woodpeckers became 'wood packers', thrushes 'thrashes'.

It was also seriously flawed, with no proper assessment of mining of material required for construction. The dam would use no less than 32 lakh truckloads of boulders, the bulk of which would be gouged out from the riverbeds of tributaries of the Dibang. Ironically, one of the stated purposes of the project is flood moderation, while it is well known that boulders are nature's first line of defence against floods.

The EIA report of the project also failed to consider the impact on downstream Assam, particularly on the fragile ecology of the Dibru-Saikhowa National Park. I visited the park in September 2013. Dibru-Saikhowa is located at the confluence of three of India's easternmost rivers—the Siang, Dibang and Lohit, which join to meet the Brahmaputra. The park is shaped by these rivers—a mosaic of forest, swamp, river, grassland. It is beautiful. We met with dolphins in the river; dung on the forest floor indicated elephants were just ahead of us; in the grasslands we had the rare opportunity to see the Bengal florican do its mating ritual—shoot up some four metres into the air, descend, and then rise again before floating to the ground. A critically endangered species, the Bengal florican is one of the rarest birds in India. We missed the other flagship bird of the park though, the black-breasted parrotbill. All of it is endangered by the Dibang project, and the other mega-hydel projects on this river system. The diurnal fluctuations will severely impact the dolphin, while the grasslands where the florican thrives are unlikely to survive the change in the water regime.

Unfortunately, such shoddy EIAs are the norm. The EIA reports are usually prepared by consultants hired and paid for by the project proponents, and hence can hardly be considered unbiased. What is also jarring is that there is no accountability for the glaringly inadequate documents that are submitted. Disregarding the blatant fallacies of the EIA, the prime minister at the time, Manmohan Singh, laid the foundation stone for the project in December 2008. In doing this, the country's highest office showed contempt for the country's laws—as the project then had yet to get forest and environmental clearance, which are statutory requirements.[22]

The Dibang Multipurpose Project was a rare case: it was denied forest clearance twice. The Forest Advisory Committee (FAC), which takes the decisions for forest regulations, rejected it in July 2013 given the 'very good forest cover'. The FAC also cited irreparable and adverse impact on the ecosystem, and the fact that there had been no study on cumulative impact of the several other hydroelectric projects proposed in the same river valley apart from Dibang.

The rejection was clearly unpalatable, and various arms of the government worked to smoothen its passage. It is reported that the environment and power secretary met and agreed to place the proposal again before the FAC. Further pressure was put by the Cabinet Committee of Investment which asked that the environment ministry 'may grant the requisite clearance for diversion of forest land expeditiously'.[23]

When the project was placed again before the FAC in April 2014, the dam height was reduced marginally by 10 m resulting in no significant reduction of the grievous impact of the project. It was rejected again, as the committee considered that such a marginal reduction of height did not make the project environmentally as well as socio-economically viable.

But within a few months in September 2014, the project was given forest clearance. While it is apparent that various ministries— coal, power, steel and environment—worked feverishly to reverse the decision; it is unclear what additional inputs or knowledge tilted the decision in favour of the project. One member of the FAC, Chaitram Pawar, vice president of Vanvasi Kalyan Ashram went on record to say he 'had no clear idea of the details. It was my first meeting so I had little experience, and did not understand many things.'[24]

And on such institutions we entrust our natural, national heritage.

The loss of forests since the economic reform process began in the 1990s has been monumental. Over the past thirty years, 14,000 sq km of forest have been diverted for 23,716 industrial and infrastructure projects including dams, mining, power plants, highways, etc.[25] This works out to approximately 250 sq km of forests felled every year.

Forests are not sterile; they are alive, rich, biodiverse. Wild species are not confined to the 5 per cent of our land, Protected Areas—small green islands in a mosaic of forests–fields–towns–cities that we have ordained for them. Wild animals also occupy forests and habitats outside sanctuaries and parks. Leopards live their life out in villages, wolves and foxes thrive in grassy landscapes we dismiss as wastelands, and tigers in some multiple-use 'Reserve' forests are present in greater densities than in many tiger reserves.

And don't be fooled when the government tells you that forest cover is increasing, or that it is greening India by planting trees—generally a very lucrative and hence desirable enterprise. Such plantations have a very poor survival rate, usually sometimes as low as 10 per cent. Most are monocultures, and have little biodiversity value, don't perform vital ecological functions as river watersheds, and are unable to support genetically viable populations of elephants or tigers. They are no replacement for old-growth forests—complex, natural ecosystems that have evolved since ancient times—that we are freely dispensing with. It is such barren plantations, plus parks, tea gardens, orchards that are also counted as 'forests' in official estimations, thus showing an artificial increase. The bald truth is that India's quality old-growth forests are declining, and rapidly so.

The environment ministry earned itself a certain—unsavoury—reputation. In the newsroom it was referred to as the 'ATM ministry': it filled the coffers of those who served it—bureaucrats, ministers, political parties—as it doled out permissions and signed away forests. And even though the ministry was never flush with funds—the allocation to safeguard the country's environment and forests has never exceeded 1 per cent of the entire budget—and was mostly a 'junior ministry', lacking a Cabinet ranking, there was hectic lobbying for its chair, especially by regional political parties.

The MoEF had also become somewhat of a rubber stamp, gained a reputation for rent-seeking and the word was, clearances could be 'managed'. It was a sad state of affairs. The environment ministry, in a sense, has the most significant portfolio—to safeguard vital ecosystems and the country's natural endowments, to which the health and livelihoods of millions of Indians are tied. Each decision it takes—should that coal mine be allowed in a forest that forms the catchment of a river? Can more industries be allowed in a critically polluted area?—must strike that delicate balance of meeting our needs for today while ensuring there is not a poverty of resources tomorrow.

In May 2009, things changed rather dramatically, when the Congress-led United Progressive Alliance (UPA) came to power for its second term, and Jairam Ramesh, from the Indian National Congress was appointed environment minister.

To say that Ramesh rocked the boat would be to understate things. He became the country's most visible environment minister, and his ministry's most vocal critic. The early days were heady for those working in environment protection. Ramesh brought in transparency, with the MoEF website giving unprecedented access to documents and government orders. He was accessible, and involved varied stakeholders—affected communities, concerned experts, scientists, etc. in the decision-making process. He was a rare politician who understood that economic growth at the cost of ecological security could not be sustained. In an interview, Ramesh admitted to me with characteristic candour that 'environmental regulations today, whether they relate to the environment or forestry, meet industrial and not environmental objectives'.[26]

The National Green Tribunal, a special environment court to hear grievances about green violations in short deadlines was set up in 2010 to address the lack of an effective redressal mechanism. Ramesh refused to give a nod to a few big-ticket projects which would have grave ecological impacts or had grossly violated environment norms. These actions became highly controversial and earned him the moniker of 'Dr No'. Among the projects that Ramesh declined to approve were a coal mine on the edge of Tadoba Tiger Reserve, a $12 billion steel project that would have been India's biggest Foreign Direct Investment Project; coal mining in one of the densest forests in the country; and a mega real estate project in the ecologically fragile Western Ghats. That most eventually got the nod—some by Ramesh himself—is another, less edifying story.

The environment ministry became a hot zone for the growth versus environment debate, and was viewed—even within the government—as the 'roadblock' ministry, accused of jinxing the reform process. Newspapers regularly headlined the environment ministry being a 'hurdle' to some project or the other. Huge amounts of money were invested in projects, often illegally—construction commenced before regulatory clearances were granted; vested in equal measure were national aspirations for economic growth.

Growth was allegedly slowing down—even as it averaged 6.5 per cent annually—and the Opposition and press pilloried the government, coining the infamous phrase, 'policy paralysis', to describe the situation. Upset with this turn of affairs, Prime Minister Manmohan Singh warned that the 'environment regulation regime was pulling us back to the hated licence permit Raj era'[27]—a reference to the red-tapeism that had plagued the economy in the pre-liberalization period. This struck a jarring note on any attempt to address the conservation crisis, effectively implement environment laws and strike a balance between conservation and growth. The message from the Prime Minister's Office (PMO) was consistent; an official in the PMO was quoted as remarking that 'the [environment] ministry has tended to lean in favour of the need to protect [the] environment'.[28]

Excuse me, but surely that was the *task* of the environment ministry?

I found it nothing short of bizarre that the environment ministry was being pilloried for—apparently—doing its job. Would the ministry of transport be crucified in the same manner for building roads or the industries ministry for promoting industry?

Meanwhile, Ramesh's outspokenness and clashes with the corporate sector, and his colleagues in other ministries, were under constant media glare; and his tumultuous two years came to an end in July 2011 when he was 'kicked upstairs',[29] as lobbyists unkindly referred to his promotion as Cabinet minister for rural development. Ramesh's departure was not unexpected. His raising the green ante had raised the hackles of powerful interests, both politically, and in the corporate sector. It was clear that the prime minister was uncomfortable with some of his decisions and positions—one of which was the 'no-go' for coal mining in dense, contiguous forest areas, which largely proved to be his undoing. Added to this were the big-ticket projects which he had objected to on environment grounds such as the Navi Mumbai airport, the Lavasa Lake City project in Maharashtra, mining in coal blocks in pristine forests, the mega steel project by South Korean giant POSCO. He was, however, to compromise on most, and in each case or project environment logic was trumped by other interests[30]—economical, political or lobbying by industry, foreign policy issues, and above all, the need to project India as an investment friendly country.

The environment *vs* development debate did not simmer down with Ramesh's exit In fact, it came to a head with *India Today*, a major newsweekly, running a cover with Ramesh and his successor, Jayanthi Natarajan, titled 'Green Terror'.[31]

Green *terror*?

I was stunned. Appalled. This was a landmark in India's conservation history: A country so deeply connected to nature—where rivers and animals and trees are worshipped—had come to a point where it considered protecting nature a hurdle, even an 'act of terror'. What made us perceive regulations that ensured clean air and water, nourished soils, provided for healthy rivers and forests—the very basis of life—as nothing less than a nuisance, best gotten rid of? Importantly, did this demonization of the environment have any basis at all? Had red tape really become a 'green noose strangling development'?[32] How much of a 'hurdle' was environment really to economic growth? How many projects had been stopped by green regulations?

As far as Ramesh—and his successor, Natarajan—were concerned, they were neither 'green terrors' nor messiahs. The rate of green approvals granted during their tenure—and through the UPA regime—continued at a very high 90 per cent. In the ten years of UPA rule over 2.4 lakh hectares of forest had been diverted for industry and development projects. The rejection rate for diversion of forest was less than 0.032 per cent![33] Still, the whittling-down of protection continued. The coastal zone regulations were drastically changed during Ramesh's tenure to allow, for instance, 'hi-rise buildings in fishing villages right on the coast'.[34]

A vital exercise to classify 'no-go' areas protecting a little over a third of dense, contiguous forest areas, rich with wildlife from coal mining, was first severely whittled down, and then eventually abandoned.

Conservation was subservient to the clearance agenda. The ministry's own guidelines to protect important wildlife corridors and elephant reserves, issued in March 2011, were withdrawn in haste within a year under the leadership of Jayanthi Natarajan, and thrown open for industry and mining. This was a body blow for wildlife, since a substantial population of India's wild creatures—elephants, tigers, leopards, snow leopards, wolves, etc.—inhabit areas outside sanctuaries and parks.

The March 2011 guidelines required projects in elephant reserves and corridors to be placed before the NBWL for scrutiny, but the then additional director general (wildlife), Jagdish Kishwan, the country's topmost authority on wildlife, seemed to view this crucial protection as a mistake by noting that, 'elephant reserves and corridors had somehow got included as requiring clearance of the standing committee of NBWL'. He was also to write that 'we should not make the process and procedure (for wildlife clearance) complicated'.[35] The solicitousness is heartening, but misdirected: Is the convenience of project proponents the ministry's lookout, or the welfare of elephants?

The architect of the original guidelines, the then deputy inspector general (wildlife), Prakriti Srivastava, who had steadfastly refused to dilute these wildlife-protective measures, was unceremoniously transferred, and also harassed.

An oft-repeated contention is that India needs coal, and that blocked forest clearances are the cause of India's coal shortage and energy crisis, as well as delay in infrastructure projects.

Here's a reality check: The MoEF has given adequate environment and forest approvals in the key sectors of power, coal mining, irrigation and steel to support project capacity till 2022. Between 2006 and August 2011, for instance, clearances were granted for thermal power capacity that was 60,000 MW or 40 per cent in excess of proposed requirement till 2017. For coal, in the 11th plan period (2007–12) till August 2011, the ministry had given clearance to 181 coal mines[36] which would double the capacity of coal mining in the country.[37] Environment regulatory process is *not* the bottleneck, the problems lie elsewhere. Capacity in power and coal lies under- or unutilized, while project proponents clamour for clearances for new projects, probably because these give them ownership of valuable natural resources: land, water and minerals.

Making environment, forest and wildlife laws the scapegoat for all other failings simply avoids addressing the real issues. A multitude of factors impact and shape an economy—the global investment climate, the monsoon in a given year, human resources, technology, consumer spending. According to the Economic Survey of India, it was unfavourable market conditions that were stalling projects in the private sector, not regulatory clearances. This is backed by data from a study[38] which said lack of promoter interest and unfavourable market conditions were stalling projects to the tune of 50 per cent in 2015–16, while lack of environment clearances accounted for a bare 2.2 per cent; in 2012 its share was 5 per cent.

To pin the blame for a sluggish economy on environment regulations is not merely incredibly simplistic, it is a false premise—a convenient untruth.

🌿

Environmental governance—or what passed for it—had become highly political, and the 2014 parliamentary elections had the not unexpected impact of taking it to a new low. The ruling Congress-led UPA was floundering; it was mired in multi-crore-rupee scams, including in allocation of coal blocks. It was under attack from industry for 'stalling growth' and, in an effort to 'appease' this lobby, a new environment minister Veerappa Moily—who, ironically, also held charge of petroleum—was appointed just five months before the election. He softened rules to facilitate industries and proclaimed he had cleared some seventy projects in the first twenty days of his tenure.[39] One of the most controversial projects that got the green nod included the South Korean steel giant POSCO's $12 billion steel plant project in Orissa, which has faced long-standing and stiff on-the-ground opposition besides legal tussles related to environmental approvals.[40]

In its ten-year reign, the Congress had well and truly shattered the green legacy bequeathed to it by its previous—and powerful—leaders like Indira and Rajiv Gandhi.

Environment issues are rarely central to electoral dialogue in India, and in the 2014 election too, green issues were brushed aside, unless you were to consider their presence in the negative sense. The BJP (Bharatiya Janata Party)-led National Democratic Alliance (NDA) government, which came to power in May 2014, promised to frame environment laws to facilitate the speedy clearance of industrial proposals. Central to their electoral campaign was the allegation that the UPA had ruined the economy, and the BJP promised to break the 'policy paralysis'. Its prime ministerial candidate, Narendra Modi, had served for over a decade as chief minister in Gujarat. Through his tenure Narendra Modi had carefully cultivated the image of being an economic miracle worker, a 'Vikaspurush' (literally, 'man of development'). He was the architect of the much-lauded 'Gujarat model' of development. The highlights of this model: Gujarat was business and investment friendly, had excellent infrastructure, greater concentration of factories and manufacturing units, and a fast-growing GDP.

But Gujarat's social index is poor, and it is an environmental disaster, point out critics: The state earned the dubious distinction of being the most polluted in the country, with the industrial town of Vapi on top of the toxic heap; it also had three of the most polluted river stretches (in the Sabarmati, Amlakhadi and Khari rivers) in the country. It is also pointed out that vital elements of the Gujarat model include easier, quicker permits, licences and environmental clearances.

When the BJP government came to power in the Centre in 2014, it made good on its promise of 'ease of doing business'. Unfortunately this mainly focused on dissolving the existing environment regulatory regimes, thus carrying forward far more aggressively the work started by the earlier government.

In August 2014, at the behest of industry, the PMO held a meeting with the ministry of environment, forests and climate change (MoEFCC)[41] authorities, and other stakeholder ministries such as coal, road transport, power, steel, etc. The PMO laid out a sixty-point agenda, submitted to it by the Confederation of Indian Industry earlier in the month, to 'streamline the process for environment, forest and wildlife clearances'.[42] Nripendra Misra, the PMO's principal secretary, who led the meeting, noted that many projects were pending for a long time for want of clearances 'due to cumbersome procedure and difficult mechanism'.[43]

Seven months later, the government had addressed at least fifty-five of those action points, according to a report in the financial daily *Mint*.[44] Some of these included relaxation of rules for constructing roads in forests and conducting preliminary surveys for projects in wildlife sanctuaries and national parks without any mandatory regulatory regime.

This also raises a fundamental question as to who drives the agenda of the environment ministry; it is the *government* who is the custodian of forests and other natural resources like water, minerals, rivers; holding the country's natural heritage, its wildlife in trust. What is good for industry is not necessarily so for the country, and its citizens.

Within the first few months of its coming to power, the Modi government sought to review the gamut of laws that protect India's wildlife, forests and environment and appointed a high-powered committee for the purpose. Reviewing laws is the government's prerogative, and perhaps this was called for, given that India's environment governance is collapsing. But the need of the hour was to strengthen governance and the law and ensure its implementation. Unfortunately, the recommendations of the committee 'seemed to be tailored primarily towards introducing changes to environmental laws—essentially relaxing procedures and standards for projects—with the primary purpose of "doing business easier in the country"'.[45] The process of review was heavily criticized as being hasty, undemocratic and lacking transparency. Its terms of reference were vague. The committee did the mammoth task of reviewing six environment laws—from those regulating water pollution to protecting tigers—and submitted its report in less than three months. Bizarrely, comments from the public were restricted to 1,000 characters—about a tweet-and-a-half per law—reducing the vital exercise of 'public participation' to lip service.[46]

Critiquing the committee's recommendations is a lengthy affair; suffice it to say that if implemented, they would have dismantled the foundation of environment protection and justice in India. Fortunately, the recommendations were struck down unanimously by a Parliamentary Committee[47] which clearly stated that these should not be acted upon, as it 'would result in an unacceptable dilution of the existing legal and policy architecture established to protect our environment'.[48] However, the idea to overhaul environment laws has not slipped from the agenda but is merely biding its time.

The environment ministry also announced a policy-based regime for a range of industries and infrastructure, including roads, railways, mining and renewable energy. This ensured that once the government announces a policy—say, regarding developing ports along India's coast, interested project developers will be assured of a smooth run, without any legal and technical issues. Environmental lawyer Ritwick Dutta terms this approach most problematic as it puts policy above laws, and undermines people's voice in a democracy.[49]

Meanwhile, the government enacted a new law in March 2016—the National Waterways Act, which marks over 100 of India's rivers as National Waterways—aquatic highways to carry cargo (never mind that most have little water left, and are more drains, not rivers). It is reasoned that such navigation is fuel-efficient, hence cost-effective and eco-friendly. Its green credentials are highly questionable, since channelling rivers into navigable water canals involves building barrages, embankments for port terminals and dredging along channels to allow ships to sail through. Such activity will reduce a river to a canal, and a noisy, filthy thoroughfare, ruining its ecology. For the Gangetic dolphin such a waterway could be a fatal blow. Our flagship dolphin species is virtually blind; it survives by echolocation, that helps the creature 'see', detect and navigate. It fishes, finds a mate, breeds, raises calves, senses danger and averts risks by echolocation. But this remarkable evolutionary adaptation to survive in a murky, silt-carrying river where sight will not penetrate may not save the dolphin now. With over 90 per cent of the Gangetic dolphin distribution overlapping the proposed waterways, its world is set to become infinitely more noisy, with the dredging and din of vessel engines and traffic. It was such mass shipping and pollution[50] that was to eventually see the end of the Yangtze river dolphin, declared extinct in 2007.

India's freshwater sources are further endangered with the government ignoring the vital hydrological component in defining an inviolate forest to enable its smooth and easy diversion for mining, industry and other uses. An important factor to define forests as 'inviolate', and thus protect them from coal mining, was their hydrological value—whether they served as catchments to perennial streams, irrigation projects, or water supply schemes, or their proximity to rivers and streams. But the government decided to prune parameters related to water, citing that 'the required data doesn't exist'. For one, to claim that the country does not have basic hydrological data on rivers, streams, catchments and reservoirs is doubtful—and unacceptable. Equally distressing, is to disregard such a vital parameter, even as the country reels under drought and severe water crisis. A pressing example of this is the volatile agitations between the states of Tamil Nadu and Karnataka over the distribution of water of the Cauvery river. Extensive deforestation along the Cauvery basin has led to an ecological imbalance in the region. Prime rainforests have been felled to make way for urbanization, plantations, agriculture, infrastructure and industry; this has contributed to decline in rainfall, flooding, soil erosion and falling water tables. Yet, even as the water wars escalate, no lessons have been learnt. A railway line and high-tension power transmission lines through the dense evergreen forests of the Western Ghats, that require the clear felling of thousands of trees have been allowed, much to the consternation of the locals who have petitioned to save the forests of Kodagu, 'the water tank of Bangalore', as these cradle the principal catchment area of the Cauvery river.

The other big problem with environment governance currently is that the central government is abdicating its role and responsibility in conservation. One indication is its view to wash its hands of wetlands—an important ecosystem that hosts waterfowl and rare mammals like fishing cats, recharges groundwater, helps in floodwater retention and supports livelihoods. The draft Wetland

Rules, 2016 proposes to do away with the Central Wetland Regulatory Authority at the central government level and replace it with a State Wetland Regulatory Authority. To justify the move in the name of 'decentralization' is to put a spurious positive spin on it, as it allows for no involvement of local stakeholders like fishermen, farmers who are directly dependent on wetlands, or independent experts. As compared to the earlier Wetland Rules of 2010, it watered down the definition of wetland, the activities prohibited in it and did away with the requirement of an EIA for regulated activities.

The government is doing the same with its national animal, the tiger, as well as other wildlife. In April 2016, Prime Minister Modi announced a whopping 80 per cent increase in the Project Tiger budget. Unfortunately, this jump is all smoke and mirrors. The central government simultaneously slashed its contribution to funding tiger reserves to 60 per cent, whereas it earlier provided for the entire nonrecurring expenditure. The rest will have to be met by the states from their larger financial kitty. But with very few exceptions, states take their own sweet time to release money, with wildlife rarely perceived as a priority sector. In fact, even funds transferred from the Centre for reserves are, more often than not, delayed. For example, when I visited Jharkhand's Palamu Tiger Reserve in February 2011, funds had not yet been released even though the end of the financial year was just a month away. The Simlipal (Odisha) director admitted that besides salaries, all other funding—for fuel to meet patrolling needs or monitoring tigers or strengthening forest roads—came from Project Tiger. It was doubtful if the state would step in if the Centre withdrew its share. When I visited the National Chambal Sanctuary, Rajasthan in March 2016, it had not received any funds at all for the previous financial year. How, then, are sanctuaries supposed to function, protect wildlife? There may be vehicles for patrolling, but no fuel to run them, or to pay the wages of contractual labour who perform the vital task of foot patrol, anti-poaching and tracking wildlife.

So, while the budget has been increased, whether the benefits will permeate to the ground is unlikely. What this also does is remove the Centre's oversight, shrinking its active role in conserving the tiger.

Another blow is the undermining of boards that regulate crucial approvals for projects in eco-fragile areas including wildlife sanctuaries. Bodies such as the NBWL were established with a view to draw on the independent views of domain experts, bring in checks and balances and transparency in the decision-making process. The reconstituted NBWL (formed in July 2014) lacked the mandatory number of independent experts and, going by its performance, has been reduced to a toothless body.

In its first meeting in August 2014, the board's standing committee cleared 133 projects, inside, and in the immediate vicinity of national parks and sanctuaries.[51] A report from the Delhi-based Centre for Science and Environment noted that, in the two-year period between 2014 and 2016, the NBWL cleared 301 projects, deferred 105 and rejected only four inside parks and sanctuaries, and in their immediate area of influence.[52]

This gives a whole new connotation to the term 'Protected Areas', which are supposedly sacrosanct, set aside as havens for wildlife.

There is something even more troubling than the high rate of clearance, of decimation of protected wildlife habitats. And this is the fact that the environment ministry crowed—there is really no word that says it better—about its high clearance rate. The environment minister Prakash Javadekar was to note in a booklet[53] highlighting the achievements of the MoEFCC in one year that, 'So far 650 Public and Private Projects worth several thousand crores and with an employment potential of over one million have been cleared.' There was nothing, though, to back claims of jobs generated or details about monetary values.

The report gushed about its achievements of fast-tracking various clearances, the expeditious disposal of projects, the easing of norms for roads and railways in forests, of governance for faster growth. The chapter on 'Protection of Wildlife' is most indicative of the ministry's current priorities. It extols as its achievements projects cleared by the NBWL's standing committee such as construction and expansion of roads through Protected Areas like the Kutch Wildlife Sanctuary, fences in tiger reserves and national parks, and the expansion of gas fields in elephant habitat.

We are at another turning point in the country's conservation history. All these years, the environment ministry had kept up a facade of its mandate of environment protection, now even this fig leaf has been shed. It still makes a few noises of 'development without destruction' but the MoEFCC has now officially declared its priority, and mandate, which appears to be to *facilitate* the clearance process, and be an enabler in India's growth story. Unfortunately, at a great, irrevocable cost to the environment. India's environment governance does need a transformation, as the NDA-led BJP government rightly said. Green laws are not intended to be 'roadblocks', or enable rent-seeking, but conserve a country's scarce natural endowment, protect its wildlife, and ensure clean air and water for its citizens. They need to be *strengthened*, and implemented effectively. The 'ease of doing business' must have in its framework *sustainability*, as promised by the government, as well as a strengthening of environment safeguards. Environment governance demands a far-reaching vision that is inclusive of intergenerational equity. That's the trajectory that governance must take, with judicious decision-making, transparency and accountability.

More than growth of the economy, it is the health of the natural environment, on which the future of India, and its citizens, rests.

Protecting the environment is in our national interest.

India's Notional Board for Wildlife

It is not quite enough to designate some areas as national parks and sanctuaries. We should ensure that they really are sanctuaries.

—Prime Minister Indira Gandhi, in her inaugural address
to the Indian Board of Wildlife, 8 July 1969

The National Board for Wildlife (NBWL) is India's apex body, represented by independent members, for wildlife conservation. It plays a decisive role in the protection of the last remaining wildlife habitats, particularly Protected Areas (PAs). Its standing committee is tasked with regulating projects—from a factory to a road to a water pipeline—within national parks, sanctuaries and conservation reserves. This is its most high-profile and controversial role, and frequently makes headlines. I was part of this institution for three years, and the following presents an insider's account of how sanctuaries and the last remaining refuges of the country's beleaguered wildlife are being dismembered by industrial, commercial and infrastructural projects with the government's tactical approval. It was these three years that led me to believe that the extinction of wildlife would be likely caused not just by the greed of poachers, but equally by the 'rapacity of developers'.

So this is how, and where, the fate of our endangered wildlife is decided, and sealed: In a closeted air-conditioned room in the hallowed halls of India's ministry of environment and forests (MoEF), miles away, geographically and emotionally, from the exquisite spaces they occupy. Huddled in that room, with captured images of tigers, elephants and their ilk staring down from the walls, were the who's who of Indian wildlife in a meeting of the standing committee, NBWL on 25 April 2011. The stated intent of the meeting was to understand the impacts of proposed projects in national parks and sanctuaries, and *regulate* the same, with the objective of *safeguarding* wildlife. Presiding over the meeting was then environment minister,[1] Jairam Ramesh, with the additional director general of forests Jagdish Kishwan, the country's top boss for wildlife preservation as its member secretary, and other senior officials from the ministry. I was present in my capacity as one of the seven non-official members.

The meeting started at 3 p.m., we were out of that room by about 5.30 p.m.—and in that span of two and a half hours, the committee had taken some fifty-eight decisions, many of which allowed for diversions for destructive projects, from PAs, and in their Eco-Sensitive Zones (ESZs). Pardon me, it might be incorrect to say that the *committee* took the call; these were largely unilateral decisions, even as our dissenting voices were brushed aside.

Given below are some of the infrastructure and other projects that were cleared in that fateful meeting:

- Expansion of highways to four and six lanes in Hazaribagh Wildlife Sanctuary (Jharkhand) and Kanha Tiger Reserve (Madhya Pradesh). Construction and upgradation of roads within Desert National Park and Darrah Wildlife Sanctuary (both in Rajasthan).
- A dam on the Parwan river was cleared. It would submerge 82 sq km of Shergarh Wildlife Sanctuary (Rajasthan),[2] destroy nearly two lakh trees and divert water from the Chambal river.

Another project of withdrawal of water for a thermal power plant from the National Chambal Gharial Sanctuary also got the nod—even as a Wildlife Institute of India report circulated in the same meeting clearly recommended that no new projects could be allowed for taking water, as the Chambal was rapidly getting deficient—depleting at 3.5 per cent per year—in water flow, shrinking viable habitat of the endangered gharial and the Gangetic dolphin.

- Denotification of the *entire* Trikuta Wildlife Sanctuary in Jammu.
- Limestone mining and expansion of a cement factory in the ESZ of Son Gharial Crocodile Sanctuary, Madhya Pradesh.
- Diversion of land from Bahu Conservation Reserve, Jammu, to lease to the army.[3]

The above list is not exhaustive, it is indicative. It wasn't just the clearances granted, though, of course, that was distressing enough. It was also the conduct of the meeting. I expressed my anguish in an email to a fellow conservationist, 'The decisions are supposed to be *collective*, but I didn't see any of us getting a word in edge ways. We were hushed. I am now a party to decisions I do not agree with. If this situation continues, the NBWL will end up as rubber stamps to the destruction of wildlife.'

I must point out here that the law is unambiguous in that there shall be no destruction or diversion of habitat from a national park or sanctuary unless it is for the improvement and better management of wildlife. If there is some way in which wiping out a sanctuary, or drowning it, or blasting and cutting through habitats where animals nurture their young, helps wildlife, it escapes me. In my three years on the board, and an exhaustive reading of minutes of various meetings, I am yet to come across a decision to divert PAs that is backed by credible reasons as to how it *benefits* wildlife.

The 22nd meeting of the standing committee was widely covered by the media, but as the demands of breaking news dictate, the stories were largely immediate, and not necessarily in-depth. Here, I will delve into the details which give a picture of the abysmal state of wildlife governance in the country.

But before I do, a quick background on the board, and its role. The NBWL is a statutory body, chaired by the prime minister under the Wildlife (Protection) Act with a mandate to frame and monitor conservation policies that will safeguard wildlife and PAs, and other important wildlife habitats. Over 650 PAs cover just about 5 per cent of India. Even this miniscule portion is severely stressed by various anthropogenic pressures, and infrastructure, and other development projects within it. It is relevant to note that we are far below the world average of 10 per cent. Even our neighbouring countries fare better—Bhutan protects half of its geographical landscape, while PAs cover roughly 17 per cent of Nepal and 10 per cent of Pakistan.

Sanctuaries and national parks play a vital role in safeguarding the country's ecological security. They are not just the last refuges of some of our rare, endangered fauna, but provide numerous ecosystem services. PAs serve as biodiversity vaults, river catchments; they nourish soil, sequester carbon, sustaining India's over one billion people.

It does not serve our national interest to sacrifice our PAs and compromise ecological integrity for short-term gains.

The NBWL has forty-seven members, with a preponderance of government top brass, and is also represented by non-official members, with expertise in wildlife conservation. This hallowed body earlier called the Indian Board of Wildlife has had many stalwarts like E.P. Gee, Sálim Ali, M. Krishnan, Anne Wright, and in its heyday made many significant contributions to conservation. The slide mainly began[4] after liberalization of the economy in 1991; over the years the original intent of the NBWL has been massively subverted, so much so that the independent nature of the board and the presence of civil society has become a greenwash for pushing 'development' projects that threaten the very wildlife habitats it is supposed to protect. In a letter to the prime minister in 1997,[5] conservationist and editor of *Sanctuary*, Bittu Sahgal, who has served as a member of the board over many terms, was to write that, 'Virtually all commercial use of forests is categorised by planners as "development",' and drew attention to the hidden, but exceedingly high, cost of such infrastructures of commerce, on wildlife.

Full board meetings were few and far between, and to ensure continuity of business, a standing committee is drawn from the board. It exercises all powers of the NBWL, subject to its general superintendence, direction and control, and meets once every three months. One of its tasks is to regulate activities within the PAs, and also any project around 10 km—the ESZ of a national park or sanctuary.[6] The law, in letter and spirit, demands that activities that are detrimental to these last remaining wildlife habitats are not allowed, or allowed only after detailed scrutiny, and backed with scientific data of its benign nature.

I learnt of my appointment in September 2010 as I was heading out of Similipal Tiger Reserve, Odisha. It had been a sleepless, magical night, spent in the company of elephants and the largest congregation of sambar deer I have seen to date, a vast herd of some 200. As soon as I got connectivity, my phone beeped a message, '*Mubarak ho*, Prerna Bindra, Member, NBWL!' To say I was overwhelmed is a gross understatement. Surely, it was providential that I was nestled in the wilderness, when I was entrusted with its responsibility?

It was this fervour that was to carry me through the greatest—and hardest—learning experience in my years of conservation work.

In the four-odd years that I worked closely with the system—albeit as an outsider—I was to realize that conservation wasn't just at the bottom of the government's priority list, it was practically a non-entity. I was a member of the standing committee of the NBWL between 2010–13, and of a few other significant government committees before and after; this was the time when the environment *vs* development debate was at a fever pitch, with environment laws being viewed as 'hurdles' to development. As was wildlife, and the habitat they occupied.

We hadn't quite come to the stage when trying to protect wildlife from rapacious industrial and infrastructure projects was viewed as 'anti-national', but we were almost there. I recall the proposal for a viscose yarn factory which would likely pour its toxic effluents into the Patalganga river, the adjoining wetlands and the Karnala Bird Sanctuary, Maharashtra. Producing viscose fibre, and presumably *only* in that precise location, was of 'utmost national interest'. Saving a national park, wasn't.

The last refuges of wildlife are bountiful, the wealthiest part of India, with minerals, water, timber, land. From an economist's perspective, a forest is a natural *resource*. The value of a forest lies in razing the trees to gouge the minerals beneath; a wetland's worth is its conversion to real estate. As I explain in the earlier chapter, PAs and forests are practically the only land available in the country and thus much coveted; most of the rest of the country has already been used—built upon, ploughed, inhabited.

In this context, the 25 April meeting was an eye-opener, the first of many hard lessons I was to learn.

The meeting had started on a bad note. At 10.55 p.m. on 22 April 2011 (ironically celebrated as Earth Day), we were emailed 'additional agenda items', over thirty project proposals for discussion in the meeting to be held a mere two days later. Each item was presented in a sheet containing very basic facts. We had not received, for any proposal, vital information such as the Environmental Impact Assessment reports or accompanying maps for us to comprehend the impact of the project. For instance, how would we grasp, say, the consequences of a proposed road in Kanha Tiger Reserve, without knowing which areas it would run through? Did it cut through the heart, or skirt the sanctuary, or impinge on a frequented tiger corridor? Did it bisect, and thus restrict, wildlife access to a waterhole? Such information is critical to weigh in on a decision, but proposals rarely, if ever, contained such vital details. Even important wildlife species in the area were omitted. Some projects had not bothered to mention the number of trees to be cut, others had underplayed it. Few, if any, gave a thought to vegetation, an integral, vital part of the ecosystem. A bald forest won't throb with life—undergrowth, grasses, shrubs bind the soil, support smaller species like ground nesting birds, reptiles, mongoose, pangolins, and also provides cover to carnivores like tiger and leopards.

There seemed to be a casual approach to submitting information on projects. Often, the information provided was incomplete, misleading and attuned to fasttrack clearances. We were duly and regularly misinformed.

Later, when trying to resolve this issue, I was shocked to learn that withholding vital information was sometimes deliberate. Officers involved with the process revealed that at times they were asked to omit critical information, 'that would show the project in negative ways'.

This was corroborated later by a statement to the Central Bureau of Investigation (CBI),[7] by a key official in the MoEF's wildlife division, Prakriti Srivastava. For much of her tenure (2009 to early 2012), the standing committee was part of her portfolio. Ms Srivastava writes that she was 'instructed (by her seniors) before every meeting of the NBWL's Standing Committee not to include information in the agenda that would be detrimental to getting clearance and that it was the job of the wildlife division that clearances are obtained'. Ms Srivastava further writes that 'the agenda for meetings sent by the Wildlife Division with comments in favour of conservation was inevitably diluted and modified so as to benefit project proponents, rather than wildlife'.

We were fed convenient untruths, while the inconvenient truths were avoided.

For example, one last minute 'item' on the agenda of the fateful meeting was an irrigation project that asked for land to be diverted from Keladevi Wildlife Sanctuary. The information that Keladevi formed almost a third of the famous Ranthambhore Tiger Reserve—which would surely have raised hackles—was missing. When we pointed this out at the meeting, the state authorities denied it!

The horror, and the extent, of such deception hit home during my site visit to the Kaimur Wildlife Sanctuary (Uttar Pradesh) just the week before the 25 April meeting. A cement plant had been proposed on the sanctuary's edge by Jaypee,[8] a construction giant. Kaimur straddles both UP and Bihar. In UP, the landscape is mainly scrub forest and then as it spreads into Bihar, it becomes the forest of our imaginations—thick, dense, riotous—what ecologists call moist deciduous forests. The Bihar part of Kaimur still sees the odd tiger, and local staff excitedly informed us of a recent visit by an elephant, which had likely made its way through the broken corridors linking Kaimur to Palamu Tiger Reserve in Jharkhand. The river Son runs alongside the sanctuary and the cement plant was proposed on the opposite bank. This sanctuary is another of our underrated, unexplored gems—we saw hundreds of blackbucks dotting lush grasslands, a jungle cat rushed across our path, and dusk was announced by the piercing howl of the jackals. A prized sighting was the increasingly rare hyena loping amid the shrub, two cubs in tow! Kaimur is one of the last places to have supported the now extinct Asiatic cheetah, and the caves we visited had prehistoric rock paintings depicting swamp deer and rhinos, giving a picture of the lost biodiversity of the region.

But what I want to dwell on isn't the wonders of Kaimur, or even the extensive limestone mining that had reached the sanctuary's doorstep, or the sludge that sullied the Son. I was accompanied by the then inspector general of wildlife (MoEF), and we had had a gruelling two-day trip meeting state authorities, Jaypee officials, forest staff, local people, and touring the mines and factories. It was only when we came back—and after digging around for information—that we found out we had been had. This particular plant was sub judice in the Supreme Court. The UP government had deliberately misled the standing committee by suppressing this crucial fact, and we had not been informed even during our site visit! In my site visit report I was to write, 'by deliberate omission, the state has misled the Standing Committee and appears to be prejudiced in the matter'. The land on which the factory was proposed was forest land. The environment clearance granted by the MoEF was on 'wrong grounds, supporting the interest of Jaypee Associates'. Nor had the company bothered with legal procedures under forest and wildlife laws but had squatted on it, constructed the plant, flattening trees, paving roads—the works.

I insisted on visiting the site of a proposed thermal power plant by the same company, Jaypee, in the vicinity of Kaimur. This project had not yet received its wildlife clearance from the NBWL, but who cared? Construction was on full swing here as well.[9]

After the Kaimur visit, I came back to Delhi, and another shock: an inbox containing a long list of additional agenda items that would place some thirty wild havens under the hammer two days later on 25 April.

I requested that these last-minute proposals be dropped for this meeting, explaining that it was difficult to carefully review the projects, understand their import or arrive at any informed decision-making on the basis of such bare facts, and in such a short period. This request was reiterated by other non-official members as the minister walked into the room, but Ramesh dismissed it, before proceeding to rush through the proposals in a tearing hurry. Each proposal was 'discussed' in as much time as it takes to make Maggi instant noodles: Two minutes!

We—non-official members—had little opportunity to voice our concerns or to object. Chief wildlife wardens, who officially represented the state, mostly rooted for the projects, a standard practice I witnessed through out my tenure (with rare, commendable exceptions). That was their brief, apparently, to go back with the 'job done'—read with the clearance in hand. This was—yet another—shock. The Chief Wildlife Wardens were usually placed on the opposite side of the table of non-official members, and with each meeting it became a bit of 'Us *vs* Them', as we slugged it out; they convincing us of the harmless nature of the project, whatever it might be, and we reasoning otherwise. Somehow, I had imagined, as wardens of wildlife of their state, we were on the same side of the table.

Nor did any of our agenda, related to matters of wildlife protection, get a hearing. The minister said, 'generic items can be discussed later, let's dispense with the clearances first'.

'Later' didn't come. Conservation issues were deferred to the next meeting. This had occurred in the past, and would occur, again, in the future.

We were appalled.

The sorry state of affairs at the MoEF was well known. While it still clung to a fig leaf of its protection mandate, the machinery in the MoEF was largely geared towards the objective of clearing and diverting forests and wildlife habitats, including PAs, for other 'non-forest activities'—for example, roads, mining, industry, power projects, bridges, hospitals, resorts, ashrams. The NBWL was expected to toe the line—increasingly perceived as a rubber stamp for India's growth and industrial aspirations, but this was a new low.

With Ramesh at the helm, this was even more of a shock. Since his appointment in June 2009, the new minister of environment and forests had ushered in hope. I am not talking of his green cred—or otherwise—here. His track record as far as environment clearances was concerned was pretty much the same as his predecessors; he himself admitted that some 90 per cent of the projects were getting cleared. But Ramesh's working was nuanced, he had an appreciation of the environment challenges that faced the country, and made an honest attempt to understand the complexities of conservation.

He took diverse opinions on board on the wide range of issues that fell under his domain—from genetically modified crops to coastal regulations. Weekends would usually find him in some remote reserve to understand ground reality, and his enthusiasm on seeing a tiger was infectious. More importantly, he had brought in transparency and shaken up a dysfunctional ministry. He was accessible, and open to diverse opinions. You could butt heads with him—it didn't come back to bite you later.

Our first standing committee meeting in October 2010 had focused on conservation issues. Proposals for diversion were deliberated extensively, site visits were recommended so that decisions would be well informed, taking into account ground reality. Ramesh also agreed to upload the standing committee agenda in the public domain. Till now, stakeholders like conservationists, local communities, local NGOs, remained in the dark about upcoming projects in their area. This would give them an opportunity to send in their suggestions, insights and objections to projects in wildlife habitats.

It's another matter that the agenda is back to being a state secret.

Well, that honeymoon didn't last long, and the pro-environment stand that Jairam Ramesh had taken increasingly began to seem like political rhetoric. It was also clear that Ramesh was under a lot of pressure. He had refused some big-ticket projects that were detrimental to wildlife, like mining in the vicinity of Tadoba Tiger Reserve, and a neutrino laboratory, that was proposed just a kilometre or so away from the core of Mudumalai Tiger Reserve, and bang on an elephant and tiger corridor.

Ramesh had taken on the coal ministry over mining in dense forests, and was opposed to the road transport ministry's plans to expand a national highway that cut through the crucial corridor linking Pench and Kanha tiger reserves. Predictably this did not make Ramesh very popular with most of his colleagues; the then Union minister of steel, Virbhadra Singh, publicly asked Ramesh to be 'pragmatic, not dogmatic'.[10] The prime minister felt that Ramesh was being overzealous. A political journalist confided that Manmohan Singh had told Ramesh to get realistic and get things going with projects stuck due to environmental clearances. Post the 25 April meeting, the media highlighted Ramesh's statement that his ministry had been forced to reverse its positions under pressure from the prime minister, a fact that the PM acceded to in a meeting with editors in June 2011.[11] Ramesh admitted that the PM admonished him on more than one occasion that 'while ecological security is all very well, what India needs most is rapid economic growth'[12].

I may have digressed, but it is important to understand how politics comes into play in conservation. Ultimately, it is the political, fiscal and economic environment that greatly influence a country's commitment to conserving nature—or not.

And it was in this political environment, that conservation had to find a foothold.

The 25 April saga did not end with the meeting; in fact it marked the beginning of our effort to streamline the working of the standing committee. In a letter to the environment minister— by this time Ramesh had exit from the ministry and Jayanthi Natarajan had taken over—we pointed out that the 'standing committee decision-making is flawed. "The usual practice is to place a number of proposals including large projects like dams, highways, mines in a single meeting, and members are expected to decide their fate in the space of just an hour or two. With little room for discussion of conservation issues, unfortunately," the role of the standing committee has been merely limited to that of a clearing-house.'

The task of the committee was to regulate; not clear, or thwart projects. Regulating activities in wildlife habitats called for a reasoned, informed debate to determine the advisability of projects placed before it from the perspective of ecological values and wildlife conservation.

There were other grave concerns with the functioning of the committee, and the way projects were presented. We found a lacklustre attitude to consider viable alternative sites and options for projects in PAs, and this needed greater attention.

Many a time projects came for clearance when they were already halfway through. It was a clever ruse: this fait accompli. Money, invariably running into thousands of crores, had already been sunk in the project, and was used to apply undue pressure on concerned committees. And, no project ever went away. Apparently our *no* was of little consequence, most rejected projects made their way back to the table, confident that eventually the committee would wear down, and nod a jaded head.

A particularly telling example was the 800 MW Kol Dam on the Sutlej river which would submerge 125 hectares of Himachal Pradesh's Majathal Wildlife Sanctuary, placed before us on 13 October 2010. Refreshingly, the officer representing the state—the chief conservator of forests (biodiversity)—advised against the dam. Majathal harbours the cheer pheasant, a Schedule I species, with the same level of protection as the tiger, though its presence didn't find mention in the proposal. This was just one among a laundry list of indiscretions; from hiding the extent of damage to not bothering with biodiversity studies. Over 51,000 trees were to be axed, yet the agenda placed before us said 'Nil' against the number of tress to be cut!

Himachal's State Board for Wildlife had also not met and discussed the project, as is mandated before it is placed before the National Board. The concerned authorities had merely circulated the project to the members, and taken their agreement.

About 50 per cent of the dam was already complete, Rs 2,197 crores already spent! When we inquired why NTPC, a public sector company, had not waited for a wildlife clearance as legally required, the response was, 'NTPC was not aware that there shall be submergence of Wildlife sanctuary.' Not *aware* of the submergence area? 'Strange,' remarked chair Ramesh, 'for the proponent agency, the NTPC to be *unaware* that the Kol Dam would submerge a wildlife sanctuary.'[13]

The project was rejected.

But, it was back again on the table in March 2013. By now some 80 per cent of the work had been completed, with more money poured in, even though the proposal had been rejected, and had not obtained a wildlife clearance, a blatant violation of law.[14] It was appalling that work had continued despite the project being rejected by the board, that too at considerable public expense. Equally distressing was the fact that there seemed to be no accountability for such transgressions.

The project was turned down, only to be placed again on 6 June 2013.[15]

We noted in our decision that the blatant, and serious, violation of the provisions of the Wildlife (Protection) Act, 1972 could not be endorsed, and that it was not fair, or acceptable to present a fait accompli to the standing committee. However, we reckoned our rejection was likely to be overruled given the expenditure already incurred and its repeated appearance at the table, in which case the project would stand recommended, provided another unprotected cheer pheasant habitat is notified as a sanctuary. This should be greater than the area to be submerged, and this must *precede* any continuation of work, or submergence. We asked that accountability be pinned on defaulting agencies, and that such fait accompli situation should not set a precedent for other projects.

On inquiring later, I found out that this process was ongoing. But I must admit, I have not been able to ascertain it.

Who would supervise if this and other such conditions would be followed through?

Monitoring compliance is the MoEF's weakest link, both the Centre and the state lack the mechanisms or resources to do so. Reports from the field indicate that once a project gets the nod, compliance to conditions is very poor. For example, if a road is granted clearance in a wildlife area, it is usually stipulated that work will stop at such-and-such time; labour will not cut wood for fuel from the PA, no material, gravel, etc., will be taken or debris dumped in the sanctuary. But rare is the instance—if any at all—where these are followed. The ministry does not have the resources, or the wherewithal, and frankly, the will to monitor compliance.

Rarely has the ministry taken any penalizing action against violating projects, let alone, God forbid, scrapped a project in the face of repeated violations.

There seems to be a standard set of conditions that are part of clearances doled out. I doubt these are taken seriously, even by those who impose them. I recall the discussion of a proposed bridge over a riverine sanctuary, with dolphins as its flagship species. Conditions proposed included building speed breakers on the bridge, so as to avoid accidents with wild animals of the sanctuary. Such touching concern was misplaced, unless the sanctuary's Gangetic dolphins had evolved to stroll on roads!

We laughed, though inside of me, I wept.

Minutes of the committee meetings were also sometimes manipulated, thereby failing to give an accurate record of the proceedings. The same statement of the CBI[16] was to say that the 'IG and ADG (WL) ensured that comments of the non-official members of the NBWL Standing Committee were not incorporated in the minutes of the meeting.' The comments of members on the recorded minutes were not incorporated in the 20th or the 21st meeting of the standing committee. For the 22nd meeting, four members, including myself, had sent comments/clarifications on some serious omissions, on receiving the 'summary records' of the meeting. Yet, the ministry was to note: 'The minutes of the 22nd Meeting of Standing Committee of NBWL were circulated to the members. No comments have been received.'[17] I wrote to the then member secretary of the committee asking for detailed minutes, and requesting that objections and comments of individual members must be taken on record.

This was important—the decisions could be legally challenged. The proceedings of the standing committee, NBWL should not leave any doubt that due process has been followed and there has been application of mind to every agenda item brought up for deliberation.

But this was to continue, and in the next meeting some of us took up the matter of 'abridged and diluted comments and objections of the members'.

We took all these issues up, repeatedly with the MoEF. In other words, we fought back. When going through my papers for this chapter, I was surprised at my (and my colleagues) persistence in taking up, and following on these systematic flaws in the functioning of the committee, and thereby governance in the wildlife regulatory procedures.

I must point out here that such issues had plagued the committee before as well, and fought with equal alacrity by previous members. Former members of the board Shekar Dattatri and Praveen Bhargav write that in the 10th meeting of the standing committee, NBWL on February 2008, an 8.6 km ghat road was proposed through the Srivilliputhur Grizzled Giant Squirrel Sanctuary in the Western Ghats, a globally recognized biodiversity hotspot. The chair was S. Raghupathy of the regional Dravida Munnetra Kazhagam (DMK) party, who was the Union environment minister. The proposal was forwarded by the DMK government in Tamil Nadu. The road would disrupt a vital elephant corridor. Non-official members rejected the proposal and recorded their dissent in a letter to the MoEF, but the 'minutes of the meeting, published later on the MoEF website, falsely claimed that, after due deliberation, the Standing Committee had decided to recommend the proposal!'[18]

Another brief point here, I was also serving as a member of Uttarakhand's State Board for Wildlife during these years. The same issues that one was wrestling with in the National Board plagued the State Board as well. Agendas reached us at the eleventh hour. There were times when the proposals did not even inform which

PA was involved! Also missing was other essential stuff: the area of the PA, maps, lands proposed for diversion, whether the matter was sub judice or otherwise, the comments of the park director, etc.

A few states had not bothered with a board—till it was realized that the projects they sent up to the National Board for clearance weren't getting a hearing. The law mandated that a project could only be placed before the NBWL on receiving the recommendation of the state wildlife board. Another ploy was to not hold meetings of the state board, lest some member ask questions and raise inconvenient objections to a project; instead the agenda—usually a collection of proposed projects—would be circulated among members, to get their consent.

That said, in Uttarakhand, we managed to drive home various conservation issues in our meetings of the State Board. It's chaired by the chief minister, offering a unique opportunity to present wildlife issues which rarely got a hearing otherwise! A major achievement was the creation of new PAs, notably Naina Devi Himalayan Bird Conservation Reserve, a pristine oak forest that harbours rare pheasants, and the occasional tiger, and was rapidly getting desecrated by large, unseemly tourism infrastructure.

So, the message I want to convey: Things *changed*. Slowly. For the better.

There were still—deliberate—slip-ups, and misrepresentations in recording the minutes, but they became detailed and largely reflected the spirit of what was said. A few critical projects were stopped. One was a missile-firing testing system on Tillanchong island, a narrow strip of island in Nicobar. The Tillanchong Wildlife Sanctuary holds the most stable population of the Nicobar megapode, which is restricted to the Nicobar Islands. The missile testing would have been particularly disruptive since the megapode is a ground nesting bird. The other was a radar installation in Narcondam Wildlife Sanctuary, a remote, tiny island in the Andaman and Nicobar archipelago, and home to about 300

Narcondam hornbills, a species that is found nowhere else in the world. In its refusal, the ministry noted that there are other viable options for installing radar, 'however, there is no such option available for the hornbill whose survival will get seriously threatened if the proposed radar installation is allowed on the Narcondam island'.

Conservation issues found place in the meetings, and I even recall discussing them first, before we got on to the 'clearance agenda'! I pushed for a renewed effort to revive the waning fortunes of the critically endangered great Indian bustard and the hangul, which were both taken up by the ministry, and followed up with the respective state governments.

We were also able to help steer the creation of a few new PAs, and expand the area of existing wildlife sanctuaries.

An important exercise was drafting the 'Rules of Business' for the conduct of the standing committee, and for defining and guiding its functioning. This was an effort to address the lacuna of the poor, haphazard conduct of the meeting which had no detailed framework for its functioning. The preamble stated, 'The standing committee in its deliberations and decisions will be guided by the long-term *conservation* interests of the country.' The rules gave due weightage to the committee's primary role of proactive conservation; and laid down sensible conservation-oriented rules such as timely availability and detailed information regarding projects, provision of proper monitoring mechanisms to ensure compliance of conditions imposed, transparency of agenda and minutes, a minimal quorum for decisions, etc.

We could make a difference—collectively and individually.

I realized it was critical to put dissent in writing, explaining— in detail—the reasons why the proposed project was unwise, and ensure its recording. I would like to cite the Girnar ropeway project here. A ropeway was proposed in the Girnar Wildlife Sanctuary (Gujarat), which harboured a nesting colony of the critically endangered long-billed vultures. The vultures are locally called

'Girnari *gidh*'[19], as they inhabit the gradients of Girnar mountain which is part of the sanctuary. The birds roosted, nested and bred in the vicinity of the proposed ropeway. This was one of the few sites where vulture populations had recorded an increase when their populations were plummeting—by an astounding 97 per cent in the country in the last fifteen years.

The site visit report by scientists and experts clearly stated that the mountain was the only stronghold of the vulture in north Gujarat. The ropeway passed through its prime habitat. If it was constructed it would cause the local extinction of this critically endangered bird, and so, must not be allowed.[20]

Nonetheless, it was recommended by the standing committee.

Lest you think we were a heartless lot to condemn a bird, never fear. A vulture cafe was suggested to serve the birds carrion before and after the ropeway whizzed along and downloaded its passengers—twenty-six times a day! Such 'cafes', feeding stations, have formed part of conservation strategy for the vulture, as the main cause of its decline is pinned to Diclofenac, an anti-inflammatory drug commonly used for cattle. This cheap painkiller is fatal to vultures—who feed on cattle carcasses—causing renal failure. A cafe would ensure safe food.

But here?

Which self-respecting raptor would hang around after blasting and drilling had blown off its nests, and with the added cacophony of a busy thoroughfare? It occurs to me that the conditions we impose are more about *ourselves*, a salve to our stricken conscience; not really to help the animals.

A wild animal's prime need is undisturbed habitat and when that is desecrated and cluttered and destroyed . . . money will not buy it a new home. Yet, when a project is cleared, almost always a tiny percentage of the cost is imposed, usually for use towards the affected PA. There has not been, however, to my knowledge, any systematic assessment of whether, and how, this money is actually spent on the ground.

Girnar is an ancient pilgrimage site, and the ropeway would carry devotees to temples. Halting a pilgrim's progress bordered on blasphemy. I had done some homework and was prepared. I had grown up in Gujarat. I tapped old networks, and learnt that devotees were not the driving force for the ropeway. Their faith believed that the physical endurance it took to climb that mountain was as significant as praying in the temple. The journey was as important as the destination—and a joyride on a ropeway didn't quite cut it.

Ironically, vultures feature in the MoEF's portfolio of Critically Endangered Species, and there is a special programme for their revival. One major component is a captive breeding centre. On one hand the ministry set aside funds and initiated efforts to revive vultures; on the other it freely dispensed with its few remaining habitats.

I penned a dissent note, which served as an impetus for the Supreme Court's Central Empowered Committee to recommend that the ropeway should not be allowed to be constructed in the Girnar Wildlife Sanctuary.

The vultures won the day.

This was another significant learning: However bleak the situation, whatever the odds and the pressures, you *can* make a difference. If you are persistent and generally used to knocking your head against a wall, some day it would yield.

Being a member of the standing committee was an unparalleled opportunity to speak up, to take a stand, where it counted. It was effective, as you had incredible access and were privy to the most opaque of government meetings and decisions. This is a serious forum that plays a decisive role in conserving wildlife . . . a nation's natural heritage. It is meant to be a force for the *good*, and undermining it—as has been happening with successive governments—simply has to discontinue.

I would like to stress here, this is not about how much we did (or didn't do). I am focusing on this period simply because as a member, I know it better and can bring in an insider's perspective.

Board members before us fought tremendous battles for wildlife, and their contributions have been seminal. And we failed as well; we had to pick our battles, and sometimes knowingly or unknowingly, our decisions must have caused irrevocable harm. It's a burden that I live with.

Unfortunately, things were to get worse.

In May 2014, India ushered in the Bharatiya Janata Party (BJP)–led National Democratic Alliance (NDA) government with a thumping majority. While the earlier United Progressive Alliance (UPA) government had been steadily weakening safeguards for India's environment, forests and wildlife, the NDA carried forward this agenda in an even more aggressive and systematic manner. The ministry of environment, forest and climate change (MoEFCC) shed its fig leaf of a protection agenda, and positioned itself as a ministry tasked with the government's mission of 'ease of doing business', and in a series of measures diluted and dissolved regulatory regimes—some of which are discussed in the first chapter. The government's intent was made clear, by the fact that the 'ease of doing business' 'was included in a meeting of state environment ministers on environment *protection* in April 2015'.[21] As part of its achievements, the government was to highlight in May 2015, the high number of clearances given by the NBWL, under the heading of 'Wildlife Protection'.

The term of the old board was over, and a new one was constituted in July 2014. In what was clearly a bid to get a pliant board, it was constituted with just three members—as against the mandated fifteen as per the Wildlife (Protection) Act. This matter was taken to the Supreme Court, which issued a notice to the Centre questioning the formation of the NBWL and asked it to put on hold the projects cleared by the board in its first meeting. Though a full fifteen-member NBWL was then reconstituted—the original three members now made up the standing committee, and would be taking crucial decisions on projects within PAs. Of the three, one is a serving forest officer,[22] and another a retired forest officer from Gujarat, Prime Minister Narendra Modi's home state where he served over two terms as chief minister.

In its very first meeting (August 2014) the committee considered 240 projects, and cleared 133.[23] The then environment minister and chair of the standing committee Prakash Javadekar went on record to say that the ministry was 'on autopilot' and 'took 130 decisions in a single day'.[24] Speed matters, but the question that begs to be asked is: Why such haste? Did the 'autopilot mode' allow time for debate and deliberations? Did such a tight time frame allow for judicious decisions on matters that can endanger rare species and our last wildernesses?

In just seven meetings the board approved 301 projects, while 260 projects were given the nod in seventeen meetings of the five years of UPA rule.

Javadekar was also to say that 'no compromise has been made in a single case. We are protecting the environment. Our philosophy is development without destruction.'[25]

We wish.

How, for instance, is a road cutting the most pristine part of Dudhwa Tiger Reserve, or the expansion of a highway and a railway line through the corridor connecting Kanha and Pench Tiger Reserves or felling 325 hectares of pristine forests and thousands of trees to make way for a dam, not destructive?

Many of the projects cleared were in crucial wildlife areas, including *within* national parks, tiger reserves and elephant corridors. In the 34th meeting of the NBWL, seventeen projects inside PAs were green-lit. As part of its analysis on 'environmental governance' of two years of the NDA government, the Delhi-based Centre for Science and Environment showed that the NBWL's standing committee rate of rejection since May 2014 was lower than 1 per cent (it was bad enough before at 12 per cent between 2009–2014!). It cleared 301 projects, deferred 105 and rejected *only four projects seeking forest land inside PAs and in ESZs around PAs*.[26]

The damaging projects that the committee allowed are too numerous to list but among those cleared included a river linking project that would drown, disembowel and split Panna Tiger Reserve; a road through Kutch Wildlife Sanctuary that would endanger the flamingos' *only* nesting site in India; housing colonies and offices in Dudhwa Tiger Reserve, and the controversial hydro project[27] near Fambong Lho Wildlife Sanctuary and the Khangchendzonga National Park—now a World Heritage Site in Arunachal—to name a few. Also to get a nod was the missile-firing testing system on the ecologically fragile Tillanchong island. The Nicobar megapodes are poised to lose their only sanctuary.

The committee's non-official members seem to be mute spectators to this destruction. In its 34th meeting, it cleared three projects in critical elephant corridors. One of these was an extension of the notorious Sevoke-Rangpo 'killer track' through the Mahananda Wildlife Sanctuary in North Bengal. Over fifty elephants have been killed on this track between 2004–2015. In September 2010, seven elephants were mowed down by a speeding train, as they tried to save a calf that got stuck in the line. Raman Sukumar, a member of the standing committee, and noted elephant expert, explained that 'there is hardly any elephant habitat after Sevoke',[28] thus paving the path for its approval.[29] Oddly, in a report[30] co-authored by Sukumar, this railway line is cited as an elephant corridor.

The standing committee cleared projects that had been earlier rejected, presumably because their impact on wildlife would be devastating, and irrevocable. There was rarely any additional input, information or further scrutiny to explain the basis of why the stance had been reversed. For instance, it approved of widening of National Highway 17 through the Karnala Wildlife Sanctuary in Maharashtra even though it had been rejected twice before. The sanctuary is small, with a high biodiversity value— and importantly, there were alternate routes available. The current standing committee had its own inexplicable logic to justify granting approval. The committee in its infinite wisdom reasoned that the road-widening will smoothen traffic, reduce foul emissions from recurring traffic jams, and thus *benefit* birds and other wildlife!

What's also trending is to ask for a site inspection *after granting the clearance*. The *ERC Journal*[31] lists six projects—in the 34th meeting—where site inspection visits were ordered after the clearance was already granted.

The very idea of a site visit is to take a considered decision based on a detailed and thorough scrutiny, after ascertaining facts from the ground. A site visit post the decision is a facade, taking away the possibility of rejection if ground surveys indicate detrimental wildlife impacts.

It waived conditions it had set earlier, indicating a lenient attitude, 'prioritising the convenience of the project proponents, over their mandate to assess proposals in conformity with the law'.[32] In its 35th meeting, it waived an earlier condition that restricted drilling operation at night-time. This was for construction of a gas processing plant near Assam's Dehing Patkai Wildlife Sanctuary, and an important elephant area. It would give animals of the forest no respite from the constant disturbance and din of drilling and construction.

The NBWL had also asked the National Highway Authority of India (NHAI) to abide by the mitigation plans proposed by the National Tiger Conservation Authority and Wildlife Institute of India for the highway, NH7, that cuts through one of India's most critical tiger corridors connecting Kanha and Pench Tiger Reserves in Central India. These mitigation plans allowed for a series of underpasses, elevated expressways and underground tunnels at crucial points to allow passage to tigers, leopards and other wildlife. NHAI refused to do so and the standing committee agreed that the mitigation plans would be reviewed, thus relaxing its earlier stance.

Conservation policy decisions taken by previous boards were also dismissed. For instance, the guidelines and rules painstakingly drafted by the earlier committee to put in place processes to ensure that decision-making was informed, judicious and transparent were dismissed. Further reforms were expected in the clearance process, and therefore, it was decided that the matter would be dropped. The objective now was to 'make clearance process more efficient'.[33] A fundamental point missed is that the objective here is not clearance, but *regulation*.

The National Board 'for wildlife' days seem to be well and truly over. It's time to redefine its mandate, in the same manner that the MoEFCC has apparently found its true calling in subverting its conservation mandate to accommodate the growth agenda.

It could be more appropriately known as India's Notional Board for Wildlife.

Lines of Blood

The best thing you could do for the Amazon is to bomb all the roads.

—Eneas Salati

Fast and Furious

I crouched, almost flat on the ground, to take a wide-angle photograph of the snake, crushed under a vehicle on the road that cuts through the montane grasslands and tropical rainforests of Kudremukh National Park in the southern state of Karnataka. That achieved, I went round the other way, grasping the snake by its tail to place it off the road and in the forest, in a bid to give it some dignity in death. That's when it jerked, reared its head and swirled around.

It was a venomous snake—one of the few such species in India. A cobra. D.V. Girish—colleague, conservationist, friend—swiftly pushed my hand aside, whipped out his snake hook, and gently lifted the reptile. No use now, the cobra has gone limp, ebbed of life.

It felt like a kick in my gut, watching the snake die. I know many of my fellow men and women believe that snakes are better dead than alive. But, like most wild creatures, snakes will only attack when harassed, provoked or surprised. Left alone, they are largely harmless and rarely pose a threat to people. Besides, snakes occupy an important ecological niche as mid-level predators eating crop pests such as rats and mice. This cobra was my ninth dead snake of the day as we drove down National Highway 13 in Kudremukh. I was to list fifteen that morning (after which we lost count), and noted at least five species (a few were crushed beyond recognition). The stunning neon-green vine snake (three), rat snake (two), sand boa (one), bronze-back tree snake (three), cobra (two), and was that the rare, endemic pit viper? We saw other squashed creatures—notably, the beautiful southern bird-wing, the largest butterfly species in India.

The road through Kudremukh, part of the Western Ghats, a global biodiversity hotspot, is a virtual animal graveyard. Other mortalities over time include the lion-tailed macaque, one of the most endangered primates in the world, and endemic to these parts, besides the sambar deer, capped macaque, leopard, mouse deer, and even the world's largest wild bovine, the Indian bison or gaur.

The problem, however, extends far beyond Kudremukh.

Highways and roads criss-crossing wildlife reserves and habitats—and speeding vehicles running over wild animals—are one of the main drivers of extinction, globally. Snakes, as well as other reptiles and amphibians, suffer the highest casualty rate, but are by no means the only victims. The big and the beautiful are easy prey too. A cursory glance at news reports showed that a tiger, a leopard, an elephant and two sloth bears had been mowed down by vehicles speeding across roads running through the forests in about sixty days between May–July 2016. A friend travelling to Nainital in Uttarakhand called in distress from the site of a hit-and-run. The photograph he mailed me depicted a disembowelled langur and two red foxes. The langur had likely been run over, and the foxes—a vixen and her pup—had moved in to scavenge on what was to be their last supper. This tragedy took place on the Nainital–Kaladhungi road, a quaint bridle path half-a-century ago, and frequently used by legendary hunter-conservationist Jim

Corbett. When Corbett was a young boy he used to go back and forth on this path from his family's summer home in Nainital, a picturesque hill station, to their winter home, Kaladhungi in the foothills.

During my years travelling in forests I have personally seen— and peeled off the tarmac—civets, squirrels, tortoises, snakes, frogs, jungle cats, blue bulls, hornbill, hyena, chinkara, blackbuck, jackal, porcupine and peafowl. It seemed a sacrilege to leave them; they were wild animals who had succumbed in an alien world, and deserved a more honourable end than being stuck to asphalt. The hyena was particularly heartbreaking: she was still warm, and her teats full with milk. Somewhere in the scrub forests along the busy highway, her cubs awaited a mother who would never return. They would starve to death. Distressed, we spent hours combing the area, trying to find them (while not really knowing what we would *do* with orphaned hyena cubs), but it was futile.

Vehicles are voracious predators, taking a huge toll on wildlife, globally. The Centro Brasileiro de Ecologia de Estradas[1] estimated in 2014 that every year about 475 million animals die in Brazil as victims of roadkill.[2] There are no such comprehensive studies in India, but the following should give you an idea of the scale: The Haridwar–Najibabad road skirts Rajaji National Park in Uttarakhand, cleaving through the contiguous stretch of adjoining forests that form the park's buffer zone. Following the death of a tiger—crushed by a speeding truck—wildlife researchers walked the road for a week in July 2016 between 5 a.m. and 7 a.m. each day.[3] The sum of fatalities they observed in that week included leopard, cheetal, yellow-throated marten, python, king cobra; and 'we are not even listing the many smaller creatures: snakes, frogs, birds, insects', said one of the researchers.

In most cases all that the animal was trying to do—like the proverbial chicken—was cross the road, when it was helplessly confronted with a monstrous piece of metal hurtling into its path. My colleagues and I have stood by a state highway that skirted a reserve one evening through to midnight, in an attempt to see which animals crossed the road, and how. We observed a herd of sambar trying to make their way across. Every time the deer plucked up the courage to walk across; its ears would perk up, and hearing a distant vehicle, it would scuttle back in alarm. It was a good forty minutes before they eventually succeeded. Animals are not programmed to match the speed, nor do they have the dexterity to escape an oncoming vehicle. Most freeze and are easy prey.

Unnatural selection by automobile is a recent phenomenon. Animals have adapted over millennia to deal with adversity and evade predators. Cuttlefish and stick insects use camouflage, changing colour and texture to blend in perfectly while sea cucumbers can solidify into lumps or turn to mush to merge with their surroundings. Animals play dead, release toxic chemicals, distract predator attention by breaking off bits of their body, group together to mob a predator or develop powerful speeds. Nature is yet to equip its creatures to match the swift evolution of the predator of the twenty-first century, the automobile, which has developed merely three–four generations ago.

In my childhood a car was a rare luxury, and if you were fortunate to have one, it was rolled out only on special occasions. We cycled everywhere, and with few cars on roads it wasn't the dangerous game it is today. With a growth of 7.64 per cent in 2015—and expected to grow between 7–9 per cent in 2017—India is the world's fifth largest passenger vehicle market.[4] From 0.3 million registered vehicles on 31 March 1951, 159.5 million vehicles were plying Indian roads by 2012.[5]

I sometimes wonder if even *Homo sapiens* have evolved sufficiently to deal with this mechanical beast that rages across rapidly expanding roadways. Science and statistics seem to think not: for instance, in India 1.46 lakh people lost their lives in road accidents in just one year (2015). While researching I came across 'Mr Graham', a rather disquieting visual representation of how a human body would have to evolve to survive a car crash. As part of a road safety awareness drive, Australia's Transport Accident Commission partnered with researchers and trauma surgeons to develop 'Mr Graham'. With his helmet-like skull, bulbous head, airbags between each rib and loads of fatty tissue to protect delicate bones, Mr Graham cuts a grotesque figure, and while he would 'find it difficult to get himself a date', he would certainly survive a car crash!

🖋️

Automobiles and the roads they require have moulded landscapes across the world: The ecological consequences go beyond the visible impact of tragic accidents that crush rare wild creatures. There are other, less obvious but equally lethal, fallouts of roads that run through forests. So much so that 'Road Ecology' has become a separate discipline under conservation biology, the focus of which is to fully comprehend the plethora of threats and arrive at appropriate solutions.

One implication is greater access—roads bring in settlers, developers, hunters. In the Congo Basin, logging roads opened up vast areas for what can only be called a 'poaching epidemic'. In about a decade more than 60 per cent of the region's forest elephant population was wiped out.[6] In the Russian Far East, studies linked roads and tiger mortality. From 1992 to 2000, the Wildlife Conservation Society studied the fate of radio-collared Siberian tigers living in areas with no roads, secondary roads and primary roads; and found that the survival rate of adult tigers living in areas with roads was about half of those living in undisturbed forests.

Noise pollution is another, not unrelated consequence. The drone of running vehicles, blowing of horns and associated vehicular sounds drown out birdsong. Birds sing to communicate, and frogs call out to their mates as well. Noise pollution changes the mating and breeding behaviour of frogs, birds and other such creatures that hugely rely on acoustics to attract mates. A few have adjusted, like belting out their ditties at times when noise is at the lowest, or raising their volumes, but populations thin, and may even die out, in sites where roads, and other invasions like noisy railway lines or factories, have intruded.

The most worrying, and vexing, issue however, is the transformative power of roads: The advent of a road marks the death of wilderness. Roads are agents of change, transforming landscapes where they go. They function as arteries, carrying growth and enabling development into hitherto remote and untouched parts of the world. Their impacts are both inspirational and distressing; empowering and poignant. If they usher in economic growth, they also erode cultures and devastate environments.

When a road opens up an area, it serves as an ancillary to further development, increasing the human footprint. The *New Yorker*[7] cites the example of the first paved highway across the Brazilian Amazon in the 1970s. It connected the 1,200-mile distance between the northern port city of Belém with the country's capital, Brasília, and was hailed for spurring rapid development in the region. The highway led to the growth of a network of smaller roads and the birth of new towns and industries. However, the ecological costs were monumental. Pristine rainforests were destroyed, 'swaths of deforestation some two hundred and fifty miles wide, stretching from horizon to horizon' and replaced by pasturelands, cattle ranches, towns and industry.

In India too, there are many similar examples. A significant one is the making of the Mughal Road—and the unmaking of the Hirpora Wildlife Sanctuary (in Kashmir), through which it cuts. The historical mountainous track was used in 1586 by Emperor Akbar to enter the Kashmir Valley from Lahore, and was used similarly by subsequent Mughal rulers. In recent memory, it was a scenic kuccha path, winding its way through fir and alpine meadows, hugging the majestic Pir Panjal range in the Himalayas. In 2007, construction began to upgrade the road for a supplementary connection between Srinagar and Jammu—the summer and winter capitals of Kashmir, respectively. For months and years, till 2013, the mountains echoed with the sound of exploding dynamite—blasting, gouging the hillsides, ripping into the hills, while tonnes of debris rolled down and turned lush meadows into sterile hills of rubble.

The zippy new Mughal Road proved fatal to the wild, rare goat that is emblematic of the mountains, the Pir Panjal markhor. The blasts caused continuous soil erosion that devastated critical markhor habitat. Once not uncommonly visible along the trail, they have retreated, from habitats that are no longer havens, to places unknown, but likely with equally fragile futures.

Only 250–300 of the Pir Panjal markhor are estimated to now survive in small fragmented populations, and the Hirpora Sanctuary is one of its last refuges.[8]

Mountain roads carry other risks: they can lead to severe deforestation, erosion and landslides. They can accelerate the devastation caused by natural disasters, and the losses can be colossal, as was seen during the floods and landslides in Uttarakhand in 2013 and Ladakh in 2010. Over half of the landslides studied following the Kashmir earthquake in 2005 in which thousands lost their lives, were linked to human activity.[9] Construction of roads was the most common cause of landslides as they steepen the slope angle. Other causes include building on fragile slopes, deforestation, construction and terraces built for agriculture.

The Mughal Road is now a hectic thoroughfare, with a constant rumble of trucks and tourists, and with ambitions to be a national highway. There is such a proposal, and were it to come through, the road will be expanded and widened further. The stretch where the road crests the once-pristine 'Pir ki Gali' is a typical tourist 'viewpoint' now, featuring a cluster of dhabas and sundry shops, littered with empty packets of chips and fizzy drink bottles, and such other remains of visitor's gluttony. Worse, it has opened the floodgates for graziers who now arrive by the truckfuls with their livestock as soon as the snows melt. This is a critical time for the markhor, who have survived the bleak cold season when grass is thin on the ground. In winters, the males expend their energies rutting, seeking and fighting with other males for a mate; the females get pregnant as the snow melts—so that they can take advantage of the first flush of the protein-rich grass.

But with quick, easy access, the graziers with their huge herds flock the meadows, leaving no feeding grounds for the markhor . . . who may simply starve to death.

Markhors are hardy animals, surviving the harshest of winters; they are the most agile of wild goats, negotiating sheer cliffs and tough terrains.

It is doubtful, though, they will survive the Mughal Road. In the past decade, numbers in Hirpora have halved to about thirty. Experts fear that the markhor may become extinct in the sanctuary.

The tragedy is, it needn't have been that way. Even with the onslaught of the road, the damage could have been minimized. Further development, structures, construction should not be allowed to come up, and any plans to expand the road are best forgotten. Most importantly, in critical markhor habitats, the grazing must stop.

It's still not too late to do this.

It will be a happy road to travel then, looking out for the rare chance to watch one of the world's most endangered goats as you drive amid the magnificent Himalayan mountains.

Broken Forests

Roads have sliced almost the entire land surface of the earth into no less than 6,00,000 pieces, half of which are less than 1 sq km in size.[10]

Such fragmentation causes havoc to natural habitats. Roads splinter landscapes, making tiny, dysfunctional fragments of a thriving ecosystem. They cut off well-worn migratory paths of wild species, caging them into small forest patches, making them more vulnerable to localized extinctions. Such isolated patches decay faster.

The spillover effects of roads are visible on either side—thinning, dying trees, sliced vegetation, intrusion of invasive species, retreat of wildlife. Biologists call this the 'Edge Effect'. A study led by Nick Haddad, of the North Carolina State University, revealed that 70 per cent of the world's forests are within 1 km of the forest's edge, which includes edges created by roads. Species in such broken forests decline, and may even disappear—the same study indicated that fragmented habitats lose an average of one-third of their plant and animal species within twenty years.

The expansion of National Highway 7 into a four-lane highway is creating such an 'edge' in Madhya Pradesh's Pench Tiger Reserve. In itself Pench's 411 sq km is inadequate for a viable tiger population, but it is connected to the more sizeable Kanha Tiger Reserve through a living corridor. The reserves and other forests here form part of the Central Indian landscape—considered the largest tiger landscape in India—which has a network of Protected Areas linked through increasingly fragile corridors. This landscape is crucial to the future of the tiger in India. If wild tigers are to survive in the long term, this is one of the few places they will flourish.

The Kanha–Pench landscape supports over 200 tigers as per the 2014 all-India estimate,[11] and they thrive here because of its contiguity. But the expansion of NH7 (and other activities, like a railway line running parallel to the highway) will irrevocably break this vast landscape. Increasing fragmentation will shatter the connectivity with small tiger populations in isolated reserves facing the risk of local extinction—in the short term due to poaching, and genetic decay over generations in the long term. The logical end of such splintering of habitat is the local extinction of tigers.

Denuded forest fragments also force unwieldy adaptations and behaviour change. I am haunted by the story of a hoolock gibbon,

India's only ape, forced aground by a road that had slashed the canopy cover of a lush evergreen forest of the North-east. The hoolock is a highly specialized arboreal creature using its long, agile arms to glide along tree branches. It is not adapted to walk. In the natural order of things, they would not be found on the ground, where they are very vulnerable. Yet, I encountered a troop—nervous, unsure, awkwardly scrambling to scurry across the road and forage for food. A far cry from the beautiful, agile acrobat of the canopy.

The fact is, roads are vital infrastructure of transport, and are 'engines of growth' that facilitate development of a region. They propel the economy and are required not just for heavy industry and commerce, but importantly, to connect hitherto inaccessible villages and communities to health and educational facilities, markets, employment and entrepreneurial opportunities. In India, where over 30 per cent of villages are not linked by all-weather roads, this need is vital. Conversely, it is argued that roads, may 'drain out wealth' of remote regions by wheeling out natural resources. For India's colonizers, it was a priority to build an extensive rail and road system in the interiors to accumulate cheap timber. Today roads are cut into remote forests (in Odisha and Jharkhand, for instance) to transport coal and iron ore, where minefields are rapidly coming up. There is another factor which drives the demand for roads: strategic interests in the country's border areas. Given the sensitivity of the issue, and urgency of infrastructure requirement on borders, environment clearances for such projects are processed on a priority basis.

But, as much as the country needs growth it also needs forests and other natural habitats, given their value as ecosystems and the local livelihoods they sustain. Sometimes, ecological concerns must take precedence.

What if the construction of a road were to lead to the death of a species, doom a tiger population, cement a wetland or murder a mountain?

This was the dilemma we faced as members of the standing committee of the National Board for Wildlife (NBWL) when the proposal for the Gaduli–Santalpur road was placed before us for clearance in June 2012. The proposed road would pass through the Kutch Wildlife Sanctuary in the Great Rann of Kutch, Gujarat.

The sanctuary harbours a number of endangered species such as the wild ass, Indian wolf, caracal, houbara bustard, desert fox, desert cat, etc. It also serves as a critical passage for migratory birds from across the globe. What caused us the greatest concern was the breeding site of flamingos in the sanctuary—the only one in the Indian subcontinent. For greater flamingos it is the only known nesting site in all of South Asia. The sanctuary was, in fact, created to secure this site. It was India's legendary 'Bird Man', the late Sálim Ali, who gave the nesting site its popular nomenclature 'Flamingo City' in 1945 when he estimated the flamingo population here to be no less than half a million. The 'City' is the source, from where the flamingos fly off every winter across the subcontinent, to wetlands like Chilika (Odisha), Pulicat (Tamil Nadu) and Sewri (Mumbai) and back to nest and breed, raise and ready their young, who then take wing, and thus continue the cycle of life.

There is a reason this site is favoured by the bird. The waters here are a unique cocktail of fresh water that flows in from the river Luni and saline water of the Arabian sea, providing a rich flow of nutrients in which microorganisms, crustaceans, algae and fish thrive—making a perfect feeding, and breeding ground for flamingos. The road construction will have a grave impact on the water regime here. This problem is further compounded as the region is heavily silted, requiring embankments and guard walls, causing artificial impounding of water on both sides of the proposed road. This will upset the region's hydrology, and the food chain dependent on it.

The ministry of environment and forests (MoEF)–appointed expert committee that visited the site gave a nuanced report. It gave alternative alignments with less ecological implications for certain sections of the road. This involved upgrading an already existing road which would be more cost-effective, easier to make and accessible through the year unlike the one proposed. Certain sections of the proposed road were rejected, given their likely impact on Flamingo City. The committee warned: 'It (the proposed road) would result in all probability in the abandonment of this breeding site, and India will thus lose the only breeding site of the flamingos which in turn could spell doom to the population of these birds in the Indian subcontinent.'[12]

The standing committee's stance was unequivocal against recommending the road.

Still, the proposal was tabled repeatedly. Perhaps 'saving some birds', was viewed as unreasonable, especially in the face of the fact that it was a strategic road. The stated purpose was to provide greater access to the Border Security Force posts guarding the Indo-Pakistan border, as the Rann runs into the Sindh province in Pakistan, as well as internal security due to illicit activities in the border areas.

Ostensibly.

The defence argument wears thin, a member of the expert committee pointed out, explaining that the proposed road is a good 50 km away from the border, and would still need feeder roads to reach the posts.

A certain ecological disaster, it does not make economic sense, either. The region remains inundated for about seven to eight months, and hence would be inaccessible. For the rest of the year, the entire flat expanse of the Rann is a road, and you could drive a sturdy vehicle anywhere! Besides, there is already an existing alternative road network, though longer, that can be extended and strengthened.

So what drove the construction of this road?

The road proposal coincided with the government's push to sell the 'white desert' of the Rann as a major tourism attraction. The site visit report of the committee also stated that, 'It is evident that a main purpose of the proposed road is to encourage tourism.'[13]

Some press reports[14] framed the NBWL concerns regarding the road as a 'stumbling block and hurdle' in the government's efforts to develop tourism along the road—the sanctuary itself; Dhordo, a tourist hub and site of an annual desert festival; Kala Dungar, the highest point in Kutch; and the ancient Harappan site of Dholavira, which is also at risk from the road construction.

Most other media organizations though took up this issue, mainly to highlight the plight of Flamingo City. One web portal, Conservation India, created a campaign around the issue, helping sustain the pressure.

On 22 July 2014, a new NBWL was constituted, and the proposal was part of the agenda for its first meeting on 12–13 August 2014. It was given the go-ahead. There was no additional insight, field visit, information or study that might have tilted the decision in favour of construction of the road.

I do not know how many of you have seen flamingos in the wild (if not, go *now*). I have yet to see a more exquisite bird. I looked up my notes and this is what they said, 'Viewed from a distance in the Rann, the flamingos were a shimmer of pink in the far horizon; closer, they seemed like long-legged ballerinas, their graceful curved necks buried in the water, occasionally lifting their heads and spreading their wings wide to perform a tight, tiny ballet. So utterly beautiful and graceful that even science takes a bow, calling them *Phoenicopterus roseus* (and *P. minor*), "crimson water nymphs".'

I cannot fathom the deliberate choice of a project that would erase the flamingo off India's landscape, even though a perfectly viable, ecologically safe option was available.

It's not just about 'saving birds', or whatever rare wildlife stands threatened—destroying an ecosystem has far wider, graver consequences. What comes to mind is the proposed road to connect Aritar in Sikkim with Khunia More in West Bengal, which would run through Pangolakha Wildlife Sanctuary (Sikkim), Neora Valley National Park (West Bengal), as well as two crucial elephant corridors. The unkindest cut would be the 15-km stretch through the Neora Valley. The road would straddle high ridges, tearing down Himalayan temperate forests and habitats of rare species like the red panda, marbled cat, takin, pheasants and tragopans. Its route would take it to Jorepokhri, the source of the Neora river. The blasting and construction would destroy the catchment and the natural water systems that feed the towns of Kalimpong and Algarah, and a number of villages downstream.

Fortunately, at the time of writing, this proposal has been shelved, and the Neora Valley and its river, live on. As an aside, the site was earlier proposed for a hydel project and was visited by an Indian Administrative Officer (IAS), Bhaskar Ghose (who has served as commissioner in the region). Ghose walked the forest during his site inspection, and in his report asked that the valley be spared. He writes in his memoirs *The Service of the State: The IAS Reconsidered*, 'if there had to be a facility to withdraw water, it would have to be far lower down, away from the sanctuary; the valley had to be left as it was, as inviolate, as tranquil and quiet. There are too few of these places left, and I for one was not going to be a party to the destruction of one of them.'

The ebb of one threat leads to the flow of another. The battle to safeguard the last of our wildernesses is an ongoing task, featuring bold and responsible decisions taken by many unsung heroes.

The Road Ahead

The scale of the problem is imposing, and clearly set to accelerate.

India's road network of 4.42 million km is one of the largest in the world, second only to the US, and equalling it in quantitative density. However, in terms of population, India has only 4 km of road per 1,000 people.

Already a priority, the roads and highway sector is set for an aggressive expansion. The financial outlay for 2016–17 was enhanced by around 24 per cent to construct an additional 10,000 km—more than a twofold jump compared to the previous year—and upgrade 50,000 km of state highways into national highways. Many of these would spread ribbon-like into forests, wetlands, sanctuaries.

To facilitate this rapid growth, rules and regulations that govern roads, indeed all linear intrusions like railways, power lines, etc., have been relaxed more in the past few years, based on the perception that environment norms are slowing down such projects. The consent of affected village bodies (gram sabhas) was done away with in 2013 by the Congress-led United Progressive Alliance (UPA) government which was in power. About a year later, the new government in power, the Bharatiya Janata Party (BJP)-led National Democratic Alliance (NDA), ushered in a major relaxation of rules for faster execution of roads. Tree-cutting, construction, etc. could now start after getting an in-principle approval from concerned local authorities such as district forest officers, whereas earlier it needed to go through the rigour of a forest clearance process as mandated by law. Surely projects that involve considerable expense and have far-reaching implications require wider consultation, varied perspectives and informed decision-making?

In 2015, the environment ministry announced its intention of creating a standard policy for all roads and other linear projects like railway lines. Such a general approval scheme would also apply to all road projects within 100 km of the Line of Actual Control (the 'border' between Indian-held lands and Chinese-controlled territory, spanning the northern Indian states of Jammu and Kashmir, Uttarakhand and Himachal Pradesh and the northeastern states of Sikkim and Arunachal Pradesh) and in areas affected by left-wing extremism (LWE) and militancy. Reportedly, there are plans to include all international borders as well. Border areas are the wild's final frontier, their very remoteness offering refuge to a variety of endangered flora and fauna—from flamingos in the marshy deserts of Kutch, to snow leopards in the lofty Himalayas, and India's only ape, the hoolock gibbon, which inhabits the rainforest of the North-east. The central-eastern belt of the country, which is affected by the LWE, is rich tiger and elephant habitat. Such a one-size-fits-all approach is ludicrous—roads impact different ecosystems and diverse wildlife differently. A general clearance to all without considering individual species, ecosystems and project-specific needs is nothing short of disastrous.

The road ahead looks bleak.

Yet, it need not be. There are ways to avoid or at least reduce the carnage, to allow animals the right of passage . . .

❧

One simple engineering quick fix is to have speed regulations in wildlife-rich areas and to properly deploy speed breakers. This has worked remarkably well in Zanzibar, where strategically placed speed bumps on a road through a forest reduced the deaths of the endangered red colobus monkeys by over 80 per cent.

Other measures involve building infrastructure: maintaining and building culverts, underpasses and overpasses, keeping in mind the behaviour and ecology of the species concerned. For arboreal animals, artificial canopy 'bridges' at vital points allows for safe passage, as will maintenance of a natural canopy and green cover along the edges of roads.

A sensible question that could be posed at this point is: Do animals actually use infrastructure that humans design for them? This point was deliberated at a meeting to discuss mitigation measures for the expansion of a National Highway cutting through Rajaji National Park, and the crucial Chilla–Motichur elephant corridor. The director of the Wildlife Institute of India was asked to weigh in with his expert opinion on whether elephants would use overpasses. 'Well,' said the director, 'we'll need to ask the elephants!'

He has a point.

The decision to construct roads cannot be driven merely by economic targets and gains but must include, at the planning stage, a deeper understanding of the landscapes they penetrate and a sensitivity towards the species that share our planet. In 2014, *Nature* magazine,[15] published a global map that pinpointed areas with high ecological value that must remain roadless, and those where benefits to human beings in terms of agricultural development, employment, etc. come with relatively little environmental harm, and vice versa.

A similar exercise should be undertaken for India, which should form the basis on which road infrastructure is planned. Protected Areas, and critical tiger corridors are already well mapped and must be strictly no-go. Pristine natural habitats, river catchment areas, wetlands, crucial wildlife, particularly elephant, snow-leopard corridors—should simply be left alone. Where unavoidable, the extent, width and type of road should be carefully planned and regulated.

A MoEF-appointed expert committee, of which I was part, issued comprehensive guidelines to this effect in 2013. The committee was constituted in response to the numerous proposals before the NBWL seeking approvals for construction of new roads, and expansion of existing ones within sanctuaries—making it a top threat to wildlife.

The expert committee called for a ban on new roads, expansions and upgradations (from kuccha fair-weather roads to black-topped ones) in Protected Areas and 1 km around them to provide a buffer. The thumb rule for Protected Areas and pristine natural habitats was to avoid new roads, and seek alternative routes.

While the ministry accepted these guidelines, there is nothing to show it has been put into practice—as road after road is being granted approval inside reserves. The guidelines are perceived as being obstructive.

But putting these recommendations into practice is not an unsurmountable exercise, nor is it 'anti-growth'.

For example, an alternative route to the contentious NH7 was recommended so as to secure the tiger population of the Kanha–Pench landscape it cut through. It added another 80 km and about 90 minutes of travel time. But it would save a forest, and its tigers. We do make, and take, bypasses through cities. So why are forests considered expendable?

Animals need *respite*. Night is when animals move the most, and when most fatalities take place: a night ban on vehicles is advised. This is currently in place on the highway that passes through Bandipur Tiger Reserve in Karnataka and links the state to Kerala. But it must be said that the ban was hard-won, and keeping it in place a constant battle. This single initiative gives the animals great relief, and room for movement.

The case of Sariska Tiger Reserve in Rajasthan is a salutary note on which I'd like to conclude this chapter. It showcases the complexity surrounding roads in forests and conservation—and that solutions can be arrived at, if there is a will to do so.

I visited Sariska in 2008, when tigers were flown in from Ranthambhore Tiger Reserve, also in Rajasthan. This was part of a programme to rebuild the reserve after the local extinction of the tiger in 2005. I was there again a year later. Both times I was witness to massive dharnas—demonstrations, though not always peaceful—protesting the closure of a state highway that cuts through the core of the reserve. The highway connects state capital Jaipur to Alwar city, and is a very busy one, particularly at night when thousands of trucks ply the road. One of the conditions for the reintroduction of tigers in Sariska was that the highway be closed to traffic (a Supreme Court order was passed to this effect in 2009).

Consequently, the alternative route was repaired and widened. Not to the satisfaction of the local inhabitants, though, as it meant an extra 12 km of travel. Their main contention however, was that the alternate road did not connect Thanagazi, a town that bordered Sariska. This would dent their livelihood. The mainstay of this small town is animal husbandry, and the locals need swift connectivity to market their dairy products. The government assured a new road would be built to connect Thanagazi. But making new roads is a slow process—and the agitations continued, at times taking an ugly turn. Forest officials were heckled—a range forest officer and his staff were beaten up by a mob of over 5,000 people, while Park Director R.S. Shekhawat barely managed to escape unharmed. It was the director who had led the effort to shut the highway, refusing to be cowed by local political pressures and the wrath of the people. One of the demands the agitators sought was his immediate transfer!

Foresters also worried about other repercussions. Disgruntled local communities living on the fringes of a reserve are not usually happy partners in a conservation project. The restrictions that a Protected Area demands can lead to tense situations. The villagers were unhappy with tigers; it was because of the *tigers* that the road was being closed. There was already some level of resentment due to the grazing restrictions—there is pressure of over two lakh cattle on this 807-sq km reserve. Tigers were preying on livestock, adding further heat to an already bubbling cauldron.

Security around tigers was tightened as a precaution. Keeping the tigers safe was critical for Sariska's future. They had been radio-collared, and were also closely monitored on foot, with two men exclusively devoted to each tiger, besides the regular patrolling by forest staff.

Meanwhile, the new road connecting Thanagazi was constructed thus giving the villagers the much-needed connectivity from their town to both Alwar and Jaipur. In my most recent visit in November 2016, the state highway was shut to commercial traffic, a precursor to gradually closing it down. With a lighter traffic load, especially at night, tigers have taken over—at least three are known to use the area.

I missed meeting one. As we entered the reserve, fresh pug marks showed that the big cat had been on the move. The tiger finally had right of way.

Sinking a Tiger Forest

*What we are doing to the forests of the world is but a mirror reflection of
what we are doing to ourselves and to one another.*

—Mahatma Gandhi

I have a confession to make. I believe I have committed a 'national
crime'. The crime of such extreme nature, as defined by India's
honourable minister for water resources, Uma Bharti, is that I
have spoken out against the Ken–Betwa river link. The first, and
flagship, project of India's River Linking Scheme, it will strike
at the heart of India's other flagship project: Project Tiger, at its
Panna Tiger Reserve in Madhya Pradesh. Bharti wasn't, of course,
talking about me personally. In an impassioned outburst to the
press on 7 June 2016, she threatened to go on a hunger strike if
the Ken–Betwa River Link Project was delayed further, and stated
that 'the attempts to delay the project by environmentalists was a
national crime'.[1]

I am now going to compound the national crime further, by
putting on record that the latter—Project Tiger—has had a degree
of proven, if measured, success, while the idea to join great rivers,
as though they were plumbing pipes or canals, is an extravagant
exercise, a 'dangerous delusion'[2] whose soundness and wisdom
need to be questioned.

The ambitious—dare I call it audacious—plan is to interlink, reshape and realign the natural flow of thirty-seven of India's rivers, by constructing thirty canals, stretching over 15,000 km, and 3,000 reservoirs—as per information from various government documents and reports. The process will redraw India's geography, and irrevocably alter its physical, ecological entity. The big idea is to dam the rivers that have surplus water and direct the flow into rivers that are not so well endowed. This is an inherently flawed premise. Experts dismiss the notion that a river can have *surplus* water: each drop performs an ecological function. To assume that a river has surplus water, just because it exceeds the demands on it, is fallacious. A river has functions to perform beyond fulfilling human needs. It supports aquatic life, recharges groundwater, influences microclimate, dilutes pollutants. Besides, most basins are heavily overexploited for industrial, agricultural and domestic use—with raging water wars between states whose cooperation is imperative for the project.

From the project's perspective, a river is the sum of its water, its value measured in its utility. But rivers are not mere storehouses of water; along with the water, flow their histories, legends and culture, all of which is now threatened. Rivers have evolved over millions of years and are dynamic ecosystems with a catchment, basin and floodplain.

During the monsoons, excess water flows in a river's aquifers and swells floodplains, rejuvenating the land. In the dry season it is this reserve which maintains its base flow and recharges groundwater. A river may begin life as a trickle of snowmelt or run-off, expanding to become a great river, as various streams merge along its course. The river nourishes the earth. The flow of fresh water as well as the silt the river carries enriches the basin along its flow, enhancing the productivity of the land, and forming the very basis of India's rich agriculture.

Another myth that the River Link Project rests on is that river water flowing into seas is 'wasted'. The river prevents saline ingress into fertile coastal lands, pushing out the sea, which would otherwise invade the land. When river and sea meet, the confluence of fresh and salty water creates the most bountiful of ecosystems—estuaries, rich with fisheries, birds and other life.

It is claimed that river-linking will irrigate 35 million hectares in the water-scarce western and peninsular regions, and produce 34 GW of hydroelectricity. It is being presented as the solution to the country's acute, and endemic, water problems; and plans have been drawn to wrap it up within a decade.

How realistic this claim is, and whether such large-scale engineering is essential to end our water woes, is open to question. Parineeta Dandekar of the South Asia Network on Dams, Rivers and People (SANDRP) points to cheaper, as well as socially and environmentally benign options which 'include increasing irrigation and project-specific efficiency, rational cropping patterns, putting to use our existing mega infrastructure which is under-performing, using water equitably, harvesting rainwater and managing demand better, among others'.[3]

It is interesting to note here that Maharashtra, on India's western coast, has the highest concentration of large dams in the country (1,845), yet only 18 per cent of tilled land is[4] irrigated.[5] If we look at the big picture, over 60 per cent of India's current irrigation needs are met from groundwater and small irrigation projects.

River-linking was first mooted in 1982, when the National Water Development Authority (NWDA) was set up to study its feasibility, but only gained momentum in the Atal Bihari Vajpayee-led National Democratic Alliance (NDA) government in 2002. It didn't make much headway in the ten-year rule of the United Progressive Alliance (UPA) that followed. With the Bharatiya Janata Party (BJP)-led NDA government coming back to power at the Centre in 2014, river-linking received a renewed push under Prime Minister Narendra Modi who promised to fulfil Vajpayee's dream, designating it as a project of 'National Importance'. It has the backing of the Supreme Court, which called for the central and state governments to work on the interlinking of rivers, and that a special committee be set up for the purpose.

The river-link venture comes at a humongous cost. The project cost estimation of Rs 5.6 lakh crores in 2002, is now likely to exceed a gargantuan Rs 11 lakh crores.[6] Even so, the *real* costs of the project—human, ecological, social, economical[7]—are much higher, have not been factored in, and are frankly near-impossible to measure.

The construction of canals and large reservoirs are likely to submerge at least 27 lakh hectares, drowning fertile lands, villages, homes, forests, wildlife sanctuaries.[8] Over 1 lakh hectares of natural forest cover are likely to be directly submerged. There are no official estimates of the number of people who will be displaced, but SANDRP puts the likely figure at over 1.5 million.

We know rivers as living arteries of our planet, the lifeblood of civilization, quenching the thirst of generations, watering our fields, fuelling our industries. And hidden beneath the shimmering surface of rivers is an extraordinary variety of aquatic creatures—from the iconic dolphin to otters to little-known aquatic insects that are vital to the ecosystem—and the economy—as important food resources for fish. As rivers are dammed, their course changed, water soldiered through canals, the ecology of the riverine ecosystems will be destroyed, and with it aquatic life: dolphins, gharials, turtles, rare freshwater fish like mahseer, commercially important species like hilsa, and birds like skimmers who nest on banks.

It will also mean the end of a way of life for the millions of fishermen whose lives, and livelihoods, are tied to that of the river.

Shockingly, a project of such enormous scale has had no thorough, robust, scientific social- or environmental-impact studies or cost-benefit analysis. One wonders if this is a deliberate omission, for it is doubtful if the project will stand up to such scrutiny.

To understand the ground situation, I travelled to Panna Tiger Reserve, where the contentious Ken-Betwa river link is expected to kick-start the project—and submerge the reserve's pristine forests.

Panna Tiger Reserve, Madhya Pradesh

At Ground Zero, in Panna Tiger Reserve, the mood was sombre; the upcoming river link is a dark shadow that stalked my visit—every beloved site I saw, animal I observed, vista I drank in—river, valley, gorge, grassland—appeared to have its days numbered. My anxiety was mirrored, manifold, in the eyes of the forest staff by my side. They have clocked innumerable hours— days and nights—to protect this reserve and its tigers; they have taken on poachers, timber smugglers, graziers. They have calmed irate villagers and faced their wrath when 'their' tigers preyed on livestock. Human–tiger conflict situations are understandably tense, and usually villagers, fatigued and frustrated by the losses, vent their ire on foresters who are the custodians of the forest, and its wildlife.

Now, though, the forest staff found themselves out of their depth. The plan to dam and draw water from the river Ken that meanders through their forest—and their villages (most of the staff is from these parts)—is incomprehensible to them, and 'terrifying'. It is bigger than them, beyond their grasp.

Briefly, both the Ken and Betwa start their journey from the Vindhya mountain range, and meander northward, through Madhya Pradesh to ultimately merge in the Yamuna in Uttar Pradesh.

The Ken–Betwa project aims to irrigate over six lakh hectares across five districts in Madhya Pradesh and Uttar Pradesh, provide drinking water to over 1,00,000 people and generate 78 MW of power. Six hundred and sixty million cubic metres of water will be drawn from the Ken river in Madhya Pradesh and channelled through a 220-km-long canal into the Betwa river. This will necessitate building the Daudhan Dam in the heart of Panna, affecting no less than 28 per cent of the reserve's core critical tiger habitat.[9]

Red paint was slashed over ancient Vindhyan sandstone, at Sundighat in the Ken Valley, where we spotted many rare, endangered vultures roosting in the nooks of the sheer cliffs. The paint indicated the alignment of the over-2-km-long and 77-metre-high Daudhan Dam that will be built on the Ken.

The red is also an indicator of the death of the river Ken, of the forest it feeds and the life it nurtures.

It occurred to me that the tigress I saw the day before—T6 (Tiger 6)—that beautiful, powerful, ethereal being, should have been splashed by a spot of red too, marring her ochre and black stripes. For the waters will swallow her as well. She is the collateral damage of the Ken–Betwa river link. She, and the other dozen-odd tigers, that reside in the submergence area. And the vultures that we saw: nesting, roosting, diving, gliding, soaring, flying. They are doomed too. Vulture populations in India have, in fact, plummeted by over 97 per cent in a matter of about ten to fifteen years. However, the minister for water resources has assured us that the vultures will be safe, reasoning that '97 per cent of the vulture nests are above the maximum water level'.[10]

It doesn't quite work that way. Here's why.

The Ken is one of our most spectacular rivers, meandering through a 30-km-long gorge amidst sheer rocky cliffs. These cliffs provide an ideal nesting habitat for five species of vultures including the critically endangered long-billed *Gyps indicus* and the red-headed *Sarcogyps calvus* besides the rare Egyptian vulture, *Neophron percnopterus*.

The Daudhan Dam will submerge this entire length of gorge, destroying the unique habitat of more than a thousand of these highly endangered avian creatures and submerging 400-odd live nests.[11]

While a few vulture nests may well be above the submergence line, it is foolhardy to assume, therefore, that the birds will survive. Vultures are one of the avian world's best fliers. They don't beat their wings to fly but glide with the wind, sometimes for as far as 100 km or more. They need heights to launch themselves and take advantage of the updraught produced when the wind blows over hills and ridges; or depths so that they can ride the thermals, which are rising columns of warm air. The gorge, and the rocky cliffs that line it, are therefore a perfect habitat for vultures.

With the construction of the Daudhan Dam a stagnant reservoir will replace a vibrant, living river. With the reservoir's water lapping at their door, the vultures won't be able to take flight, and will have to learn to flap their wings, in the manner of ducks, as they hop off and on their nests. The problem is, vultures can't evolve into ducks, not even for the greater common good of the country, not even to spare honourable ministers the inconvenience of a hunger strike.

We have also been reassured about the national animal. In fact, the water ministry, the nodal ministry for executing the River Link Project, assures us that 'the tiger population will increase, with the region getting more water'.

If it weren't heartbreakingly tragic, it would be rip-roaringly funny.

Here is a summary of what the project will do to tigers: The dam of the Ken–Betwa link, power house and a large part of the reservoir are *almost entirely* located within the Panna Tiger Reserve, directly submerging 89 sq km. Over 58 sq km is in the core critical tiger habitat, deemed inviolate and sacrosanct as per the Wildlife (Protection) Act, 1972. The impact area will be far greater. Construction, quarrying, mining, blasting, staff colonies, etc. will drown, disembowel and dissect over 200 sq km of the reserve—and the wildlife within it. The reservoir will bifurcate the reserve. The shrunken, fractured landscape will not be able to host a viable population of tigers, who are territorial and wide-ranging. Added to this is the impact of the construction, blasting, tunnelling, quarrying, and movement of men and machinery—all of which is expected to last for a decade.

We know tigers are rare, endangered and hence precious. The tigers of Panna are, in a way, even more special. After Panna's tiger extinction debacle (tigers were declared extinct in Panna in 2009 mainly due to poaching, compounded by the management's refusal to acknowledge the crisis), tigers were translocated from March 2009 onwards from other reserves in Madhya Pradesh in an unprecedented exercise. There was a massive, concerted effort to rebuild the Panna tiger population led by Field Director Rangaiah Sreenivasa Murthy, backed by the state government, the National Tiger Conservation Authority and the Wildlife Institute of India. Monetary support was extended as well, the project cost Rs 478 lakh over five years.

The Panna team worked 24x7 to monitor and protect the tigers, and keep them safe. The translocated tigers were uncertain in this alien territory, and the spectre of poaching continued to haunt the park, for which constant monitoring was required. (Incidentally, the Panna team includes its elephants! Especially the tusker Ram Bahadur, who played a pivotal role in this exercise. He has been there, on the job, since the first tiger was relocated to Panna. The management relied on Ram Bahadur to help them monitor tigers in the toughest of terrains, under all weather conditions, as well as in tricky situations like steering a tiger back to the forest when it ventured into human territory.) Thirteen villages were voluntarily relocated from the rich Ken Valley, a mosaic of forest and grassland, and a prime habitat for tigers. Three of these relocated village sites are now directly in the submergence areas. The ongoing monitoring and radiotelemetry study of tigers in the reserve has shown that at least three tigers occupy that area now.

The authorities recognized they needed the support of the local communities if Panna was to have a future, and reached out to the people in an effort to instil in them a sense of ownership and pride for the tiger and the reserve. While the villagers living on the fringes of the forest are remarkably tolerant, the reserve and its tigers are a source of simmering animosity. Tigers and leopards prey on livestock, while deer and wild boar routinely raid fields, causing loss of livelihoods. Farmers are monetarily compensated by the government but payments are invariably delayed, and the process is complex and bureaucratic—and there have been efforts to rectify this as well.

'Friends of Panna' is a diverse group of naturalists, writers, students, teachers, foresters, farmers, journalists who have come together to support the park. Nature camps are being organized, local children taken on tours to see the reserve. When I visited the reserve in November 2015, I landed bang in the middle of an enthusiastic procession winding its noisy way through Panna town, which borders the forest. Exuberant cries of *'Bagh Bachao, Van Bachao!'* (Save the Tigers! Save the Forest!) rent the air. Some 500 young students were rallying for their tigers, whose forests, they said, 'gave them water and fresh air, and had made their town famous'!

Such a strong message of hope.

The hard work of the Panna management paid off in the field as well. Their dedication was rewarded when the tigers bred, raising cubs—and the next generation of Panna's 'new' tigers. From zero, there are about forty tigers in the reserve at the time of writing this in November 2016—and they are charting new territory, dispersing outside the reserve and populating the landscape. Panna's tigers today have spread out to an area of about 30,000 sq km in this landscape. This success has won it international fame, and it is cited as a model of conservation success, which other countries want to learn from, and replicate.

It will all go to dust—the effort, the expense, the resolve, the pride in this extraordinary achievement.

The proposed reservoir, the canals, a network of 221 km, and the construction will wreck crucial wildlife corridors towards the south and southwest of the reserve. Tigers use these corridors regularly. When 'T3' (Tiger 3), was brought to Panna from Pench Tiger Reserve in November 2009, he almost immediately started moving out of the park and travelled about 450 km through three districts, back towards his home range—Pench! In this, T3 taught us that tigers have a strong homing instinct. Meanwhile, at least four tigers traversed the southwest corridor through the patchy forests of Chattarpur–Sagar–Lalitpur. Among them was the pregnant tigress 'P222' (Panna 222), who eventually had her cubs on the park's southwestern tip, reiterating the critical importance of the connectivity this corridor provides.

It is not just tigers, and vultures, that the project will obliterate. The reserve has other rare wildlife—wolves, chousingha or the four-horned antelopes, sloth bears, leopards, pangolins, foxes, wild dogs—who now face an equal risk, and an equally uncertain future.

Besides the impact on wildlife, there are other fundamental problems with the project.

'But Where Is the Water?'

If you think drowning tigers is of little concern, then consider the fact that vast forests which form the catchment of the Ken river will be destroyed. How will the river rejuvenate itself if the forest vanishes? The project will divert nearly 1,074 million cubic metres of water from the Ken river to the Betwa river basin every year. Experts opine that the river Ken falls short in meeting the water requirements of the people along its course, so it is bizarre that it is expected to have 'excess' water to feed another river.

Data to back the claim that the Ken has excess water is shrouded in secrecy. Both the rivers, Ken and Betwa, are tributaries of the Yamuna and Ganga, and being international rivers the data related to them is classified.

The NWDA does not give data to support the view that the Ken basin has surplus water[12]—especially if it is to maintain its *aviral dhara*—the continuity of flow to keep the river alive. River ecologist Brij Gopal says the assumption that the Ken basin is water surplus is entirely erroneous and farthest from the reality on the ground as possible.[13]

The Ken flows for over 270 km downstream of the proposed Daudhan Dam: how will it sustain the people, and their livelihoods of farming and fishing, with its water siphoned off? Besides, river water is crucial for groundwater recharge—changing the course of the Ken will deprive the rain-deficient areas downstream leading to severe water shortages.

A visit to Panna in early summer shows a shrivelled Ken, a riverbed so dry you could walk on it. I also found a palpable disaffection among the people, that the project will seek to transfer the Ken water to irrigate other districts in Madhya Pradesh and Uttar Pradesh, even as they are water-starved. What about their needs and aspirations? How will this river-link fulfil its ambitious plan of flooding lands stricken with drought, when the Ken has no water to offer? There were other reasons for the sense of discomfort, and they have to do with the people's cultural connection to the river Karnavati, the ancient name of the Ken. The Pandavas, of the Indian epic Mahabharata, are believed to have spent part of their exile in these forests, and legend has it the river disappeared—the water vanishes into a deep rift at Pandavan, the place where the Mirhasan river joins the Ken—as it did not want to disturb the Pandavas.

The tragedy is that such monumental decisions which lay to waste our natural heritage, and destroy lives and livelihoods, are based on shoddy Environmental Impact Assessments (EIAs).[14]

The Ken–Betwa project's EIA is a study in incompetence. It is factually inaccurate, inept, mala fide and misleading. It dismisses the area under submergence as 'neither a home nor an important habitat for wildlife. There are no known breeding grounds within the project area'—even as there is documented proof of at least three breeding tigresses here, and about a third of Panna's tiger population. Such riverine habitats are preferred haunts of tigers, more so in dry, deciduous forests like Panna.

In failing to mention the barrage to be constructed in the Ken Gharial Sanctuary on the Ken river, the EIA overlooks the impact on the sanctuary, which is downstream of the dam site.

Incredibly, the EIA also discovers new species in the park—the slow loris (residents of evergreen forests in the North-east), the Manipur brow-antlered deer (its habitat is self-explanatory, except to the learned EIA consultants) and finds a sal forest (another absurdity; no sal here in fact, Panna forms the northern boundary of natural teak forests in the country). It mentions tree species like kaju (cashew), which flourish in coastal climes, and the Chir pine, a resident of the Himalayas. It also lists as an advantage that animals 'get plenty of water'! Another benefit pointed out is that the reservoir will prevent encroachments and invasion by livestock—but won't the dam, and the resultant havoc, be the biggest invasion of the park? What will be left to conquer?

There are appalling discrepancies in the EIA on the issue of mining for the dam. At one point it is mentioned that 'all the quarries are within the PA [Protected Area], both upstream and downstream' but then later says, 'Adequate care has been taken not to locate quarries and burrow area in Panna Tiger Reserve areas.' For the record, the first statement is correct—quarrying will be within the reserve.

Nothing quite sums up the callousness of the EIA than its estimation of the number of trees required to be cut—it had counted 32,900 trees, and when this incongruity was pointed out, revised it to an astounding 13.96 lakh.[15] Of these, over 11 lakh trees are within the national park.

I will take this opportunity to point out that such substandard EIAs are routine. Most are based on rapid, one-season assessments and secondary information that is lacking in critical details and transparency. They are heavily biased in favour of the projects, as the consultants are employed by the project proponents themselves! Ritwick Dutta, who heads the New Delhi-based non-governmental organization (NGO), EIA Response Centre, says: 'None of the EIA reports present a true picture of the environment impacts. Nor has a single report has ever said that a project should not come up.'[16]

The End of Panna

Meanwhile, the Ken–Betwa River Link Project is on the fast track. It is a National Project. Madhya Pradesh chief minister Shivraj Singh Chouhan has announced that it is his top priority. Predictably, facts were suppressed, dissenting voices were disregarded, rules circumvented and manipulated to accommodate, and fast-track, the project.

Panna Field Director Murthy, who had refused to recommend the Ken–Betwa link, stating that the project, 'if approved will lead to the death of Panna Tiger Reserve'[17] was transferred—though officially, of course, the transfer was said to be routine. He was replaced by a more pliant director, who while saying that 'due to heavy ecological losses it is difficult to recommend the project', left the 'decision to competent authorities'. The chief wildlife warden—top boss of wildlife in the state—retracted his earlier decision of not recommending the Ken–Betwa river link.

As Panna is a Protected Area, the river link requires clearance from the State Wildlife Board before it goes to the Centre's National Board for Wildlife (NBWL). Madhya Pradesh sought to denotify 90 sq km of the Panna National Park in the wildlife board's meeting on 11 August 2015 but met with stiff opposition from some of its members. The minutes of the proceedings conveniently failed to mention the issues raised concerning the Ken–Betwa link.

Two non-official board members, Belinda Wright, who heads the Wildlife Protection Society of India, and M.K. Ranjitsinh, who has served as secretary in the ministry of environment and forests, submitted a strongly worded note penning their objections to the Ken–Betwa link as the August 2015 state board meeting 'minutes had been manipulated to facilitate the clearance of the Ken–Betwa Link Project'.

The note is an unambiguous, clearly worded and gutsy statement at a time when most independent institutions are being rendered pliant and toothless. It clearly details the impact of the project, and the inherent flaws, fallacies and malicious intent of the EIA report. It is also a startling record of the abysmal governance of our wildlife and forests. Wright and Ranjitsinh point out that 'the State Wildlife Board is a statutory body created under the Wildlife (Protection) Act to advise the State in the *protection* of wildlife. It is not envisaged as, nor should it be misused as a project clearance committee.' They add that, 'most of the inconvenient facts were hidden and not put before the Board'.

They ask the chief minister, the chair of the state board: 'Kindly do not allow the manipulation of the Board to facilitate the clearance of a project (Ken–Betwa), without a genuine Environmental Impact Analysis and the assessment of the viability of the project.'

On its part, all that the government has done is make empty assurances about mitigating the damage to Panna (how, when the habitat itself is drowned?), and of tigers being translocated 'elsewhere'. Frankly, in a land-scarce, densely populated country like ours, there is no elsewhere where tigers can breed and thrive. Tigers are apex predators; they are also territorial and have a home range that they have familiarized themselves with over years. They cannot be ferried around. We haul them to Panna (after we have finished off the earlier lot), and when they settle and breed—with considerable investment of time, money, energy and effort—we now plan to dump them someplace else.

The National Tiger Conservation Authority gave its seal of approval to the project[18] and recommended that the loss be compensated by adding Nauradehi, Rani Durgawati (both in Madhya Pradesh) Ranipur and Mahavir Swami (both in Uttar Pradesh) wildlife sanctuaries as 'satellite cores' of the reserve. Hogwash. All four are already sanctuaries—no new area will get protective cover by this grand scheme. How will these 'satellites' survive if the main forest which holds the source (breeding) population of tigers and connecting corridors is pillaged? And how, pray, will these far-flung sanctuaries serve as satellite cores? Rani Durgawati, for instance, is a tiny 25-sq km park—and about 150 km away from Panna, with fragile connectivity.

The standing committee of the NBWL too approved the project on 23 August 2016.[19] Speaking on the issue, the Union environment minister, Anil Madhav Dave, who is lauded for his 'contribution to river conservation' made his intent clear on the Ken–Betwa link. In an interview to *Outlook*, a newsweekly, Dave dismissed the concerns regarding the impact on Panna: 'These (apprehensions) are all based on speculations as the project is yet to begin. My stance is that we should start with one project and do a profit-and-loss assessment within five years. If we see more profit, we should then move ahead . . .'[20]

So are we to understand that the Ken–Betwa river link is an *experiment*? Which we are expected to stand by and hail (its opposition is a national crime, remember?) as it destroys in its wake forests, gorges, valleys, villages, vultures, tigers?

Unlike a profit–loss balance sheet, the losses cannot be recovered later.

The losses are irrevocable. Forever.

The tiger, in case the nation has forgotten, is also our national animal, which we are committed to conserve. But this is about so much more than tigers. What about *Panna*? How does one 'compensate' for the loss of pristine forests, gorges and grasslands that will be submerged and annihilated? Consolidating tiger habitats is the need of the hour, but no amount of compensation can alleviate the damage that will ensue by drowning Panna's heart.

It will simply mean the end.

The Real Tiger Story

Do not cut down the forest with its tiger, and do not banish the tiger from the forest. The tiger perishes without the forest, and the forest perishes without its tiger.

The tigers should stand guard over the forest, and the forest should protect the tiger.

—Mahabharata, 'Udyogaparvan', 29, 47–48 (400 BCE)

The mood was lazy, the afternoon, languorous, the environs, sublime. After a morning drive, we—I was accompanied by O.P. Tiwari, the deputy director of the park—were sitting in a jeep by the edge of a meadow in Kanha (Tiger Reserve) quietly taking in the forest, the vast expanse of the meadows, dotted with spotted deer, hearing the murmur of leaves, soft coos of doves, the occasional sharp cry of the crested serpent eagle.

In a fraction of a second, the mood shifted. A langur emitted swift, sharp cough-like calls in ascending levels of panic. The cheetal followed suit, raising their heads, stiff little tails perking up as well, as the denizens of the jungle erupted in a cacophony of alarm calls.

A tiger was *here*.

A twig cracked, just beside us. Something moved behind the foliage, masked by a curtain of grass, then that *something* broke cover, stepping out, languidly, velvet paws padding softly on the path. A tigress . . . so powerful—and so utterly beautiful.

She took my breath away.

She padded on, either unaware of or completely indifferent to our presence, though her taut muscles gave her away: I sensed she was alert. Tense? As she glided by, she made soft moaning calls. She was calling to her cubs (Tiwariji whispered she had three), telling them she was coming to them . . . perhaps telling them not to come to her?

She walked past, almost away, but then she stopped, looked over her shoulder, her amber eyes staring straight into mine for a brief heart-stopping moment . . . before she mingled with the shadows of her forest.

As someone who has roamed India's forests for many years, I have been fortunate to meet tigers a number of times—though never enough! Each encounter is a blessing, seared into my memory and my heart. But this one was extra special: the tiger and I had *communicated*, or so I like to believe.

The tiger is the greatest of all the great cats, the most powerful, adored, revered and feared throughout history. Few other animals inspire such awe and devotion, no other animal has inspired such worldwide concern and efforts for its conservation. Yet, the tiger remains endangered, three (the Javan, Caspian and Bali) of its sub-species are extinct, and two—the Malayan and Sumatran—are listed as Critically Endangered.

Tigers have been wiped out from 93 per cent of their former habitat which once stretched from Turkey in the West to Russia in the East. Tigers once roamed in twenty-three countries, but now survive in only a dozen. Breeding populations exist only in eight. Tiger fire is burning out. It recently vanished from Cambodia, hangs by a thread—and a prayer—in China, Laos and Vietnam. Worldwide, tigers have suffered a 'range collapse' having lost 40 per cent of their range, since 2010.[1] In seven short years, nearly half of the area occupied by tigers earlier is now emptied of them.

The habitat has become hostile, unsuitable; or the tigers have been hunted out.

Current global populations are estimated at 3,900, split between five subspecies.

India remains the tiger's best hope.

The trajectory of *Panthera tigris*—the royal Bengal tiger—in India's conservation landscape is well-documented. At the turn of the twentieth century, it is believed India had some 40,000 tigers. But the cat was considered both a pest and a coveted trophy, and hunted with ferocity—by some accounts 80,000 tigers were killed between 1875–1925.[2] Post Independence, tiger shikar was a major 'sport', attracting hunters who brought in much-needed foreign exchange. The Government of India Tourist Office advertised, 'The sportsman's greatest trophy. Thrill to the excitement of tiger shikar found only in the lush jungle of India . . .'

Trade in tiger skins was rampant. In 1967, Kailash Sankhala (a forest officer who would later head Project Tiger) helped expose the extent of the trade in an article in the *Indian Express* that showed tiger, leopard and snow leopard pelts being sold openly and in great numbers in bazaars—including in Delhi's hip Chanakya market. A year later, export of tiger skins was stopped. In 1970, then prime minister, Indira Gandhi, banned tiger shooting silencing the powerful shikar lobby with these words: 'We do need foreign exchange, but not at the cost of the life and liberty of some of the most beautiful inhabitants of this continent.'[3]

It was a timely call given that the first all-India tiger census conducted in this period showed that only about 1,800 tigers were left in India.

Indira Gandhi enacted stringent laws to protect wildlife and forests, and in 1973, she launched Project Tiger, the biggest conservation initiative of its time, globally. Nine tiger reserves were carved out in various ecosystems, from the mangroves of the Sundarbans to the dry forests of Ranthambhore to the sal forests of the Terai-Corbett. Managers were hand-picked to run the initiative and protect these key tiger habitats. India's 'Mission Tiger' was backed with strong political commitment and tremendous zeal, and the great cat responded. Its numbers stabilized.

Then, in the 1990s, the tiger was hit by a double whammy. Poaching spiked. With an escalating demand for tiger bone used in traditional Chinese medicines,[4] killing tigers became extremely lucrative. This demand coincided with sagging political will; wildlife had no support at the top, and had ceased to be a priority. Success had also made the country smug, and this complacency manifested on the ground, where protection slackened. The tiger bore the brunt. In Rajasthan's star reserve, Ranthambhore, tigers routinely sighted had vanished. Rumours of poaching swirled around. In his book *The Last Tiger*, conservationist Valmik Thapar writes that in 1992 'the arrest of a poacher led to revelations that from late 1990 poaching gangs had wiped out 15–20 tigers and endless other animals'. Thapar estimated a similar loss in the neighbouring Sariska Tiger Reserve. Billy Arjan Singh, legendary conservationist and architect of Dudhwa Tiger Reserve (Uttar Pradesh), was acutely worried for Dudhwa—in his estimation the park barely had a fifth of the official claims of 100 tigers.

This scandal could not have hit at a more inopportune time. An international tiger symposium was planned in 1993 to celebrate two decades of Project Tiger, and to announce the new numbers of 4,300 tigers, more than double the number when the project began. The numbers were bravely announced—not that anyone believed in them. Despondency had set in, and the then forest secretary candidly admitted that this was a time for 'introspection not celebrations'.[5]

The 1990s also saw a change in economic policy that ushered in a free market economy—which sidelined green concerns. India relaxed environment safeguards that had been built over the previous two decades in order to promote industry, investment and infrastructure. Prime wildlife habitats and forests were increasingly razed for industry and infrastructure development.

India's mission to save the tiger faltered, and the cat never really recovered. As the new millennium dawned, the true enormity of the crisis was made public in the year 2000 by then Project Tiger director P.K. Sen, who revealed that India was losing a tiger every day[6]—though the government chose to dismiss it as dramatic exaggeration. Then in 2005, all hell broke loose when tigers completely disappeared from two of India's most famous reserves, Sariska—a mere three hours away from Delhi, the seat of power, and shortly after, from Panna Tiger Reserve.

Those were the Manmohan Singh years. As an economist and former finance minister, Singh was the architect of a series of economic reforms during the 1990s. His stated intent to safeguard ecological concerns within the growth paradigm rarely translated into concrete actions. But the spectre of a tiger-free Sariska ballooned into an international embarrassment. Global media pressure and outrage from conservationists and even from within the government forced a reticent administration to act.

The prime minister made his maiden visit to a tiger reserve, Ranthambhore, to assess the situation and convened a Tiger Task Force to advise on the growing crisis. The report was problematic inviting criticism and dissent even from its members— one contentious point being the promotion of the 'coexistence agenda' which among other things suggested relaxing wildlife laws that govern Protected Areas, a disastrous idea, given the extreme extractive pressures from local communities, and even more so from development agencies and commercial interests. It failed to address or take note of the immense threats faced by tigers because of the increasingly industry-friendly clearance procedures for diversion of forests.

It, however, gave two significant recommendations. One was to incentivize, by way of fair compensation, villagers willing to relocate from core tiger habitats to create inviolate space for tigers. The other was to replace an inaccurate (and easily manipulated) census method that counted footprints—pug marks—with a more scientifically robust one that used 'camera traps' to photograph tigers, identifying them by their stripe patterns that are as individual as a human fingerprint.

And the tide turned again with the tiger recovering in both these reserves—Panna and Sariska—and countrywide numbers rising an astonishing 50 per cent in eight years from 1,411[7] in 2006 to 2,226 in 2014.

2,226—and the Real Tiger Story

It was a crisp January morning in 2015 when India's then environment minister, Prakash Javadekar made a generous offer, buoyed by the 2014 census that counted about 2,226 tigers, a 30 per cent leap from 2010 of 1,706, 'India is now in a position to donate some tigers to other countries which are not faring so well and where tigers are on the decline,' he said.

India was obviously doing something right to give the tiger a secure home to live, hunt and breed. There is, deservedly, a tremendous pride in this achievement. More so that a country like India with its 1.3 billion people, grinding poverty, yet galloping economic growth and its consequent pressures, harbours the maximum—over 60 per cent—of the world's remaining wild tigers.

While tiger-estimation methods were contested by some of the world's leading tiger scientists (and the arguments continue), it is an undisputed fact that there are definitely more tigers in the wild than were previously estimated, new areas were censored, and conservation initiatives had paid off, particularly in some habitats. The Wildlife Institute of India attributed voluntary relocation of villages from core areas of tiger reserves and the consequent creation of inviolate habitats to be one of the key factors in restoring tiger populations. Coupled with better on-the-ground protection, some habitats revived. Over the years, tigers have recovered, remarkably, in some reserves such as Nagarhole and Bhadra in Karnataka,

Pench and Satpura in Madhya Pradesh, and Ranthambhore in Rajasthan, to name a few.

Nagarhole is a true success story. In the 1960s, you could barely spot deer or cheetal in a forest that was overrun with hunters, loggers and local people who had encroached into reserve lands. Today, Nagarhole is a relatively secure reserve, with robust tiger densities of ten to fifteen cats per 100 sq km. A few lesser-known parks have flourished as well. Valmiki in Bihar was a write-off. But it has resurged, and with thirty-odd tigers, Valmiki has earned a place on the world's tiger map. A committed state and management, supported by the non-governmental organization (NGO) Wildlife Trust of India, made all the difference.

No other country has invested so much to recover tiger populations as India. New reserves have been created, growing from Project Tiger's original nine to fifty. The bereft landscapes of Sariska and Panna were repopulated with translocated tigers from other reserves. The process had political backing, and with good leadership, constant monitoring of tigers and strict vigilance, populations in both reserves were rebuilt. The central government earmarked funds for a Special Tiger Protection Force, and while the going has been very slow, a few reserves now have guards specifically trained to take on poachers.

As someone working in conservation, I am frequently asked—or rather, told, 'You must be *happy*, since it's all good with tigers, isn't it? After all, we now have more tigers than before.'

I will refrain to comment on the happiness quotient or its correlation to tiger numbers, and focus instead on addressing the real issue—how secure is the tiger's future? And try to present the real tiger story as it plays on the ground, and in the corridors of power, whose priorities shape the tiger's future.

The problem with 'increasing' numbers is that they breed complacency, taking attention and urgency away from conservation action. They serve as a smokescreen, glossing over the real threats that tigers face, such as spikes in poaching and the shocking decline in tiger habitats. Tiger numbers don't jump overnight, a stable population is the outcome of years of protection.

Lost in the 2,226 euphoria was what was left unsaid. The mood spoiler that was whisked under the red carpet of dignitaries that flooded the room: that the wild tiger is facing its worst crisis ever. That the tiger's domain is shrinking, splintering. The national animal is slowly retreating to small islands, isolated by roads, railroad tracks, canals and power lines; the land carved up by dams that flood entire ecosystems, by massive mining projects that reduce forests to a muddy moonscape, by industry and other development that is rapidly obliterating tiger habitats and the corridors that connect them. Even as Environment Minister Prakash Javadekar made his jubilant announcement that India now had 2,226 tigers, his ministry was orchestrating the destruction of the most pristine, protected, tiger habitats.

The success of relocating tigers to reserves from where they had gone extinct was toasted, but not a word was said about the fact that the same relocated tigers were going to be swallowed up, along with their new home in Panna, by a dam that would link the Ken–Betwa rivers, destructing and bisecting about a quarter of the reserve. Nor was there any discussion on how tiger conservation would be integrated—or not—in plans to expand the network of highways, railway lines and mines that are fragmenting one of the finest tiger habitats in the world: the Central Indian landscape.

There was no reference to the fact that the legal framework that protects the tiger is unravelling, endangering the tiger, all of the country's wildlife and human health as well, as our forests fall, waters are polluted and overused, and air becomes unbreathable.

❧

In another era, tigers roamed vast forests, unfettered by human habitation. But as human population boomed, forests gave way to fields and factories. Livestock edged out ungulates in jungles. The tigers' realm dwindled—today they are confined to only 7 per cent of their original range.

Development activities are turning once-verdant tiger landscapes into fragile islands, with sanctuaries and reserves ringed by mines, highways, canals, reservoirs, resorts, towns and factories. So much so that during his tenure as environment minister, Jairam Ramesh (not known for his tact!) remarked at a private function in October 2010 that the obsession with a double-digit GDP was a bigger threat to the tiger than the poacher. His comment caused an uproar, especially since a staunch GDP proponent, Montek Singh Ahluwalia, then chief of the erstwhile Planning Commission, was among his audience. Ramesh took pains to drive home his point explaining that this ambitious growth target with the consequent demand for more energy—principally coal, as well as infrastructure and industry—is the single biggest threat to the tiger today. Pointing to a photograph of a tigress with four cubs taken in Maharashtra's Tadoba Tiger Reserve, Ramesh said that their future was cloudy, with some forty current and proposed coal mines, and washeries encircling the reserve, threatening to block the tiger's passage to connecting forests.

Tiger reserves are protected by law, and any non-forest activity—from withdrawal of water to expanding a road to laying transmission lines—has to go through an environment regulatory process, which is being framed as 'anti-development'. For example, if a mine is proposed in a tiger landscape, more often than not, headlines in the media say, 'Highway Hits Wildlife *Hurdle*'. Pause here for a moment. *Think*. Tigers and other wild creatures have been reduced to 'hurdles'?

Had things come to such a pass?

India's Prime Minister Narendra Modi strongly and categorically refuted this when he delivered the inaugural address of the 3rd Asia Ministerial Conference on Tiger Conservation in Delhi on 12 April 2016. 'Tiger conservation is not a drag on development,' he stated, stressing 'the need to factor in tiger concerns in sectors where conservation is not the goal'.

His words had tremendous import, signalling support from the highest political office. For the tiger, they spelled *hope*.

Unfortunately, it was nothing more than the usual grandiloquence that politicians dole out routinely. What was happening on the ground is very different—tiger concerns are being brushed aside, even where tiger conservation *is* the goal, within tiger reserves.

A telling example of the dichotomy between feel-good speeches and reality is the aggressive push for and approval of the Ken–Betwa river link, the first of the countrywide river linking scheme. As detailed in an earlier chapter, the project is almost entirely *inside* the pristine forests of Madhya Pradesh's Panna Tiger Reserve, prompting Jairam Ramesh to call it a disastrous idea, and say that it would never get environment clearance from his ministry. Located in the heart of the reserve, it will drown a chunk—58 sq km of the core, and its tigers Panna's plight has at least gained public attention.

Palamu in Jharkhand suffers a similar fate in silence, with plans to revive the Kutku Dam, a project that has lain in abeyance for over thirty-five years. This is one of India's original nine reserves, notified in 1973, and has a rich history. It is here that the first-ever tiger census took place in 1934; I found a mention of the same in Sir John Houlton's account of Bihar, 'the area of forest covered by the census was 115 sq miles and there were 32 tigers'. The author goes on to say that 'the two biggest tigers whose footprints are well-known to forest officers were absent on this occasion'![8] Though numbers have thinned over the years, the habitat is still fairly pristine.

Given a chance, the big cat will recover here. Instead, 120 sq km of the forests could be submerged. When the then environment minister Prakash Javadekar visited in August 2015, his focus was not on tigers or wildlife; he spoke instead of the 'biggest wonder'—the Kutku Dam—which he said had been stopped by 'obstructionist governments by raising non-issues like irrelevant forest laws'.[9] Soon after his visit, a task force was set up to expedite the project, and push for speedy environmental, forest and wildlife clearances for the Kutku Dam.[10]

If dams threaten the future of some reserves, others like Ratapani in Madhya Pradesh are being cleaved by a developing network of roads and railways. National Highway 69, which cuts through the proposed Ratapani Tiger Reserve, was slated for expansion. As part of the standing committee of the National Board for Wildlife (NBWL), I visited the Ratapani Sanctuary in November 2011, accompanied by an officer from the National Tiger Conservation Authority (NTCA), to assess the wildlife impact of this project. We found the ecological costs to be too high. The staff said all manner of wildlife crossed over the road, waiting late into the night for traffic to thin. Some did not make it. Like the sloth bear who failed to escape the speeding ongoing trucks. The 907 sq km of sanctuary has three other highways criss-crossing it—and a railway line that runs parallel to NH69 is also being expanded, creating a nearly insurmountable barrier. We advised against the expansion, instead asking for the current artery to be repaired and strengthened.[11]

Ratapani spills into Madhya Pradesh's capital, Bhopal; and as the sanctuary is further fragmented, it will unsettle its wildlife, including tigers and sloth bears, escalating conflict with local people, which at the present time is minimal.

At the time of our visit, a tigress was bringing up cubs in an area not too far from the road. As cubs grow older they move away from natal areas to claim their own territories. What future did the cubs have with ever-expanding roads—and the assorted dhabas, shops and petrol pumps that inevitably followed—shrinking their forest, limiting their movement?

Not disheartened by the rejection, the proposal is being reconsidered. On a recent visit I drove on NH69 through Ratapani and noticed that work to broaden the highway has begun on both sides of the sanctuary. This is the usual trick when applying for green clearances, when the proposal will be put forth the work would likely be well under way and would have reached the doorstep of the sanctuary. The funds already sunk into a project are a tactic to add pressure for approval.

Reality bites even harder in Assam's Manas Tiger Reserve, one of India's most picturesque reserves and a place with a turbulent past. Manas was racked and ravaged by insurgency in the 1980s and 1990s, decimating wildlife. The park was emptied of its tigers and rhinos. Hundreds of elephants were slaughtered. Even 'department' elephants, employed for patrolling during the heavy monsoons were shot, burnt, killed. An incredibly heroic staff stayed through this traumatic period to protect wildlife, and tragically, a few paid with their lives.

Manas—a World Heritage Site—is now healing. Tigers are making a comeback. The rebuilding and protection of a forest is no small achievement: it has taken a decade, sheer grit, and the collective effort of authorities who partnered with various NGOs. Problems and pressures persist, and the peace is still fragile. We *cannot* be knowingly endangering Manas further.

But we are.

A new road is set to tear through the reserve, running along the India–Bhutan border. Manas straddles both countries. Wildlife doesn't respect political boundaries or international borders. Sitting in the Mathanguri Forest Bungalow, I have seen great hornbills fly across the river Beki to eat the fruit of fig trees in the Royal Manas National Park in Bhutan, while wild buffalos wallowed in the waters below; sometimes here, sometimes there.

Environmental destruction has the same traits: its insidious impacts also know no boundaries. Power projects in Bhutan can potentially devastate Manas—affecting its waterbodies and forests in ways which would render the ecosystems less supportive of wildlife. The existing Kurichhu hydroelectric power station (HEP) (60 MW) and the proposed Mangdechhu HEP (720 MW) power projects are particularly worrying, as both Kurichhu and Mangdechhu are part of a larger river system which sustains the park.[12]

A similar threat is playing out in the Sundarbans, the world's largest, unbroken mangrove forest, which traverses India and Bangladesh. The tiger of this swamp forest is a creature of both land and water—swimming between islands, feeding off fish, lapping up saline water to survive in this tough terrain. And now, this fragile ecosystem may have poison seeping into the soil, lacing its waters, and the aquatic life it sustains—fish, dolphins, turtles, crocodiles, etc. Bangladesh is setting up a 1,320-MW coal-fired thermal power plant on its fringes, in partnership with India's National Thermal Power Corporation. Huge cargoes of dirty coal will ply the Sundarbans. Dust, grime, oil, ash, hazardous wastes containing lead, mercury and more will pour into its pristine waters. The impacts will be dire and far-reaching. The project has stirred huge opposition from displaced farmers and fisherfolk, as well as environmentalists, both locally, and across the globe.

The Sundarbans is a shared heritage between both countries, yet governments have shrugged off the real threat the Rampal plant poses. Bangladesh prime minister, Sheikh Hasina, has dismissed concerns regarding the power plant as 'baseless and fictitious'[13]—despite robust evidence to the contrary. During his June 2015 Bangladesh visit, India's prime minister Narendra Modi also reportedly endorsed the Rampal project, pledging his support and cooperation.[14] Both countries are signatories to the Global Tiger Recovery Plan which has a lofty 'Tx2' goal to double the number of wild tigers by 2022, a commitment that was reiterated in the April 2016 summit inaugurated by the Indian prime minister. Yet the countries are set to jointly embark on a power plant that will endanger the world's largest mangrove forest, and the only one with tigers.

How do you double tiger numbers when you fry and drown their home?

Evidently, *nothing* is sacrosanct.

Core tiger areas are gifted away for the flimsiest reasons, including projects that could easily be accommodated elsewhere rather than destroying old-growth forests. Among them are offices and housing colonies for customs and paramilitary forces in Dudhwa. A particularly spurious example is from Rajaji (Uttarakhand), which is set to hand over nearly 20 hectares of core critical tiger habitat—also inhabited by elephants, leopards and other threatened species—to an influential spiritual group. Why? For a herb garden! The Shri Raghavendra Sewashram Samiti has applied to the NBWL under various pretexts no less than four times since 2002, and has been rejected each time.[15]

It was on the agenda twice during my tenure as a member of the NBWL standing committee. In April 2011, the project proponents did not bother specifying the reason for wanting the land; nor was there information on the number of trees to be cut, or a map delineating the area required. What was mentioned though was the presence of tigers, elephants and leopards in the area. At the time, the proposal was not even admitted for hearing, with the chairperson, Jairam Ramesh, categorically stating that 'proposals which had earlier been rejected by the Standing Committee should not be included in the agenda'.[16] But it was back on the table a year later in June 2012, this time ostensibly wanting to build a hospital in the national park. It was rejected, but the ashram/hospital/herbal garden appears to have finally gotten its way. A site visit report by representatives of the NTCA, the state forest department and Wildlife Institute of India (WII) said that 'the proposal would benefit wildlife conservation'. This is justified as the park would get land in lieu of the loss.[17] So, we will be giving away prime tiger and elephant habitat with no less than 10,000 trees to 'gain' a piece of barren land along Rajaji's southern boundary.[18] Are national parks so expendable?

While tiger reserves are becoming increasingly moth-eaten, the corridors that serve as crucial linkages between these reserves are even more vulnerable. Tigers are wide-ranging animals with an urge to roam, seeking territory, food and mates. They are also great travellers, covering vast distances. A genetic study[19] in the Central Indian landscape established that a tiger can disperse over 650 km, navigating a landscape of forests and countryside with areas of dense human populations. A tiger found hiding in a betel nut plantation in Karnataka's Shimoga district in May 2011 was identified as a former resident of Bandipur Tiger Reserve; it had travelled about 300 km.

Along these journeys, tigers hazard anything from towns to highways and canals to mines. They would have walked fast, increasing their stride even three times as compared to a confident stroll in an unpeopled forest. They would have hidden during daylight, trekking at night, preferring the cover of darkness to avoid confrontation with people and traffic.

Even so, some meet horrific deaths—like the tiger in Bijnore in Uttar Pradesh that was clubbed to death by a mob when he entered a hen coop and killed a chicken or two. Another victim was 'Broken Tail,' the star of a BBC film who took off from his natal Ranthambhore Tiger Reserve only to be crushed by a superfast train in Rajasthan's durra forests, about 150 km away.

But travel they must. It's a question of survival. Genetic exchange and vigour is critical for all species, including *Panthera tigris*. A population of about eighty to a hundred tigers in an inviolate space of 800 to 1,000 sq km is essential to ensure their safe future. However, only four of India's tiger reserves—plus the contiguous Mudumalai–Nagarhole–Bandipur tiger reserves—are capable of sustaining such genetically viable, breeding tiger populations on their own.[20]

The rest are small, containing few tigers. If isolated, small populations suffer 'inbreeding depression' and are prone to local extinction. These reserves need to be linked, allowing tigers passage, an opportunity to disperse, establish and reproduce. Corridors help recolonize habitats where tigers have become locally extinct and rescue declining local populations from extinction through migration.

This can be better understood by what happened at Rajaji National Park. Rajaji is the northwestern tip of the tigers' range. It's an extremely fragile park, with low tiger numbers due to immense anthropogenic pressures and being fragmented with highways and railway lines. Poaching has also taken a heavy toll on tigers. In 2002–3, settlements in Chilla range were removed, and the gujjars[21] voluntarily relocated outside the park. With the removal of human habitation and livestock, an inviolate, undisturbed area was created allowing wild prey—cheetal and sambar deer—to return. Tigers followed suit, and within a few years, fourteen individual tigers were captured on camera. Corbett, which has one of the highest tiger densities globally, lies to Rajaji's east and is linked through the forests of Kotri and Lansdowne, allowing tigers passage. As soon as Rajaji's habitat was restored, tigers looking for suitable territory, moved in . . . and the park flourished.

Corridors do not have to be pristine parkland but could in fact include agricultural areas, orchards, coffee or tea plantations, and other multi-use landscapes—just as long as they are 'tiger permeable,' and can be traversed in relative safety. Yet, corridors are increasingly turning into stretches which tigers cannot navigate. Rajesh Gopal, who served as the chief of India's NTCA for over a decade, said if the corridors collapse, the numbers will not matter. 'Tigers will find it hard to survive.'[22]

Nonetheless, tiger concerns are not factored into development activities in these vital genetic linkages.

Nothing explains this better than the expansion of NH7 through the corridor connecting Kanha and Pench tiger reserves, which together are home to over 200 tigers. The highway will split the 16,000-sq km Kanha–Pench landscape, and also splinter the larger Central Indian landscape, identified as one of four regions in India where tigers are expected to persist in the long term. But only if the links remain, otherwise tigers will not survive into the future. Not a single tiger population in the Central Indian landscape is viable in the long run by itself.[23]

All concerned agencies, including the NTCA, the Supreme Court's Central Empowered Committee and a number of experts including from the WII, advised against the expansion of the highway. The consensus was that the project would irreversibly damage the tiger habitat and should not be implemented under any circumstances. No amount of safeguards would restore the present status, and the alternate route (some 70–80 km longer) would save this priceless habitat. However, both the NTCA and WII seem to have capitulated under sustained pressure, and ultimately yielded to expanding NH7 at the cost of one of the country's most vital tiger corridors. Even the mitigation measures they advised were brushed aside, citing shortage of money. As then environment minister Prakash Javadekar explained, 'We will try and conserve, but we cannot allow something crazy [in the name of conservation]. We are a poor country and must be practical.'[24] It was this same minister who had repeatedly avowed the mantra 'development without destruction'.

The mitigation measures finally agreed to were done on the basis of a rapid fifteen-day survey and were not backed by robust science. They were whittled down to under 40 per cent of what had been originally advised, from a series of flyovers at sensitive crossings allowing ample room for animals to cross, to miniscule underpasses which may allow a jackal to sidle through, but could scarcely accommodate a tiger, or herds of gaur, a solid one-ton animal. These underpasses could serve as easy snares for poachers, and also flood during monsoons, rendering them ineffective.

'NH 7 is splintering one of the most important corridors in one of the finest tiger landscapes of the world. If we cannot save the best . . . what hope is there for the rest,' questions Milind

Pariwakam, a wildlife biologist who is at the forefront of a legal battle to protect the Kanha–Pench landscape.

The loss of these vital linkages spells doom for the tiger, as does an increasingly dismissive attitude towards tiger conservation, along with the erosion of authority and independence of wildlife institutions.

Even the country's Supreme Court, a long-time champion of green causes, undermined tigers, pitching our national animal against 'development'. Hearing a case challenging the NH7 expansion, the Supreme Court on 20 January 2015, said that 'conservation of tigers was important but could not be at the cost of general economic development of the country'.[25]

The real tragedy: there was an alternate route for NH7, but we chose not to take it.

Even to save tigers.

The local extinction of tigers in Panna and Sariska is well-documented, but there are other landscapes from where the tiger has vanished, unheeded.

Satkosia Tiger Reserve lies some 100 km northwest of Odisha's capital, Bhubaneswar. Satkosia was a historic stronghold for tigers, and was also renowned for its robust tuskers. I first visited in 2007, just a few months before it—along with the adjoining Baisipalli Sanctuary—was notified as a tiger reserve. It was on the decline with a low tiger density even then; still, I saw pug marks of a tigress, followed by tinier prints. Cubs! I also encountered a few herds of cheetal, sambar, wild boar and elephants. The reserve gave good vibes: the leadership was strong, staff was buoyant and vigilant.

I visited next in 2010, and the difference was stark. Satkosia was sinking. The mood was listless, protection was perceptibly weaker—and the tigers? Not one pug mark, no scat, no scrape, no clue. Even signs of prey were scant, and it was only on our way out that we spotted a few cheetal.

By 2013, all that was left in Satkosia was a tiger or two.

Satkosia's story has another sad twist. Around the same time (2012–2013), a young male tiger was found wandering in the vicinity of Bhubaneswar. He had likely made his way here from Satkosia through the Narsinghpur–Athgarh forests and crossed vast agricultural landscapes and the river Mahanadi before entering Chandaka Sanctuary and reaching the city. Wisdom lay in translocating the tiger to Satkosia, with such low numbers, it could have contributed to repopulating the reserve. But the then reserve director requested 'to release the tigers elsewhere', citing a number of lame reasons for shrugging off responsibility that having a tiger in a landscape brings. A tiger in a forest calls for increasing protection, monitoring and greater accountability.

So, rather than seize the opportunity to rebuild Satkosia, the state government opted to pack the tiger off to a zoo—'to increase the genetic vigour'—of *caged* tigers!

One suspects there was another game at play: Did the state want to write off Satkosia Tiger Reserve?

Satkosia is being cut up. A proposal on the table would denotify some 160 sq km of the heart of the reserve breaking it into two desolate pieces. The Brutanga irrigation project is expected to come up on its southern fringes, effectively blocking a critical tiger and elephant passage—over 100 elephants use it in the dry summer months to migrate to lush forests in the south. A barrage has already obstructed wildlife passage to the north, reducing Satkosia to slivers of disjointed forests.

A wise man said that if you cut up a fine Persian carpet, its value is torn to shreds as well. It's the same with a forest.

Northwest of Satkosia, in Jharkhand, lies Saranda—'the forest of seven hundred hills'—and the finest, largest sal wood forest in the world. Saranda has been a training school for generations of foresters for over a century. It is a prime elephant habitat, and once harboured both (Asiatic) cheetahs and tigers. The cheetah vanished well over a century ago, while the tiger slipped away unnoticed in the past decade or two except for an occasional transient one. Villagers sometimes complain of cattle kills, rangers report pug marks and there is the odd sighting. But the tiger's presence is shrouded in apprehension, lest it be inimical to the mining industry. Saranda is one of India's largest reservoirs of iron ore, and mining is ongoing. The state has signed contracts with a number of mining giants, and large swathes of forests are slated for destruction. Acknowledging a tiger's presence could put such plans in disarray.

Jharkhand is not the only state which failed to acknowledge the national animal. India's famous coastal paradise, Goa, refused to admit to tiger presence, again because it would endanger mining interests, even though the forest department itself had counted five tigers.[26] But the state maintained that its tigers were not residents but transients who visit Goa, not unlike its many tourists!

It is not just the eroding of forests that kills the tiger, it is *apathy*. If we refuse to even acknowledge the tiger's presence, how will we protect it?

The other dark threat shadowing the cat's future is poaching of tigers for their skin and bones, eyeballs and penises—and just about every other body part. This relentless demand for tiger derivatives from the brutal black markets of (mainly) China has ensured that tigers are not safe in India or anywhere across its range.

India is extremely vulnerable, simply because of higher densities and easy visibility of tigers. In 2016, tiger poaching in India surged to its highest levels in fifteen years, with fifty confirmed cases.[27] Actual numbers could be much higher, even ten times of recorded seizures.

Tigers are not secure, even in the finest of our reserves. On the night of 13 March 2016, five tiger skins plus 125 kg of bones were seized by the Uttarakhand Police's Special Task Force in Haridwar district bordering Uttar Pradesh. The poachers confessed to killing the tigers in Corbett[28] and subsequently burying the skins in Kot Kadar in Bijnore district which abuts the park's southern boundary. Scientists at the WII matched four of the skins to tigers captured in camera traps in Corbett's core area.[29]

About two weeks later, in Madhya Pradesh's Pench Tiger Reserve, a poisoned waterhole killed, 'Baghin Nala' (Tigress of the Streams), a favourite of the tourists, and her young cubs. The next week, a poacher was arrested in the same reserve with four tiger paws. The tiger's mutilated body was found buried two days later.

These poached tigers feed into a global illegal wildlife trade. The United Nations Environment Programme estimates the global illegal wildlife to be worth US$50–150 billion per year.[30] Along with loss of habitat, poaching is a key cause for population collapse and extinctions, of not just tigers but most wildlife species from pangolins to otters to elephants. Powerful, vicious international cartels control this organized crime. Illegal wildlife trafficking is linked to other illicit activities, including the drug and arms trade, and connections to global terrorism have been well established. So much so that in November 2012, then United States secretary of state Hillary Clinton noted that illegal wildlife trade is 'more dangerous than ever before'[31] and called it a 'national and an economic security issue'.[32] This was important, as the US is the second-largest destination market for illegally trafficked wildlife in the world.

With its wealth of biodiversity, India is the 'source' of illegally traded wildlife products. The agency to tackle the trade in India, the Wildlife Crime Control Bureau, is woefully undermanned and underpowered. Our frontline defence is equally unequipped and most reserves suffer from acute staff shortages—about 30 per cent—often leaving reserves and their wild creatures defenceless. In some cases, they are almost unmanned, like Palamu in Jharkhand, which has an astounding 97 per cent staff shortage.

Yet, wildlife crime can be controlled to some extent, perhaps even minimized. Determined, committed, united governments *can* step up protection on the ground—and control the demand of tiger parts and products. Controlling such a crime is an enormous task, but if governments resolve, they can challenge the threat head on. It has been done. When poaching imperilled the Asiatic lion in 2007, then Gujarat chief minister Narendra Modi moved the state's machinery to resolve the problem. The investigation was entrusted to the Crime Investigation Department, outside expertise was brought on board and all resources and support were made available, ultimately leading to the timely conviction of all thirty-nine accused[33]—unprecedented in a country where only 1 per cent of wildlife crime cases lead to convictions.

That's the character of this threat: the accused or the 'enemy' here is obvious: the poacher, the trader, the seller, the consumer—entities we can paint in black. But what can we do if governments sell out their tigers cheap by failing to hold reserves sacred, sacrificing their habitat, and diluting laws and policy that protect them?

It is not just about governments: are we willing to quell the enemy within? It is we as a society that has chosen to prioritize 'development', unmindful of the consequences, indifferent to its cost to the environment, to other species with whom we share Planet Earth—and to our own health and survival. Where will we draw the line? Will we mine the last forest in our endless quest for coal and diamonds? Squeeze the last drop out of rivers to quench our thirst for water? Will we question the arrogance with which we live, assuming our overwhelming, sole right over *all* natural resources, unmindful of the catastrophic consequences on other lives on the planet. And on us?

Will India have space for tigers amongst its 1.3 billion people, with a rapidly growing population, the pressing needs for their survival, and their rising aspirations and ambitions?

To Save a Tiger

Future generations would be truly saddened that this century had so little foresight, so little compassion, such lack of generosity of spirit for the future that it would eliminate one of the most dramatic and beautiful animals that this world has ever seen.

—George B. Schaller

In her lifetime, she had an award[1] bestowed on her, and her face graced a stamp. When she breathed her last on 18 August 2016, she was given a ritual bath, draped in white, a red tika marked her forehead and her face adorned with petals of rose. Uniformed pall-bearers escorted her on her last journey, and as she was placed on the pyre, a stream of people laid wreathes on her lifeless body, heads bowed, hands folded in respect. The pyre was lit, and as the flames engulfed her, the soldiers of the forest raised their hands in a final salaam for their ward . . . a tigress the world knew as Machali.

Not all tigers carry a name, nor do their deaths cause paroxysms of grief. Machali, however, was an icon among icons, and earned her fame as the most photographed resident in, arguably, the most visited of the country's tiger reserves—Ranthambhore. Few, if any, tigers have been granted a state-sponsored ceremonial farewell. After all, Machali did nothing more—and nothing less—than what a tiger mom does: Raise a healthy brood of cubs that contributed to the reserve's population. Defend her turf, and her young, including a fierce face-off with another powerful predator, a crocodile—which was captured on camera and contributed to her legend.

There are naysayers to this ceremonial episode, of devotion to tigers that is personality driven, a concentration of highly strung emotions on one tiger, while it is the conservation of the *species* that demands urgent attention. I have my reservations as well, and my doubts on presenting this as an exemplar of the support that the tiger commands; yet it must be admitted, even by the most cynical, that the powerful head hoisted on khaki shoulders is a potent statement of the extraordinary status of the tiger in India.

It is revered as the vehicle of the Goddess Durga, considered the harbinger of fertility in tribal cultures, protected as our national animal, is a cynosure for tourists and a star among our galaxy of diverse, magnificent wildlife. Unlike most other creatures on the brink, this big cat has a constituency that cares. When Project Tiger was first mooted, saving the big cat became a global goal. The World Wildlife Fund (WWF) launched a drive to support the project, and funds poured in, including from little children who donated their piggy-bank money! Forty years later in 2006 when the horror of 'only 1,411 tigers' became part of sustained media campaigns, it stirred a nation, and forced governments into action.

It is this veneration and support that has to be harnessed, to become a force for tigers, to ensure that conserving the national animal *remains* a national priority.

I am cautious in giving the Machali example for another reason: Is the Machali fan following—often fuelled by social media—far removed from the reality on the ground of people who live in close proximity with tigers? I cannot be the judge, though it must be said that saving the tiger is not a fad, or an elitist cause, as it is often dismissed. The ecosystem services that the tiger forests bestow—birthing and nourishing rivers, conserving soil, and sequestering carbon—are equally vital to all of us regardless of geography, or artificial distinctions of income and class.

Still, India has many parallel worlds. What is a cause *célèbre* for many can be a source of despair for others. Not very far from where Machali was laid to rest, in Kailadevi, part of the same Ranthambhore Reserve, two subadult tigers were poisoned. The 'Chiroli Cubs' had recently left their natal area in Chiroli range, and were finding their feet in new territory. They were young, inexperienced, yet to master the art of the hunt. They killed two goats, an easier kill than nimble wild prey. Distressed, the villagers retaliated. They scared the cubs off their meal, injecting it with a mammoth dose of an easily available, cheap pesticide. The tigers stayed away for a day, then hunger drove them back to the goats, which they consumed, and died.

For the villagers, who are dependent on their livestock to survive, the value of the two goats (about 50–100 USD) is far greater than two live tigers.[2]

That's the reality of tigers in India (indeed across its range).

Most of our Protected Areas are ringed by dense human habitations—a population which is dependent on these forests to meet their needs for fuelwood, fodder, etc., and are exerting immense pressure on the forest. For instance, the 800-odd sq km of Sariska Tiger Reserve, has over two lakh cattle within it, and the villages in its immediate surrounds.

It is within this complex framework of people, their needs, aspirations, and the pressing demands of a fast-growing economy that a path must be carved for the tiger's secure future—a future which ensures inviolate, undisturbed core areas for tigers like Machali where the big cat can breed and flourish. Barely 2 per cent of India's land is reserved for the tiger, and at least in these places, the tiger must be the only stakeholder. Not mines, not dams, not roads, not people. The law ordains that these core critical habitats be sacrosanct, its tigers zealously safeguarded. The law should be followed in letter and spirit, rather than exploiting its gaping loopholes and circumventing it to allow new projects or expansion of existing infrastructure, as is being witnessed today.

But the heart—the core habitats—cannot exist in isolation: a network of arteries—corridors—must knit them together, allowing tigers to travel and mingle, keeping the populations genetically strong and viable. The arteries must be secured too, or else the heart will cease, taking all life with it.

Crucial tiger corridors add up to 19,400 sq km of land, as per Rajesh Gopal, the former head of the National Tiger Conservation Authority (NTCA).[3] At least here, land use must be regulated so that it allows tiger safe passage.

The third imperative is to recognize the gravity of wildlife crime, to treat it as a national security issue rather than a sundry offence involving the mere murder of an animal. To tackle this crime, the Wildlife Crime Control Bureau has to be empowered, and we need on the frontlines, a strong, motivated, well-equipped force to take on a vicious enemy that profits from killing tigers.

The good news is that India has already traversed this path. It has saved tigers once, pulled them back from the brink. The rest of the world looks upon India for its leadership in tiger conservation, but we are faltering, increasingly lacking the strong political will and public pressure essential for their continued survival. Unless governments prioritize conservation, tigers cannot be saved.

We cannot waver. With more than half the world's wild tigers, we hold the big cat in trust for the rest of the world.

*

For many years, the montane evergreen forests—sholas—of Kudremukh National Park were tarnished with a deep red scar. A gigantic iron ore mine operated in the forest, hollowing a mountain that once harboured munjtac, sambar, gaur, tiger . . . and one of the rarest primates in the world, the lion-tailed macaque. A town housed the mining staff, roads cut through the pristine grassland to move men and machinery, blasts ripped the mountains. And this was a *national park*, the most protected of all Protected Areas.

It took the advocacy group Wildlife First, guided by renowned wildlife scientist Ullas Karanth, a six-year legal crusade to get a Supreme Court order to shut down the operations of the mining giant, Kudremukh Iron Ore Company. The battle was fought by a team of passionate conservationists that included D.V. Girish a local planter, Praveen Bhargav an advertising executive with a passion for law, Shekar Dattatri a wildlife film-maker and Niren Jain a budding architect. They all paid a heavy price—they were defamed, intimidated and harassed through multiple cases of criminal trespass, all dismissed, after a trying eight years, by courts as being of mala fide intent. They didn't just save a national park with the national animal; they saved the river Bhadra which carried the mine's silt and dust, ruining the fields and drinking water of the people downstream.[4]

Further east in Chikmagalur district lies the Bhadra Tiger Reserve, which might not have remained as pristine without its most fierce protector, D.V. Girish, a coffee planter and Wildlife Conservation Society (WCS) conservation partner, who has rallied together a band of local people—farmers, students, accountants, journalists—all united by a common cause to protect the forest in their backyard. They have through the years stopped three dams, illegal mines, mega tourism complexes, mini-hydel plants and wind farms, within and in the immediate vicinity of Bhadra.

Many of the people I list above are not biologists or conservationists by vocation, most are professionally employed in different streams, but have brought to the table their skills and commitment and have waged long battles to save forests.

Each of us can make a difference—if we choose to act.

On a visit to Valmiki Tiger Reserve, I noticed that the Valmiki Nagar–Bagha State Highway that cuts through the reserve was being widened to twice its breadth. The work was almost complete, though the project had not even sought mandatory approval from the National Board for Wildlife (NBWL). I wrote a complaint to the NTCA, on the basis of which a colleague made an application to the Supreme Court's Central Empowered Committee (CEC).[5] The work was halted.

In Maharashtra, Tadoba Tiger Reserve set an example by closing down its official rest house as well as canteen in the reserve's core area because of the disturbance it caused and the trash it generated. The tiger also gained ground in Pench—in the same state—when a sizeable colony of the irrigation department inside the reserve was vacated. Such struggles would try the patience of a saint: the order to vacate the illegal colony was passed in 2002, but it was only after a writ petition was filed in court by the non-governmental organization (NGO), Nature Conservation Society, Amravati, that things finally got moving in 2015 and the bulk of the colony was handed back to the tiger reserve. This could serve as an example for Corbett, where the Kalagarh irrigation township—with residences, colleges, engineering academies—continues to squat within core tiger habitat for the past three decades, even *after* the Supreme Court ordered the encroached land to be returned to the reserve.

The most vital of these initiatives is voluntary relocation of people from core critical tiger habitats, which the 2014 Wildlife Institute of India (WII)-NTCA report[6] cited as a primary driver for the rise in tiger populations. But relocation is understandably sensitive, fraught with tension—people moving away for *tigers*? Rooted in past experience of coercive displacements, social advocacy groups propagate it as a scenario where wildlife takes precedence over the right, of communities and indigenous people. It is argued that forest-dwelling people and tigers can coexist in harmony, as they have for eons. Another school of thought believes that the interest of people and tigers is always inimical, and that the tiger and its habitat can only be conserved at the cost of the people. But my years of experience in the field tell a different story, and present a unique win–win solution for both people . . . and tigers.

Faith can be found in the most unlikely of places.

I found mine in an empty cowshed in a tiny village called New Dhain which lies near Madhya Pradesh's Satpura Tiger Reserve. A man named Budhman Mangal had plans for a buffalo or two to occupy that cowshed, and was convincing the accompanying forest officer to help him realize the dream. Both put their heads together, discussed the loan process and a time was set for a visit to the bank. Budhman is one of the most successful farmers around these parts; rotating three crops a year and harvesting a startling variety of fruits, vegetables, millets, grains and legumes. His venture into agroforestry, growing eucalyptus trees, had recently yielded his first bumper crop. He has mastered a high-yield technique to make manure, and was exploring new markets for his premium organic produce. The buffaloes would be a foray into the dairy business. 'It will help pay for their college,' he said, smiling at his two little boys who were zipping dizzily around us, unaware of their father's dreams and plans for their futures.

Nothing out of the ordinary, weaving ambitions around children, investing in their future. *Future,* though, was not in Budhman's vocabulary in his previous life in Old Dhain, a village that was located in the heart of Satpura Tiger Reserve—until he and the town's other residents moved.

In 2004 the residents of Old Dhain decided to accept the government's voluntary relocation proposal that provided a compensation package for villagers to move out of core areas of tiger reserves—leaving their past behind, creating a new life for themselves—and leaving undisturbed, inviolate spaces for tigers to flourish.

Budhman prefers not to dwell on the past. His mother died in childbirth, which was not an uncommon occurrence when the nearest medical help was over 30 km away. There were no roads connecting Old Dhain to the world outside, only muddy paths. During monsoon the river raged and streams swelled with water, cutting the village off for months. When rations ran out, the villagers dug for roots and ground mango kernels to stave off starvation. While the village had a school, there was only a very occasional teacher to instruct the children. They lost half of their crops to wild pigs, gaur and cheetal, and predators preyed on their cattle. There were only two sources of livelihood: working as labour for the forest department or selling minor forest produce such as *amla* (gooseberry), *aritha* (an ingredient in shampoo), *tendu patta* (used for bidi, a type of cheap cigarette made of unprocessed tobacco wrapped in leaves)—even though collecting forest produce from a national park is illegal.

This was the thread of conversation as we made our way through the 'new' villages, whose residents had all been relocated from within the reserve over the past twelve years. At 'new' Ratibundar—shifted only the previous year—people gathered, cups of chai were passed around and freshly roasted corn on the cob was served. Discussions ensued. Voices rose, each straining to be heard as they told stories of their previous life, citing the reasons they had moved.

Walking the forest had its own dangers—they weren't so worried about tigers, or leopards; but the sloth bear could be *so* ill-tempered. Bimla Kumari's father-in-law had accidentally bumped into one with a cub, and was brutally injured. The forest ranger rushed him to the hospital, but it was too late. An old woman grumbled that they couldn't get their sons married: Who would, knowingly, push their daughter deep into a jungle? *She* gave her daughters outside! Phoolwati grabbed my hand and marched me to her home to show me her neon green paddy field, just beyond her *doorstep*. I could not grasp the import, or the excitement shining in her eyes, till I realized that in her village, Old Ratibundar, their 'fields' were 12 km away! The entire village would decamp till the crop was harvested, living in makeshift shelters to protect them from being ravaged by wild animals.

Meanwhile, the spaces they left behind have been occupied by tigers. I visited Old Dhain, where I spied pug marks in the sand. In

Old Churna, the watchers at the chowki excitedly spoke about the exploits of the resident tigress and her three young cubs. Camera traps show four different tigers have occupied Old Pattan which shifted out in 2014. It only had occasional feline visitors before. A mating pair was being spotted by one of the forest guards on patrol.

In Satpura, thirty-two villages in all have been relocated since 2004. Satpura is part of the Central Indian highlands, a largely hilly terrain of rugged ridges that plunge into gorges, ravines and valleys. Most of these grassy valleys were occupied by villages, with the related disturbance suppressing tiger populations; with villagers gone, the tigers are returning.

Remarkable tiger recovery after voluntary relocation has been documented in other reserves across the country. Within five years of the Gujjars, a pastoral tribe, moving from Chilla in Rajaji National Park (Uttarakhand) in 2002–2003, tiger densities doubled from three per 100 sq km to seven.[7] In Bhadra (Karnataka), WCS scientists have observed a doubling of prey numbers in a decade after the village relocations, and an increasing trend in tiger numbers.

In India, village resettlements to promote conservation date back to the 1970s, when the government relocated people to reduce pressures off wildlife. Some of these relocations remain controversial, some perceived to have been forced and having disadvantaged the people. A basic tenant is relocation cannot, must not, be forced, but be *voluntary*.

While one can understand and appreciate the concerns surrounding relocation, those who believe that tigers and people can live together in harmony have little notion of the harsh reality of people marooned in remote forests. Both suffer when they live in close proximity. There is no such 'harmony' when tigers kill cattle, and are clubbed to death or poisoned for their 'crime'. Villagers in Satkosia Tiger Reserve have given up agriculture, as most of it was lost to wild pigs, ungulates and elephants. I visited Raigoda village in the reserve's most verdant valley, where villagers told me that they spent entire nights atop machans, hollering and beating utensils to drive off wildlife, but they still lost about half their produce. They have been petitioning to be relocated for over a decade, but have met with empty assurances. Taking note of their plight, the National Human Rights Commission took the Odisha state and the NTCA to task, asking it to rehabilitate Raigoda and four other villages to ensure the basic human rights of the villagers.[8]

As much as it is a grave injustice to forcibly evict people from their ancestral homes, it is self-serving, if not callous, to condemn them to live in a state of perennial indigence—if they wish to go. Most nurse the same aspirations as any of us: good education for their children, connectivity, employment opportunities, medical care and entertainment. But such social services and economic development opportunities do not exist in the heart of Protected Areas; if we 'develop' these areas, allowing industry and infrastructure, the forests will be lost to the people who depend on them, and for wildlife.

Many such moves are now driven by communities who have petitioned courts and governments asking for speedy relocation. These people want to be part of the mainstream, and it is up to us— governments, organizations and civil society—to ensure that they are given the opportunity to exercise their choice in a fair, sensitive manner, giving them the best possible facilities and advantages to ease the difficult transition.

Voluntary relocation offers an incredible opportunity to revive wildlife by arresting habitat fragmentation in reserves through proactive, fairly compensated and voluntary resettlements. Equally, it is an opportunity for human welfare. The central government enhanced its relocation package in 2005, and while this did add momentum, the funds made available are woefully insufficient to meet the urgent demands coming in from villages marooned within reserves.

A few state governments have stepped up: Maharashtra and Madhya Pradesh have allocated state funds to relocate villages from a number of reserves and sanctuaries. They viewed the move as *pro-*

people, not only pro-wildlife, and thus gained political mileage. In Kerala, it was the state's chief minister who approached the Union environment minister to garner funds for relocation from Wayanad Sanctuary. The local political representative from Melghat Tiger Reserve in Maharashtra, Kewalram Kale, urged the ministry responsible for tribal welfare to allocate funds urgently for relocation of tribal people from within the reserve so that the 'children (of villagers inside Melghat) are not condemned to perpetual hardship, and can have a bright future'.

There are currently 578 villages within core critical tiger habitats. People living in forests outside of Protected Areas are also keen to relocate. Lacunae of funds should not be the limiting factor for a move that helps us achieve the twin goals of human welfare and wildlife protection. Funds should be made available not just from Project Tiger, but from other flush ministries including those governing tribal welfare and rural development. These, and other concerned departments, can also strengthen the effort by providing health, education, vocational training, irrigation and other such facilities in relocation sites. Forest departments currently coordinate with such departments to facilitate these services for people in relocated villages, but this should be made institutional.

Another niggling concern is that the government seems to have written off some reserves, a few due to problems of insurgency, others through sheer indifference. Tiger populations are far below their optimum density in Satkosia (Odisha), Palamu (Jharkhand) and Achanakmar (Chhattisgarh), a situation that can be turned around, *if* there is the will to do so.

Nagarjunasagar–Srisailam Tiger Reserve (NSTR) that spans Andhra Pradesh and Telangana has shown the way. In earlier times, this forest was flush with wildlife, prompting India's legendary 'birdman' Sálim Ali to write of his visit here in 1931, 'It stands out vividly in memory for its wealth of wild animals, including a greater number of tigers than I had ever experienced before. I recall the thrill of seeing the forest roads covered with the fresh pug marks of tiger, panther, bear and other wildlife.'[9]

Over the years, NSTR's fortunes dwindled, and by 1990, the reserve fell in the grip of left-wing extremism. It was under siege for the next sixteen years, and was written off as a 'sanctuary for naxalites'.

The lawlessness that prevailed saw the massive destruction of protection infrastructure, and also the tragic killing of forest staff. There was large-scale timber smuggling, encroachment, intrusion of cattle, illegal hunting. With the loss of their natural prey base, tigers took to killing livestock, and many were poisoned in retaliation.

After a state-led operation that saw the end of insurgency, the process of recovery began. Today, a network of anti-poaching camps polka dot the reserve, providing protection 24x7. The tiger's prey is recovering. To my utter delight, I now get camera-trapped pictures of tigresses followed by cubs from there. In 2011, I visited NSTR with pioneer conservationist George Schaller, who noted that, 'Wildlife is there in fine variety, especially large predators of whose signs we saw. The local staff were knowledgeable and dedicated to their task. The fact that the area has been rehabilitated after years of turmoil indicates this.'

The NSTR has come full circle. It has shown that even the most hopeless places can become safe havens. So what is stopping India from pulling neglected reserves from the brink?

Animals don't know the concept of boundaries . . . the tiger that wanders over from Uttarakhand's Corbett Tiger Reserve, squeezing past the almost insurmountable wall of resorts that border it, towards the river Kosi and into the Ramnagar Forest Division, has little knowledge that the land beneath its feet has lost its benign protective cover, that it is now a little poorer, more vulnerable. The Ramnagar forest is categorized as a reserve, 'multiple-use' forest and is not a designated Protected Area, even though it has an incredible diversity of birds at over 500 species and a tiger density far greater than many tiger reserves at 14 per 100 sq km.

Paramjit Singh, a forest officer in Uttarakhand a long champion of such big cats calls them 'Below Poverty Line—BPL tigers'! And so they are—the 'lesser tigers', deprived of the funding, or special staff attuned to wildlife protection that is provided for big cats within reserves. What is also referred to here is the poverty of initiative and will on the part of the government to protect wildlife outside of PAs. Individual officers like him have brought in much-needed wildlife orientation into such areas—stepping up protection, monitoring tigers, reviving degraded meadows; but what is required is a policy that is sensitive to the needs of tigers who must negotiate forests and human-dense landscapes outside the boundaries of protected reserves.

This is critical as no less than a third of India's wild tigers live outside PAs. A reserve forest like Ramnagar has minimal protection as land use can be easily changed by governments for development purposes.

Such tiger habitats outside of Protected Areas need to be secured. One way forward is to carve out forests with high tiger density, and no human habitations, and bring them under protective cover, as was done in the case of Nandhaur Valley in Uttarakhand, which I was personally involved with.

❦

While I am certainly prejudiced, it is no exaggeration to describe Nandhaur as the most beautiful of valleys. Its wilderness—700 sq km of verdant forest nestled between the rivers Gola and Sharda, with no human habitation and a galaxy of wildlife that includes elephants, sloth bears, Himalayan black bears, hyenas, serows, pangolins, sambar deer, and tigers! A WWF-India's camera trap survey had captured eight individual tigers here, and there was 'tremendous potential for rebound and a greater density of tigers, given adequate protection', believed Amit Verma, who was the Divisional Forest Officer at the time, and single-minded in his determination to secure Nandhaur. The valley is also a critical link in the Terai Arc landscape, a 810-km arc stretching from the Kalesar Wildlife Sanctuary in Haryana to Valmiki National Park in Bihar. This network of Protected Areas, though fragmented in many places, and amid dense human population, is one of the most important tiger and Asiatic elephant habitats in the world.

I visited Nandhaur Wildlife Sanctuary soon after its creation in November 2012. I had walked only a few yards from our base—the Chorgalia Forest Rest House that sits on the edge of the Nandhaur Valley—when I spotted pug marks. They were large, squarish, not tapering but broad towards the end—possibly a male tiger? They were fresh prints . . . the dust was yet to settle, a tiger had walked this path just minutes before.

Pug marks are my messengers of hope, conveying the tiger's presence. The elation that I feel when I see a tiger's footprints is unparalleled. Seeing them here, though, meant so much more. As I bent down to see, feel and revel in the signs of a tiger, I felt a rush of intense emotion: elation, gratitude and peace; as though the great cat had walked down that path towards us, to convey a word of thanks for securing its forest home.

There was more good news to follow. After dragging its feet for a decade, the neighbouring state of Uttar Pradesh created Pilibhit Tiger Reserve. Nandhaur, the reserve forests of Surai and Pilibhit form a solid 2,000 sq km of tiger–elephant landscape which further extends to Shuklaphanta Wildlife Reserve in Nepal. Buoyed by the potential of the area, Uttarakhand is now working on strengthening protection in Surai, and last heard, declaring Nandhaur a tiger reserve is on the agenda.

I believe that the creation of a Protected Area is one of the biggest contributions to conservation. It takes extraordinary vision and commitment on the part of governments to set aside land for wildlife in a land scarce, populated country like ours, and for this I thank them. While one is well aware of the dire need to protect forests for the tangible and intangible ecosystem services they provide, the immediate costs are high, demanding sacrifice of land that could be put to immediate, alternate use say, for industry or infrastructure.

Not surprisingly, it is getting increasingly difficult to acquire more area under protective cover, and it's exciting to see that in recent years, private conservancies and reserves have begun to come up across India. Such private initiatives cannot match or replace sanctuaries protected by governments but offer a great opportunity to supplement and buffer protected forests.

One such remarkable initiative is by Poonam and Harshawardhan Dhanwatey, Tadoba Andhari Tiger Reserve's dedicated defenders, who turned degraded farmland into a forest that partially supports tigers, leopards, dholes, wild dogs, bears, wild boar, etc. This seven-acre plot of land in the village Ghosri sits on a chicken neck connecting two parts of the reserve, and is therefore a vulnerable patch for passing animals. The Dhanwateys bought the land in 2001 and set about securing it for wildlife. They employed a local man to keep a watchful eye on the land, and keep off the cattle. Stopping the grazing and lopping saw the emergence of native trees and grasses, greatly aided by birds, bees, bats, butterflies—pollinators, all—and in a few years, the land was lush with indigenous grasses, shrubs and trees, such as palash, also called 'flame of the forest' for its brilliant red flowers, and tendu. The tendu, Poonam informed, they owed to the sloth bear, from whose droppings sprung the saplings. Once the land was fairly protected, Harshawardhan set about making a waterhole—and this was not unlike sending an engraved invite to the denizens of the forest, who started dropping by for a drink, especially in the dry season. Within a few years, the waterhole was shielded with a virtual wall of thick vegetation, offering skittish wild animals 'privacy' and a sense of security. One of the first, and most regular of visitors, was a sloth bear—a very genial sort contrary to their reputation of ill-tempered beasts, whom the locals took to calling 'Bakul'. The next major guest to come, and intermittently stay, was a tigress with her three young cubs, and it is in her honour that the waterhole was named 'tiger taka', and the lodge tigress@ghosri.

The conservancy also serves as the base for their NGO, Tiger Research and Conservation Trust, through which they have helped mitigate and minimize the acute human–wildlife conflict in this region—there were sixty-five fatal tiger attacks, between 2005–11. Among a series of initiatives was to train the first line of defence against big cat conflict—teams of trainers, developed from within the seventy-nine villages in Tadoba's buffer, and beyond into the Brahmapuri forests. The team assisted in reducing conflict by providing an early warning to their community about the presence of large carnivores and promptly informing authorities when their intervention was needed. The villagers were also taught how they could decrease their vulnerability to attacks simply by altering their code of conduct while in the bush.

The state stepped in by prioritizing villages in Tadoba's buffer zone to provide LPG to reduce their dependence on the forests—maximum tiger attacks were when villagers went inside forests for fuel and fodder. These were among a slew of facilities provided to buffer villages under a special scheme, Jan Van Yojana,[10] which included provision of sanitation facilities, building toilets, providing solar lights and inputs to improve their marginal agriculture. Parallely, protection was strengthened in the buffer, tigers monitored, the staff oriented in wildlife and sensitized to handle conflict situations. Gradually tourism was also developed in the buffer areas, and is backed by a policy which facilitated the benefits to accrue to the local communities.

Naturalists and guides have been trained, and slowly, local homestays are opening up. And while it is critical that such tourism has a light footprint, there is no denying that this has turned the story around for the tiger. Tigers have brought in an economic vibrancy here, and other facilities are being accrued as well. The five buffer tourism zones in Tadoba are managed by the locals with the financial benefits going directly to the communities.

Buffer zones literally provide a shield to the core, inviolate areas in reserves, and here wildlife and people coexist. Tigers are most vulnerable here, and communities bear the brunt of living in such close proximity to wild animals, with ungulates raiding crops, and carnivores feeding on livestock. It's critical that local communities don't bear the cost of conservation, they must *benefit*—which is what this initiative aims to do.

Tigers can only be protected if the people who live with tigers do not bear the cross of being the predator's neighbours.

Even better was my experience in Sindhudurg district in Maharashtra—a mosaic of fields, cashew plantations and forests, which form the northernmost limit for tigers in the Western Ghats, a global biodiversity hotspot. I had gone to the region to investigate the impacts of proposed thermal power plants and iron ore mining on the ecology. I was in Kalane village, located on a thin strip of land that connects Maharashtra's Radhanagari Wildlife Sanctuary to Goa's Mhadei Wildlife Sanctuary—and a proposed tiger reserve. A forest officer confirmed the presence of tigers in Kalane. I could see the ravages of mining, entire mountains stripped and laid bare, raw red in sad contrast to the dense semi-evergreen forest, and the paddy fields around. A farmer took me to his fields where the tiger had visited a few weeks earlier. He had photographs of the pug marks which he had submitted to local activists and concerned officers, with much hope. He believed that the presence of the national animal would save his fields which were slated for mining. The tiger had to be saved, no? Some days, he confessed, he hated the tiger—it had taken the buffalo of a neighbouring farmer, and the loss was crippling. Still, it was one they could cope with. They would recover, by and by. But if their land was gouged out for the ore, everything would be lost. Their lives, and livelihood, were tied to the land.

The tiger would save them.

He is so right . . .

Saving the tiger is not a 'luxury', and the loss of a tiger is not just the loss of a tiger. It is the snapping of yet another strand of the ecosystem on which we all depend. Tiger forests sponge the short, sharp monsoon, thus feeding the aquifers that, in turn, feed over 600 rivers and streams. India's forests absorb about 11 per cent of our annual greenhouse gas emissions. Saving the tiger is an ecological and existential imperative.

It is not about us saving the tiger, it is about the tiger saving *us*.

Failing Our Gods

. . . For the animal shall not be measured by man. In a world older and more complete than ours, they are more finished and complete, gifted with extensions of the senses we have lost or never attained, living by voices we shall never hear. They are not brethren, they are not underlings; they are other Nations, caught with ourselves in the net of life and time, fellow prisoners of the splendour and travail of the earth.

—Henry Beston, *The Outermost House*

1 January 2016, Betakholi, Athgarh Forest Division, Odisha

'Raha, Raha, Raha!' urged Panchanan Nayak, a short, wiry man whose voice rose barely above a hoarse whisper—yet his sense of urgency to 'stop' reached the three-ton, eight-foot tall cow elephant. She ground to a halt then extended her trunk to encircle her young son to contain him. She is a wild elephant, even if she goes by the name of 'Lakshmi'. She is the matriarch of a herd of twenty-five-odd elephants who followed her lead, and paused—impatiently—just short of the busy Bhubaneswar–Athgarh highway and the paddy fields beyond.

It was surreal: twenty-five wild elephants contained in their path by Panchanan or Panchu as he is known and his three colleagues: Sanatan Nayak, Dileep Sahu, Santosh Sahu. Together they form the 'Athgarh Elephant-conflict Mitigation Squad' which tries to keep people, their crops and the elephants safe by influencing their movements. Not by force, no, of course not. Not by blank-firing guns, bursting firecrackers, burning *mashals* (live torches) to drive away harried animals—which are the methods usually deployed across India to contain or get rid of 'conflict elephants' as they enter towns, bazaars, fields—places that were once forests that these animals lived in, and migrated through seeking water, food or avoiding monsoon flooding.

Here, man and beast *communicated*.

Calling this group a 'squad' is a bit grandiose. Panchu and his gang, a ragtag group of daily wagers employed by the forest department are armed with nothing more than lathis, and mobile phones to coordinate their movements, call in forest staff reinforcements, or summon the police to control crowds that form when elephants enter human settlements, crowds that all too frequently turn into angry mobs.

The elephants had approached the road in the late afternoon, a time when traffic was heavy, children were racing home from school, and cowherds were herding the cattle back to their paddocks. People were still at work in the fields and milling around doing brisk business in the dhabas and shops that line the highway. On the edge of the road, barely hidden within a fragment of forest, the elephants were restless. On the other side of the road was one of the few sources of water within this dry landscape, and the paddy was ready for harvest—offering an easy, power-packed snack for the pachyderms.

The scraps of patchy forests that the elephants are confined to do not provide enough food to sustain them.

❦

These elephants are refugees, driven away from Chandaka, a sanctuary on the outskirts of Bhubaneswar, the capital of Odisha, on

India's eastern coast. Chandaka was once connected to the Kapilas forests further north. Westward along the left bank of the Mahanadi, the forests extended towards Narsinghpur, and into what is today the Satkosia Tiger Reserve and Mahanadi Elephant Reserve.

Once upon a time the elephants traversed this entire landscape. Ancient instincts and knowledge dictate their movements, decide the paths they take. They know they must move to strengthen their bloodlines, and not to overburden a forest—given that an elephant may consume about two quintals[1] of plants a day. But these animals are not just copious consumers. Elephants are the gardeners of the forest, shaping the ecosystem they thrive in. They disperse seeds as they travel, smartly packaged in fodder—dung—sprouting new plants, contributing, in a major way, to a forest's regeneration and plant diversity. Unlike other seed dispensers—say, birds or monkeys, who have smaller ranges, elephants travel vast distances, sometimes planting seeds far from the parent tree. In one study, scientists in the Democratic Republic of Congo found that forest elephants disperse about 345 seeds per day from ninety-six different species, typically more than 1 km from parent trees and shrubs—and as far as 54 km.[2] Confining elephants to small islands and pushing them to feed in fields will slowly but surely wither a forest, which is now happening in Chandaka.

Chandaka lies at the northern tip of the Eastern Ghats, a discontinuous range of biodiverse mountains that run along India's eastern coast. Chandaka had tigers once, with the last resident recorded in 1967. Even as the big cat vanished, the forest harboured other rare species—elephants, leopards, sloth bears, pangolin and the rusty-spotted cat, the smallest wild cat in India. The region was protected as the Chandaka–Dampara Wildlife Sanctuary in 1982, mainly to protect the more than eighty elephants who roamed the 190-sq km reserve until 2004—and to serve as Bhubaneswar's green lungs.

Bhubaneswar has grown rapidly, changing the dynamics of both the city and the forest. An ill-planned expansion is transforming

Bhubaneswar from a quaint, post-Independence capital into an urban conglomerate that could one day replace Kolkata as the 'hub of the east'. Gated colonies, large institutes, tech parks, colleges and malls have sprouted, decimating and engulfing the sanctuary and the surrounding forests.

There have long been problems within the sanctuary itself. Chandaka was neglected and mismanaged, overgrazed by cattle, exploited for firewood, encroached on by village settlements. From a densely wooded, mixed sal[3] forest, it has now been reduced to a dry scrub forest with some bamboo. The encroachers were hostile to the animals and there were cases of elephants being shot. Aditya Chandra Panda, a Bhubaneswar-based conservationist recalls how the first wild elephant he had known—a one-tusked male named Ganesh, was killed. Aditya has known the Chandaka–Athgarh elephants for over a decade. 'All the big tuskers in Chandaka had names back then. Abhimanyu, Ganesh and Master Bull were legendary. Master Bull was an outsize animal who had tusks that even he struggled to carry, while Abhimanyu was foul tempered,' he reminisces. Ganesh, on the other hand, was calm, introverted and a very tolerant sort of animal, 'particularly towards curious young naturalists like me, who spent hours just watching him', says Aditya adding that Ganesh was shot dead a few years after in 2008, allegedly by a villager whose paddy he was feeding on. It hit Aditya hard, and spurred him to take up their cause, as the city swallowed the sanctuary, and wilderness turned into concrete, pushing the elephants out.

They raided fields, blundered into residential colonies and other human-occupied areas that not long before were forests. Crackers, shotguns, crowds, mobs and mayhem invariably followed wherever they went.

The desperate, bewildered elephants were on the run, hounded by mobs, harassed by hostile villagers. A few fell on the wayside: some from sheer exhaustion, a few were poisoned; others electrocuted. Six, including two calves, were crushed by a speeding train in December 2012 as they travelled southwards toward Chilika.[4] Lakshmi's herd waded through the river Mahanadi, moved through towns, villages, industrial areas and crossed highways to reach Athgarh.

The elephants were chased away from their home, chased everywhere, hemmed in scraps of forest. Wild, cornered, desperate. Pushed into conflict with man, they have retaliated by killing about ten people since 2010. Yet, they 'listen', and respond to the 'squad', who are literally, their shadow.

Why? I ask the trackers.

The answer is as simple as it's complicated: 'The elephants know we help them,' they say.

When the elephants are harangued by a mob, the trackers lead them to safety, freeing them of the terror only a trapped wild creature knows. If the elephants are near railway tracks, the squad warns the stationmaster at the Raj Athgarh station who then signals trains to slow down. They have notified authorities at power utilities of sagging power cables; running into electrical lines poses serious danger to elephants. Death may be accidental, but avoidable, if simple measures are taken. Occasionally, it is deliberate poaching or retaliatory killing by villagers who set high voltage live wire traps or erect electrified fences.

In Odisha alone, electrocution has killed over 150 elephants in the last fifteen years, according to an analysis of forest department records and newspaper reports by the Wildlife Society of Orissa.[5] Three months after I visited them (January 2016), two elephants—a mother and her calf—were electrocuted.

Panchu and his group once rescued Lakshmi's five-year-old calf, Nungura ('the one who teases'), when he fell into an open well. Nangura is a bit of brat, naughty, curious, whimsical, 'actually not unlike my own son, Pintu,' mutters Panchu as his mates holler in glee. The calf whimpered and shrieked as he flailed in the depths, with the herd desperately trying, and failing to lift him out with their trunks. The inevitable crowd gathered. Curious onlookers who tried to get close to watch the tamasha were charged at by an enraged, distressed Lakshmi, some moving particularly close, unmindful, even mocking of the animals. Many held mobile phones aloft, clicking selfies—not an uncommon occurrence these days in volatile situations. Lakshmi charged, stopping just short of the crowd. She bellowed in warning, once, twice, thrice; maybe more, but heedless, the men jostled ahead, peering into the well. Tormented by the crowd, and terrified for her calf, Lakshmi struck, killing one man.

The situation was fast becoming explosive when the squad arrived. They admitted to a brief moment of fear—after all Lakshmi had just killed a human—before it flickered out. 'The elephants are not killers,' said Panchu. 'They will not harm intentionally. We knew it was only because she was provoked, cornered, and like all mothers, fiercely protective.' So, they talked to the distraught Lakshmi, calming her, reassuring her, 'that we would get her child back. But she had to let us do our job,' said Panchu.

The matriarch moved away, a silent sentinel, and with the deployment of earth movers, the calf was pulled from the well and reunited with the herd.

In the alien, inimical world that the elephants have been tossed into, they know that they have these men on their side.

However, this man–animal relationship is taking a toll on the trackers. Their affinity for the elephants has alienated them from the other village folk, at times, even their families, who bear them a grudge for crops damaged by 'their' animals, as well as the havoc they create. Sanatan, another member of the squad, says his father is fed up with being at odds with his community, and fears for his son—with his strange job, and at odds with his people. Besides he worries, 'who will marry my son who chases elephants?' He offered to pay Sanatan the 200 or so rupees that he gets as his daily wages, if he left the job, and the elephants!

But Sanatan won't leave his job. Like the rest of the squad, for better or for worse, he feels bonded to the pachyderms.

It wasn't always so. They were hired in 2011, positions that were created because of escalating human–elephant conflict, with three human mortalities in rapid succession. Panchu and his men were unacquainted with elephants, knew little about them, and were apprehensive. They were also clueless. 'We didn't know how we were supposed to control the situation, much less the elephants. They were, are wild! And *enormous!*' remembers Panchu. In the beginning they followed the elephants at a 'very safe distance', joining the crowd in firing crackers, shouting, and wielding lathis to scare them away. But it didn't work, in fact, it had quite the opposite effect. The uproar spooked the animals, sparking greater chaos and damage.

The turning point came when they discerned that the elephants were just as terrified, yet didn't misuse their immense strength and power. 'They could have caused us grievous harm as we bumbled behind, trying to chase them away,' said Panchu. 'This gave us courage.' It also sparked empathy for the beleaguered pachyderms. As they monitored their charges 24x7, they learnt elephant behaviour and individual characteristics. They identified those who were calm—and those who could be unpredictable. They knew that Lakshmi was gentle and wise, yet if she felt threatened, or if provoked, she could become aggressive.

Elephant societies are close-knit and led by matriarchs, who are a repository of wisdom, and the hub of a complex, multilayered society. As the matriarch, Lakshmi would put her life at risk, and even kill, if her herd was threatened.

The men also realized that it was hunger and thirst that drove the animals. They understood that the animals were intelligent, emotional beings.

They saw them grieve. When one of the elephants was electrocuted, the group tried to rescue the dying animal, trampling the live wire and getting hurt in the process. They surrounded the carcass, circling it, touching it with their trunks, shaking their heads back and forth, calling out in distress.

The trackers' stories are backed by science: Elephant societies are cohesive, complex, empathetic. They stick together and cooperate to resolve problems. In North Bengal, five elephants were mowed down by a speeding train in 2010 while trying to save two of their young who were trapped on the Siliguri–Alipurduar track. They are known to comfort a grieving mate. In Corbett National Park in the state of Uttarakhand, a mother carried the wasting body of her stillborn calf for days, and through this period was comforted by others in her herd, particularly the matriarch. Corbett veteran and conservationist, Brijendra Singh, who witnessed this remarkable incident in February 2009 writes that, 'The matriarch of the elephant herd continued to caress and say something to the younger cow. Not by infra-sound, with which they normally communicate, but by the more endearing expression of touch. The tip of her trunk wandered to her wet eyes and then into her mouth and then along the length of the trunk. This expression and ceaseless caressing and fondling and the body language itself was her way of consoling the younger cow—perhaps even more touching and humane, than what we humans are capable of, in times of bereavement.'[6]

Elephants are one of the planet's most intelligent species. Their brains are comparable to ours in terms of structure and complexity. They are adept tool users. Elephants cooperate and coordinate with each other to solve problems and work together for the greater good.[7] Forest officers in Palamu Tiger Reserve narrate how elephants would 'test' the stability of flimsy wooden bridges across nullahs with their feet before they let the calves walk on them. The adults swam across. When a calf was swept away in the Baitarani river in Odisha in September 2016, the elephants joined their trunks and carried the calf to safety to a tiny isle, where they were all stranded, as the river swelled with continual rain. The adult elephants could have made their way back to safety, but chose to stay—and risk starving—rather than endanger their young.[8]

Elephants understand and respond to people. Researchers in Amboseli, Kenya speak of individuals recognizing them after a gap of many years, at times well over a decade. In Assam's Manas Tiger Reserve, guards recall that elephant herds would gravitate towards their quarters during the period of insurgency (between the late 1980s and 1990s), which saw brutal violence and poaching. Did they feel safer? We don't know, but in times of peace such behaviour diminished. A severely dehydrated tusker in Kaladhungi—famous as the home of legendary hunter–conservationist Jim Corbett—Uttarakhand allowed forest officials and vets to help him, even pour gallons of glucose water down his throat. 'When he was better, the pachyderm calmly walked off into the forest . . .' says Paramjit Singh, a senior forest official who directed this operation.

Conserving such large, nomadic animals in what will soon be the most populous country in the world[9] is a challenge enough, but when one considers the intelligence of elephants, the issue takes on more complexity. Conflict mitigation squads like Panchu's, however dedicated, can at best diffuse a crisis, but it's not unlike applying a Band-Aid to a festering, bleeding wound. The elephant in the room—literally—is the relentless destruction and fragmentation of habitat, squeezing these gentle giants into small islands.

In India, the elephant is god: Ganesha, the lord of good fortune, remover of obstacles, whose name is invoked before commencing any work or deed of significance, be it laying the foundation of a new home, or setting up a business. In some parts of India, it is believed that after death, the human soul travels outside the body and moves into the souls of elephants.

But today, as human populations continue to skyrocket and habitations edge into elephant territory, the tolerance of the people to share space with the elephant is being tested, now more than ever. Even as we venerate Ganesha in temples, in the real world—in forests and fields, villages and towns—*Homo sapiens* are locked in conflict with the lord's earthly avatar, *Elephas maximus*, that has taken a heavy toll on both species, killing nearly 400 people every year. About 100 elephants are killed by people in retaliation.[10]

As a conservation journalist, I have been aware of the conflict. The horror stories from across the country keep trickling in: Villagers in Assam riding a baby elephant that was accidentally left behind when her herd was chased away, then beating her to death as the police and media looked on.[11] In an incident in Uttarakhand, twenty-seven bullets were pumped into a tusker after it killed a man near Rajaji National Park;[12] in another, an elephant reportedly trampled a man after it was attacked and stoned by a mob (the elephant died too).

And so on, and so forth.

I thought I'd seen, heard and read enough to understand the gravity of the problem. Until I came across a photograph capturing an incident shortly after 9/11 and the terrorist attacks on the US Twin Towers. The image was of an elephant, lying lifeless in a pool of its own blood in a field in Assam. Scrawled on the carcass was 'Dhan Chor Bin Laden'—Paddy Thief (Osama) Bin Laden.[13] The message was disturbing: God had morphed into a thief and a terrorist.

The human tragedy, of course, is monumental. One can empathize with the angst and the anger of the villagers who lose their harvests and livelihood when elephants trample their fields. Crop damage can be crippling. When a marginal farmer has borrowed heavily to sow his crops, which are flattened overnight by a herd of elephants he cannot be expected to feel kindly towards the animals. And how does one even measure the aching tragedy of a child killed, or the loss of the family's sole earning member by panicked and enraged pachyderms?

But what is the elephant to do, where does it go, what does it eat, with humans having flattened and invaded its forest? The 'Bin Laden' photograph was from Sonitpur (Assam), the district with the highest rate of deforestation in the country. The elephant reserves in Sonitpur–Kameng were massively encroached post 1990s. By the year 2002, about half of the region's prime elephant habitat was lost, leading to a surge in human–elephant conflict. Between 1991 and 2003, ninety-three people were killed by wild elephants in the Kameng–Sonitpur area. During the same time frame, fifty-two elephants were found dead, twenty-five due to poisoning.[14]

Loss of forest cover directly causes and increases conflict. In North Bengal, elephants have lost nearly 70 per cent of their original habitat, taken over by tea estates, housing, fields, defence infrastructure, hydroelectric projects, highways, rail tracks, tourist resorts, etc. Pushed into human habitation, elephants have killed about fifty people each year in the two districts of Jalpaiguri and Darjeeling. Elephants have been killed too; many bear scars, burns from lighted mashals, their bodies limp and pockmarked with bullets. It wounds the spirit as well. Calves born in, and living, with conflict are not unlike children raised in war zones. Anxious, traumatized; and having never known peace, they are more capricious, prone to get into conflict. Indeed, scientists say that constant stress is also a potential trigger for conflict. Driving elephants with searchlights, crackers or guns only makes them more aggressive. A 2005 essay 'Elephant Breakdown' by Bradshaw et al.[15] published in *Nature* says that elephant populations are suffering from a form of chronic stress. Elephants are being poached for their ivory, poisoned, electrocuted, crushed by trains. They are watching their kin being slaughtered. The authors say, 'Wild elephants are displaying symptoms associated with human Post Trauma Stress Disorder—depression, unpredictable asocial behaviour, and hyper-aggression.' While their paper is based in Africa, this likely holds true for the Asian elephant as well.

❦

Athgarh, indeed all of today's Odisha, is rich with elephant lore. It was part of the ancient Kalinga Empire[16] famous for its magnificent tuskers who were coveted for wars. The Kalinga rulers were called 'Gajapati', Lord of the Elephants: they commanded huge elephant cavalries earning a formidable reputation. The Greek writer Diodorus was to write, 'Their country [Kaling] has never been conquered by any foreign king, for all other nations dread the overwhelming number and strength of these animals.'

About 20 km as the crow flies from Chandaka is the ancient elephant sculpture at Dhauli, where the emperor Ashoka embraced Buddhism, and ahimsa.

The region has now become a battlefield between people and elephants. Tuskers are being slaughtered for their ivory, and conflict is taking a heavy toll on both humans and elephants. From 2005 to 2015, 685 elephants lost their lives, while 660 people were killed in human–elephant conflict in Odisha.[17]

The slivers of forest in Athgarh where Lakshmi's herd of twenty-five-odd elephants are confined cannot sustain them. They have tried to go back to their original home range in Chandaka, but were obstructed by barriers—moats and walls built as part of management plans by the forest department. The elephants were turned away from a sanctuary created to protect them. Aditya says that the real solution is not chasing elephants or walling them in, or out, but restoring habitats. There is no effort, however, to restore Chandaka. Barely ten elephants survive there now. The big idea, it is gathered, is to make the region 'elephant free', freeing the land for yet more construction.

Even the remaining fragments that elephants inhabit in Athgarh are threatened. The grassy meadows which the pachyderms prefer are being plotted, paved and built upon. One of the critical water sources, a natural pond in the region, was slated to be filled up for a 'Picnickers Paradise Park'. No one bothers to consult the 'squad' when an elephant habitat or a crucial waterhole is signed away for a power plant or shopping complex, or any such use. The trackers form the lowest rung—in fact as contract labour, they do not even exist in the official hierarchy of the forest department.

Yet, Panchanan Nayak's squad and others like it in conflict hotspots across the elephant range are the only buffer between elephants and people, essentially suspended in a constant state of war. Sometimes they are the elephants' only saviours, even as the government forsakes them.

🍃

The elephant was the first wild creature to be given protection in India in the *Arthashastra*,[18] often described as a handbook, or an ancient Indian treatise on running an empire and on good governance; and in contemporary times under the Elephant Preservation Act, 1879. The elephant is listed under Schedule I of the Wildlife (Protection) Act, giving the highest level of protection the law can offer. Established in 1992 'Project Elephant', is dedicated to its conservation, but the initiative is underfunded and has been largely disempowered. In recognition of the deep cultural and religious significance, the elephant was declared the National Heritage Animal in 2010. Paradoxically, the land the elephant inhabits is not protected: elephant reserves have no legal sanctity, with barely a third of them covered under the Protected Area network. Elephant corridors—ancient migration paths that animals use to traverse from one forest to another—are unprotected as well, and rapidly being blocked by mines, dams, roads, railways, canals, real estate and other construction.

Efforts to secure elephant habitats have consistently been resisted and thwarted by the powerful political–bureaucrat–business–mining nexus. In some ways the human–elephant conflict is a metaphor for the 'development *vs* conservation' debate that is being played out in India, and indeed globally, today. The battle to conserve the elephant has become Ground Zero for the war over natural resources. The pressure to clear forests for mineral resources is immense in a country looking at an ambitious rate of economic growth, and for power to fuel this growth and provide electricity for its people. Elephant forests are storehouses of minerals, particularly so in the Chhotta Nagpur plateau, primarily spread across Jharkhand and parts of Chhattisgarh and Odisha. The vast forests across this plateau are prime elephant habitat—and also great reserves of mineral wealth with over 60 per cent of the country's iron ore.

In fact, former environment minister Jairam Ramesh cited coal and iron ore mining as the 'single biggest threat to elephant habitats and corridors',[19] especially in this East Central Indian belt, encompassing the states of Chhattisgarh, Jharkhand and Odisha.

In the battle between elephants and coal, the animals are expendable. Tragically, so are the people caught in the crosshairs of the conflict.

In July 2007, the Odisha government withdrew its intent to notify two proposed elephant reserves—South Odisha and Baitarani Elephant Reserve—as it would lead to lack of industries and mining.[20] The brunt of such decisions and indiscriminate mining are felt on the ground. At Hemgir in Sundargarh in northern Odisha, conflict escalated as the forests were torn to mine coal and iron ore, extracting a toll on people, and elephants. An elderly villager I met there expressed his bewilderment: Why had the *haathi* turned against them? Why were they destroying their homes, and fields? They knew the elephant as benevolent, had peacefully lived with them for years. But in his younger days, there were jungles as far as the eye could see, and rivers flowed free and clear. Now the forests are ravaged, the rivers bleeding as the mining wastes pour into the water.

In neighbouring Chhattisgarh, a similar story was played out, with the issue ultimately reaching the Prime Minister's Office (PMO) and causing a disagreement between former prime minister Manmohan Singh and his environment minister, Jairam Ramesh.

In March 2005, Chhattisgarh's assembly unanimously voted for the creation of the Lemru Elephant Reserve to resolve the escalating human–elephant conflict. Between 2005 and 2014, 198 people were killed and there were over 8,500 cases of property damage in the state. For generations, Chhattisgarh hadn't seen elephants. In 1988, eighteen elephants from Jharkhand and Odisha migrated into present-day Chhattisgarh, pushed by the extensive deforestation in both states.[21] It marked the start of the migration. From 2001 to 2009, huge tracts—an estimated 75,000 hectares—of prime elephant habitat in Keonjhar in Odisha and Singhbhum Elephant Reserve in Jharkhand were cleared for mines,[22] forcing the animals to seek refuge in Chhattisgarh.

The proposed Lemru Elephant Reserve is part of the lush jungles of Hasdeo Arand or 'Aranya', meaning forest. Hasdeo Arand is spread over 1,500 sq km in north Chhattisgarh, and is connected to Achanakmar Tiger Reserve, and onwards to the famous Kanha Tiger Reserve. Towards the east, it is contiguous to Sundargarh forests in Odisha. Along with Saranda in Jharkhand, these are one of the last remnants of the great sal forests that once clothed most of the Chhotta Nagpur plateau.

Chhattisgarh conveyed its intent to the central government which sent its team to assess the area. Its inspection team was enthusiastic in its assessment, noting that Lemru was characterized by 'dense cover, perennial water sources and moist riverine forest especially suitable for elephants . . . There is an added advantage of having nearly 400–500 sq km free from human settlement.' The team also cautioned that the only threat to the area was 'in terms of mineral importance for coal'.

Even as the Centre extended its support, Chhattisgarh quietly shelved its plans to protect Lemru as an elephant reserve. The reason can likely be pinned to a February 2008 letter by the Chhattisgarh state unit of the Confederation of Indian Industry[23] sent to the state's forest department allegedly stating that the 'the area in and around the [elephant] sanctuary has been established to be coal bearing'. The letter reportedly gave details of coal blocks that had been allocated and requested that the forest department 'shift the sanctuary to another location'.[24]

As if the sanctuary, that unique ecosystem evolved over millennia, with ancient trees of sal and mahua, grasses and fungi, rivers and streams, hills and caves, elephants and bears, hornbills and woodpeckers, were a mall or a car park that could be demolished, and propped up elsewhere. It was the biodiversity-rich Lemru forests that needed protection; drawing boundaries elsewhere, with coal in mind, would fail its purpose. But Chhattisgarh obliged, first redrawing boundaries which deleted the coal blocks then shelving the Lemru reserve altogether.[25]

The federal government failed the elephant, too.

As part of a larger initiative, the Jairam Ramesh-led environment ministry had earmarked Hasdeo Arand as a 'no-go' area for coal mining, steadfastly refusing to open it for coal even under relentless pressure from various ministries, particularly coal. Newspapers headlined that the prime minister and Ramesh were at odds over this issue. 'These mines [in Hasdeo Arand] can simply not be cleared without the loss of thousands of acres of dense forest and biodiversity-rich areas,' Ramesh was to write in a letter[26] to the prime minister on 26 March 2010.

Hasdeo Arand was contentious with more than five billion tonnes of coal reserves. In a meeting held on 21 May 2010, T.K.A. Nair, then principal secretary to Prime Minister Manmohan Singh said to Ramesh that, 'An unbroken forest is not a justified word for Hasdeo Arand and there was a need to review the approach to coal blocks.'[27] In 2011, Ramesh relented, opening up three coal blocks—Tara, Parsa East and Kante Basan blocks—in Hasdeo Arand, contradicting his own stand of a year before of never opening this heavily forested, mineral-rich region to miners.[28]

The central government also failed to act on the recommendations of the Elephant Task Force (ETF) it appointed in 2010.

One key recommendation was to create an empowered National Elephant Conservation Authority on the lines of the National Tiger Conservation Authority, which has statutory powers under the federal Wildlife (Protection) Act. The PMO is reported to have struck down the proposal, purportedly because the elephants would be inconvenient for mining interests.[29] Ramesh says that it failed because of a lack of support within the government. At a cabinet meeting, a minister dismissed the proposed elephant authority, saying that 'there are enough elephants', so much so he 'could even see them on the streets', referring to the sorry sight of India's begging elephants, an outdated and cruel practice that allows domestication and trade of a protected wild animal. Equally ludicrous is the myth of 'enough elephants'. As per official estimates India is home to about 29,000 elephants, and it is claimed that the population has been steadily rising, but these numbers have not been substantiated by a credible scientific census. An increase in population seems doubtful with the multiple threats the creature faces, from revenge killings and poaching for ivory to railway accidents and ever-shrinking, splintered habitat.

The elephant may not be facing any immediate extinction crisis, but they are threatened by attrition, with their habitat under assault.

While some cosmetic recommendations of the ETF like *Haathi Mera Saathi*,[30] an outreach campaign for its conservation and welfare, was initiated with much fanfare; substantial recommendations of bringing crucial elephant habitats and corridors under some kind of graded legal protection and regulating land use were not taken on board. Instead, the environment ministry reversed its own guidelines to conserve elephant habitats and corridors, leaving them vulnerable to be cleared for mining, industry or other projects.

The state failed its god . . .

Many miles from the corridors of power and its stink of corruption, in the hamlet of Betakholi, Athgarh, the elephant trackers braced themselves for another long night. Dusk had fallen and the pachyderms were headed to the fields, negotiating dense human populations. I worried about their future, grappling for a solution to this contentious, complex issue—both here and across India. I turned to Athgarh's 'elephant men', and we discussed the matter. They noted that it is we, *Homo sapiens*, who are at fault and I quote their collective response, 'It is not the elephants who are the problem. It's *us*. Elephants are wise, intelligent, peaceable beings with a heart and a conscience. We have wreaked havoc in their lives, taken their home, their food, blocked access to water. We have killed their families, destroyed their society. So they are pushed into being something they are not: aggressive, erratic, belligerent. Whatever "solution" we think of, *has to keep the elephant in mind*, and should not stress them further. Only then there is hope.'

The trackers may be 'nonentities' in the conservation aristocracy, but in their earthy wisdom is the crux of the solution to this complex issue: Any strategy to conserve elephants must incorporate elephant ecology, its intelligence, needs. The solution has to consider the *elephants' point of view*.

But do we have such a strategy? And can a country of 1.3 billion people accommodate elephants?

My answer would be a *very* cautious yes, we can. *If* we want to. My first beacon of hope is this Athgarh elephant squad, and others like them. There is a message in the way elephants trigger such fierce devotion in the hearts of those who protect them, against all odds, and in spite of antagonism from their own people. Secondly, there are such squads and trackers in many conflict hotspots. Our primary task is to empower, equip and motivate them, to instil in them a sense of pride. They are *heroes*, negotiating elephants in a tense, hostile landscape; saving lives of both elephants and people.

We need to *understand* elephants better. People need to be made aware of the animal's basic behaviour in relation to the precautionary measures they need to take to avoid confrontation and for their safety. The way conflict is handled must change. When you have elephants in your backyard—stay calm. Shouting, chasing and crowding the animal, bursting crackers will further panic the already traumatized pachyderms who may lash out in self-defence. What should be done, instead, is to control the frenzy, possibly calm the animals by sheltering them from the crowd, and allowing them safe passage.

A peaceful situation can turn explosive in minutes. My colleagues were recently in Odisha, with Lakshmi's herd, which had wandered over to another area, away from the watchful eyes of Panchu's gang. They were trying to cross a dirt track for well over an hour but were thwarted by the frenzy of a mob that had surrounded them. The men shouted, yelled, lobbed rocks, threw lathis.

Writes conservationist Cara Tejpal on what she witnessed, 'They [the crowd] was not acting in defence or retaliation. There are no standing crops and no homesteads to be protected. This was their evening entertainment. The grace and restraint of the elephants is humbling. The younger females of the herd were a fortress around the babies. Two others, the matriarch and her second-in-command held the defence. Every time the crowd got too close they mock-charged. It's obvious that they were exhausted, and in between bouts, they caressed each other with their snaking trunks. As though in comfort, and to draw courage.'

They are grace under fire. They could have killed a dozen men, maybe more. But all they did was wait for the cover of the dark, wait for the mob to disperse, and then, quietly, softly slip away.

This wasn't *conflict*. This was abuse.

This has to stop.

At the same time it must be said, that people are very accepting towards elephants in their midst. This is more so in traditional and tribal societies who have been living with wild animals for generations. In many places I have visited, they work their way around the elephants' movements. And extend a helping hand in times of need. When elephants got stranded on an isle in the Baitarani river in Odisha, forest officials and farmers provided them with paddy and fodder to tide them over till they could make their way across the swollen river.

There are other extremely dedicated people who work diligently to ease the friction. Ananda Kumar and Ganesh Raghunathan have done exemplary work in the Valparai region in Tamil Nadu where over 200 sq km of prime rainforests have been cleared for coffee and tea plantations. About 70,000 people live here in an area that is also used by 100–120 elephants in a year. A study by the Nature Conservation Foundation of which Ananda is part, showed that surprise encounters with elephants can often lead to human injuries or fatalities. So Ananda created an 'Elephant Information Network', and an early warning system with the involvement of stakeholders. Elephant movements are tracked during the day, and alerts are flashed in real time through text messages, phone calls, on TV, automated announcement systems in public transport and through warning lights. The state forest department has built a disaster mitigation centre, with sound alert systems, a toll-free helpline number for people to report elephant sightings, or in case of potential confrontation. There is a rapid response team that disperses to the scene quickly to protect property from elephant damage and to ensure that local people do not attack the elephants with fire crackers and stones. When given space, elephants usually move off into the forests of their own accord. As a result of these efforts, conflict in the region has minimized: three people used to die on average every year in confrontations with elephants between 1994–2002, which is now down to one per year. These collective efforts also halved the property damage incidents by elephants over the past six years.

Still, these are supplementary responses to a chronic issue. The root of such conflict lies in rapid destruction and fragmentation of forested corridors, and unless this is addressed, such efforts may flounder in the long term as habitats degrade and fragment further.

This is where we are failing, abysmally, conserving elephant habitat is nowhere on the government's priority. It is absolutely critical to expand Protected Areas and regulate land use in elephant habitats and corridors.

Both elephants and their habitat can still be saved—and this is happening one forest at a time. One example is Wayanad Sanctuary in Kerala, part of the Nilgiri Biosphere Reserve which extends across three states and harbours the largest remaining wild population of the Asian elephant. With 107 settlements, Wayanad is one of the most densely populated Protected Areas in India. Kurchiyad, in the core of the sanctuary, is one such settlement. I first visited it some fifteen years ago. Time had forgotten the tribal people living there. The muddy 'roads' were awash with rains. Kerosene lamps and the stars lit up the night. The huts were constructed with mud and thatch. Education was no more than a dream. Few children dared venture to schools, miles away, through dense forests, populated by elephants, tigers and other potentially dangerous animals.

What was most shocking were the machans perched on tall trees. These flimsily covered platform-like structures were where many families spent their nights to escape the elephants who raided the fields and occasionally destroyed their huts, attracted by the smell of grains and salt. The villagers had given up agriculture. Almost nothing was left after elephants and various types of ungulates ravaged their crops. Occasionally, they lost their cattle to predators.

The forest, too, was severely degraded. It looked starved, thinned out—trees were cut down or lopped; grasses ground by cattle, hutments and squalor had turned meadows to dust. The water source, a pond, had turned putrid.

The villagers wanted to move to a place where they did not live in perpetual fear, which offered jobs and educational opportunities. So they took matters into their own hands. They approached forest officials and petitioned their chief minister, who took their case to the central government to avail of funds from a voluntary relocation scheme that offers a compensation package for people who are willing to move out of Protected Areas.

In October 2012, residents of Wayanad sanctuary moved court. The petitioners said the residents were living in utter poverty, an 'animal–like existence'[31] without electricity or access to hospitals, schools, grocery stores or markets. Noting that it would be a grave injustice if they were not relocated, they also said the forests must be kept pristine, and undisturbed, for wildlife.

While 185 families from four settlements have moved out of Wayanad, over 600 still await relocation.

I met Shibu A.P., a teacher, the only graduate from Kurchiyad and at the forefront of the relocation effort. He told me that those who have moved out have a 'new lease of life'. In their new home, the residents have pucca houses and roads, electricity and running water, as well as medical care and education for their children.

And the forest is now abundant with wildlife. Shibu showed me a photograph of the site from where the settlement had moved. It had elephants wallowing in the water, others quietly feeding in the forests around. They now roam free and wild. The elephants had reclaimed their forest.

The Shadow Cat

And I think in this empty world there was room for me and a mountain lion.

And I think in the world beyond, how easily we might spare a million or two humans

And never miss them.

Yet what a gap in the world, the missing white frost-face of that slim yellow mountain lion!

—'Mountain Lion', D.H. Lawrence

The leopard is one of the world's great cats. Shy, secretive, smart and resilient by nature, the leopard is arguably the ultimate survivor of the animal kingdom, living above 15,000 feet in the Himalayan snows and in searing heat in parched deserts. It thrives in the remotest of regions, and in the densest of human populations. It lives in peace, and at war, with people. It is maligned, misunderstood and persecuted. Public opinion has not rallied in its favour, and it lives in the shadow of its charismatic kin, the tiger, around which most conservation efforts are centred.

My quest to understand the leopard led to some clarity and even greater mysteries and an immense appreciation and respect for this enigmatic, extraordinary feline.

And while the sun shines on the tiger, this other cat—utterly beautiful and graceful—lurks in the shadows. A rare sighting in the wild, the elusive leopard more often than not enters our mindscape when it's making news as a 'menace' on the prowl, presumably bloodthirsty. And stoned, beaten, burnt for the sheer audacity of being in spaces that were once forests, but are now the gated domains of *Homo sapiens*.

My interest in leopards was, in part, a response to such horror stories of human–leopard conflict that seemed to be occurring all across India. The leopard was everywhere—in places where you would least expect it: villages, towns, cities. It entered bedrooms in Guwahati (Assam), attended school in Bangalore (Karnataka), watched TV—and fell asleep on a couch—in Chandigarh (Punjab), entered a hospital in Meerut (Uttar Pradesh), was an—unwanted— guest in a hotel in Nainital, strolled the bazaars of Siliguri (North Bengal).

There was a cat among the humans, leading to mayhem, mobs, murder.

Newspapers and news breaking on TV routinely covered 'leopards on a rampage, prowling streets for human victims'. While I understood some reportage as amateurish (one report enthusiastically revived the long-extinct cheetah[1] with a 'family of three cheetahs prowling in Hosur, Karnataka')[2] and mostly sensational; there was no denying that human–leopard conflict existed, if erratically, across its range; occasionally with tragic, fatal fallouts.

In the early years, my reportage, too, focused on conflict dictated by the editorial diktat of 'good news is not news' journalism. I wrote on the dire—in this case, the conflict between man and leopard. It existed, it grabbed eyeballs, and I honestly believed that the issue called for attention from the public, and policymakers, alike. Besides, positive interaction, peaceful sharing of spaces between man and beast wasn't fodder for media. A war between the two, is.

My first port of call was Rudraprayag, Uttarakhand, where Jim Corbett—the most widely read author of hunting lore—had shot the 'Rudraprayag Man-Eater', the leopard who in its eight-year career had spread terror in nearly 1,300 sq km, killing at least 125 humans.

It was Corbett who pretty much established the term 'man-eater', but after a long innings of tracking and hunting man-eaters, he took to shooting with a camera, and put forward a moving case to rally support for the fast-vanishing tiger. His thrilling accounts, however, left a troubling legacy, imprinting, in popular imagination tigers and leopards as ferocious beasts, as though it was only their ferocity that defined them.

The region continues to be a conflict hotspot.

I visited—well over fifteen years back—Rudraprayag and Pauri-Garhwal in the upper reaches of Uttarakhand, and found that the tragedy had not abated. My first stop was a village where a woman had been killed by a leopard recently. Understandably, the mood was sombre, anxious, tense, vengeful—the leopard could not, would not be spared. I heard other disturbing, heartbreaking stories. A young woman harvesting her crop was mauled, a little girl snatched while sitting with her grandmother, a boy picked up on the way to school. In the decade spanning 2001–2010, leopards had caused 198 deaths, and over 100 leopards had been declared man-eaters, as per a survey by Titli Trust and Wildlife Conservation Society-India (WCS-India).[3] To deal with the conflict, this hill state has a home-grown profession in the tradition of Corbett. Local hunters, empanelled by the state forest department, are called to hunt the 'problem' leopard. I met one of them, who had clocked over thirty leopards in his fifteen-year career. He said he did not enjoy the killing, and had taken to the gun after a few children were killed by the leopard in his village. Yet this hunter, and most like him, showcase images, where they pose—in the style of sahibs—over the trophy of slain leopards. There is something odious in this show of conquest, of human triumph in these pictures. The fatal flaw in this 'strategy' is that

Photograph by Rashid Naqash

There are fewer than 200 wild hanguls in the world. Here Rashid Naqash captures two of these rare deer in their only sanctuary, Dachigam National Park in Kashmir.

Photograph by Roni Chowdhury

One of the six elephants crushed by a train on the Siliguri to Alipurduar track in North Bengal in November 2013. More than 1,200 trains cut through Protected Areas, taking a huge toll on wildlife.

A road through the Kutch Wildlife Sanctuary threatens the only nesting site of both the greater and lesser flamingos in India, possibly dooming the birds to extinction.

This dead hyena on the National Highway 16 in Odisha was a lactating mother. Somewhere in the scrub forests that lined the highway were her cubs, doomed to die.

A young tusker being chased and harassed by a mob as it attempts to cross a path that cuts into the fragmented forests of Athgarh, Odisha.

At our arrival, the little hatchlings clambered on to the male gharial who protectively kept a close watch over the young ones. In National Chambal Wildlife Sanctuary.

Female turtles land on the Rushikulya beach off the Odisha coast for mass nesting, or the arribada. Rushikulya is one of the two beaches in India where arribada occurs, and is threatened by development of ports and other constructions.

With fewer than a 100, the great Indian bustard is one of the most endangered birds on the planet. This male is captured in its mating plumage.

This one-month-old tiger cub faces a precarious future as its forest, Panna Tiger Reserve, is earmarked to be submerged by the first of India's ambitious river linking project, the Ken–Betwa link.

The population of the critically endangered long-billed vultures have crashed by 97 per cent in recent years. This nesting site at Panna Tiger Reserve is threatened by the Ken–Betwa river link.

A wild leopard walks through the narrow alleys between houses in Aarey Colony in Mumbai. This photograph sends a powerful message of leopards living in harmony with humans in one of the most densely populated cities in the world.

Leopards are adept at being 'invisible', avoiding humans at all costs. The mere sighting of a leopard, unfortunately, is viewed as a threat, and panicked, enraged mobs like this one in Guwahati, Assam, could trigger fatal conflict.

Coal mines likes this one, fuelled by escalating energy demand, are turning our forests to dust. This mine borders Tadoba National Park, one of the finest tiger habitats.

One of the two sub-adult tigers, the 'Chiroli Cubs', who were poisoned in retaliation for killing wild goats in the Ranthambhore Tiger Reserve, Rajasthan.

Photograph by Prerna Singh Bindra

Sparrows are fast vanishing from our lives and the urban spaces they once thrived in. Attracted by the garden foliage, as well as the seed and water I put out, this one here has made my home, his.

Photograph by Mayank Ghedia

The global skimmer dragonfly is a world record holder of the insect world for length of migration, flying thousands of kilometres across oceans.

there is no foolproof method to identify the 'man-eater', before it is shot. Its slayers claim that the guilty animal is identified by its footprint—but it is near-impossible to identify individual leopards by pug marks. In all probability the area would have a number of leopards, and sometimes a few may move together (for example a mating pair or mother with subadult cubs), leaving more than one set of footprints along the path. How does one identify the 'guilty' leopard? Usually, the first animal spotted is the unfortunate victim, the idea being to appease, and assuage, an angry public, and calm an explosive situation.

Other regions are also afflicted with such conflict, from neighbouring Himachal Pradesh and Uttar Pradesh, across the Terai (Himalayan foothills), stretching up to the tea gardens of North Bengal and Assam, and in the west in Gujarat, and southwards to Maharashtra, Andhra Pradesh, Karnataka but none are perhaps as severely and chronically affected as Uttarakhand.

The retaliation is equally distressing.

Looking up reports over the past year or two, I saw that leopards were being hounded in states spanning its range from India's northern tip Kashmir, to the hill states of Uttarakhand and Himachal, Gujarat in the west to Odisha and Assam in the east, to southern Karnataka. It was stoned to death, hacked to pieces, burnt to ashes: Occasionally for attacking humans, more often than not for preying on goats and dogs . . . or simply for the sin of being wild, and in 'civilization'.

In June 2015, a leopard was spotted in a village in Purulia (West Bengal). It was chased, cornered, mobbed. Panicked and terrified, it struck back. You would too, if harassed and thrashed by a frenzied mob of over 3,000.[4] A cat has claws and canines, and a villager or two got injured, none fatally. The forest department team that arrived to help the leopard was woefully outnumbered by the mob. The leopard was lynched, killed, mutilated, paws and tail chopped off. Its battered body was hung from a tree, not unlike a grotesque trophy.

In Dhamdhar village in Kalagarh, part of Uttarakhand's Corbett Tiger Reserve, in 2011 a leopard was mobbed and beaten. The forest department rushed in to the rescue, capturing the cat in a cage to be taken away. But the leopard—trapped, terrified and helpless—was doused with kerosene and set ablaze. Kerosene was poured over the forest staff too, lest they try to help the leopard.[5]

The leopard is the most persecuted of big cats.

The Kalagarh leopard's charred visage, frozen in agony, unguarded by its hapless protectors, will haunt me till the day I die, as will the fact that even as the Purulia leopard was being bludgeoned to death, rioters and onlookers were trigger-happy, filming, holding mobiles aloft to record the brutality. This clinical indifference, even glee, at the pain of a tormented creature makes me despair.

Tellingly, it indicated India's rising intolerance to wildlife. It also indicated our deficiency to deal with such situations in a proactive manner, giving rise to intolerance among tolerant people. Has the government really understood the gravity of this pervasive issue?

These horrific, tragic incidents, however, are just a part of the story. This implication of leopards as an aggressive 'conflict-cat' made me uneasy. It is too black and white, with leopards and humans boxed in, alternately, either as the aggressors or the victims. But the issue is complex, with many shades of grey.

🖋

In my years in the field, I have seen the resilience of the leopard living, if in a furtive manner, in human-dominated landscapes, primarily rural areas. There were no attacks on humans. Admittedly, both species lived on the edge, largely in peace, than at war.

I have witnessed the remarkable tolerance of villagers towards most wild creatures even when they caused damage: Elephants that broke homes, wild pigs that dug fields, deer that feasted on crops, tigers and leopards that preyed on livestock. The losses, sometimes, wiped out almost their entire livelihood but while villagers retaliated at times, it is not routine. Partially due to the country's strict wildlife laws, aided by a tolerance, reverence for all life that is uniquely Indian.

Many countries lethally control carnivores which are potentially dangerous, or as a—misguided—strategy to deal with livestock depredation. Europe has almost eliminated most of its big predators. Unlike in India, in some countries, ranchers and farmers pretty much have a licence to kill wildlife—cougars, wolves, coyote, bear—which is damaging their livestock. In August 2016, in Washington state, US state biologists shot down from helicopters part of a wolf pack for attacking livestock,[6] even as recent studies establish that there's little scientific evidence that killing predators actually accomplishes the goal of protecting livestock. Authors of the study call predator control 'a shot in the dark'.[7] There are other, frivolous, reasons to eliminate predators. In December 2016, Colarado (US) kicked up a controversy when it embarked on a 'Predator Control Program' to euthanize mountain lions and bears to revive the state's dwindling population of deer. Conservation groups assert deer populations were declining due to development in the region, and this move was aimed to serve hunting interests—to ensure enough deer for 'sportsmen' to hunt![8] In Canada, hunting bears is still considered recreation.[9]

India has one of the highest population densities globally at over 380 people per sq km; and a greater diversity of carnivores than most countries—fifty-eight, and all still largely manage to live as fellow residents.

In this context, a visit to a remote hamlet in Jharkhand's Palamu Tiger Reserve taught me an important lesson.

I was in Palamu in October 2010 as part of a team to assess the management of the reserve. Palamu is one of the poorest and driest districts of the region, and has been ravaged by years of strife, being a region impacted by left-wing extremism. One morning, a ranger informed us that a leopard had killed a couple of cows in a tribal settlement on the edges of the park. When we reached the hamlet, there didn't seem to be anything out of the ordinary. The household had five cows and a few goats. They were corralled, but the fences weren't very secure. It was hot and the family slept outside too. Sometime after midnight, the leopard had sneaked in and killed two calves. The loss was acute for a family living off the land, and their cattle. Yet, in a manner, peculiar and especial to my country, they were calmly philosophical about the cataclysm. If you lived in a jungle, this was not unexpected. The forest gave them food, water, medicine, wood, fodder—*everything*; so occasionally, you had to pay up. Sort of like the tax, that you pay the sarkar, the government, someone remarked with a wry laugh. And, no, the leopards—or tigers—do not kill people; you just had to give them right of way. Respect their boundaries. Animals do not attack unprovoked.

I was astounded. These wonderful, warm, wise people were abjectly poor, certainly in the way we define poverty. They did not have access to medical care, their children walked some 3 km to government schools; and of course, they had no luxuries that we view as necessities—cars (or roads to zip around on), TV, air conditioners (only bulbs lit by solar electricity). Yet, they seemed curiously content. The forest and the land provided; their children did not go hungry. I learnt that for these communities, it wasn't *tolerance*. Wild animals were an intrinsic part of the landscape—ecologically, socially, culturally; and one lived with and adjusted around them. Like city people do with say, vehicles, which were convenient, but had this nasty habit of running you over.

Similarly, wildlife had its uses, including some in a very consumerist way, like wild pig for meat, sambar deer for a special feast![10] Carnivores kept the ungulate population low, thus saving crops; but their presence had its risks as well.

Conflict is not just a *wildlife* issue. Human–wildlife interactions have a social context that needs to be addressed, on priority, if we are to contain the friction. In a country where people and wildlife live cheek by jowl, unless those sharing space with the wild can live in peace . . . they are not going to want to conserve the wildlife around them.

This tolerance, nay acceptance, is fraying as we get more globalized, as we become more distant from nature, as our understanding of fellow creatures dims, and as we limit our world only to ourselves—me, and mine. The tide is turning, slowly, even in places like Palamu, as communication erodes the remoteness of the region—and the connection with land and forest diminishes. In the younger generation the intolerance is more pronounced. They do not have the same intimate relationship as their forefathers with the forest. In their aspirations, they gravitate towards the urban, and all that it signifies. The acceptance of animals as intrinsic to the fabric of life is diminishing.

In urban areas, nature is increasingly the 'other', outside of us; and rarely appreciated unless we can 'control' it—like a manicured garden, or animals in a zoo. In cities, people have been abused and beaten for being kind to a dog; perceive cattle as vermin as it clogs up the roads; and spray beehives with pesticides lest a bee stings their kid. And in one such city that I endured (I cannot honestly say *lived* in), I know the leopard did too; the wonder of its presence was contained in the soft impressions on sand, and in the terror-stricken whine of my dog. I wiped off the pug mark, held the secret close to my heart, along with a prayer for its invisibility.

But, wait, what on earth are leopards doing amongst humans? *And* in crowded cities? Had they all 'strayed' from forests and sanctuaries? Why (and how) should they be invisible? What caused some leopards to attack humans, while most shy away from people? Why was it that some regions with leopards saw—deadly—conflict, while in others, humans and leopards had each carved their own space, drawn invisible boundaries?

Seeing the trajectory of conflict, and coexistence, it appears that this wild cat has redefined the concept of *wild*, and our preconceived notions of the place of wild things.

But before we trace its geographies or delve into its ecology, let's get the basics straight. Like its name, and numbers.

We call it the *common* leopard. Probably because it has the widest range of all big cats, globally, and in India. The numbers seem reassuring, though how the figure is arrived at is hazy; and frankly, confusing. The Wildlife Institute of India (WII) census in 2015 counted 7,910, an extrapolation from 1,647 individual leopards that were actually photographed. From this, it was derived that there are 12,000–14,000 leopards in India.[11] It might be less, it could, probably, be more, since the estimation piggybacked on the tiger estimation exercise. Only leopards in tiger habitats (were) counted, whereas the leopard range is greater. It survives where the tiger doesn't—or can't—scrubby jungle, tiny, patchy forests on urban fringes; and in entire states like Himachal and Kashmir.

Lest we get smug about 'oh, *enough* leopards'—as we are wont to—here is another statistic: In the last decade preceding 2012, four leopards have been killed each week,[12] as per TRAFFIC-India, an organization that monitors illegal wildlife trade. This is only the detected skins, the actual off-take would be much higher. Investigation agencies estimate that for every tiger skin, at least six leopard pelts are seized, and ten times more smuggled out, unnoticed.

Leopard pelt with its dazzling pattern and excellent drape is fashioned into coats, trimmings, hats, shoes which are in great demand in a thriving black market—spanning from China to the US. Leopard bones are ground into traditional medicines. Its derivatives serve as 'proxy' for tigers, which are increasingly difficult to source, more so as tiger cases have become 'high-profile', thus attracting more attention and scrutiny. Usually leopard bone is passed off as the tiger's. But it has its uses as well. As per traditional Chinese medicine, it strengthens tendons and bones, and dispels wind. And so, for our smooth flatulence, leopards are trapped, slaughtered, chopped and sold.

Leopard derivatives are easier finds, cheaper (with good profit margins), and low risk. An undercover investigator told me that in the higher reaches of Garhwal in Uttarakhand, you could obtain them from the local chaiwallah, if you hung around long enough. Claws are believed to be good luck charms. At the onset of the new millennium in January 2000, 18,080 leopard claws—representing about a thousand dead leopards—were seized in Khaga in Uttar Pradesh, making this the largest ever seizure of leopard parts globally. There are other examples that indicate volumes; in October 2003, the haul of thirty-two tiger skins and 579 leopard skins in Tibet was said to be sourced from India.

Like most of India's wild creatures—from elephants to pangolins—leopards are definitely on the hit list. That's the leopard's first truth.

Here's another: the leopard's seeming ubiquity is misleading. It has lost 75 per cent of its historical habitat throughout Africa, the Middle East and Asia.[13] Living with humans could likely be a desperate survival tactic; as its domain diminishes, the leopard has carved for itself newer, unlikely territories.

Tigers too can, to a certain extent, live amongst people, but unlike leopards, they must subsist in the margins, they may not *thrive*, their demands for survival are more extravagant—in terms of territory and food. About a third of India's tigers—the official count is 2,226 currently—live outside of Protected Areas, but these are largely in places with good forest cover. Tigers need inviolate, undisturbed space to breed successfully.

The leopard, meanwhile, is infinitely, more adaptive. It will reign like a king in a forest where it is apex predator—like the tropical jungles of Sri Lanka; feasting on an array of natural prey like sambar, spotted deer, wild pig, langur. It can live like a pauper on degraded landscapes eking out a living on whatever is available. Its diet is varied, with about 100 items on the menu. It eats what it gets—frogs, rodents, insects, crabs, and if living on the edges of human habitation, chickens, goats cows, dogs. It can survive without water for days, meeting its requirement from the juices and fluids of its prey.

The leopard is the most secretive of animals. Most animals avoid contact with humans—but nothing like this cat. A tiger may walk away, or be supremely indifferent to your presence. A sambar will bolt, but has this tendency to first give you a look-over to, I imagine, satisfy its curiosity! A leopard is extremely shy, and stealthy. On sensing humans—and it will see you before you spot it—it will duck undercover, hide, vanish into the shadows.

It is a master at camouflage, and has this eerie ability of rendering itself invisible. This is another of the leopard's survival traits, which has stood it in good stead in forests where it must live in the fringes, and in the shadow of larger cats, the tiger here, and in Africa, lions. This is its key to survival in human landscapes too, for a visible leopard is likely a dead leopard; if 'lucky', it will be 'rescued', and carted off in a cage—and denied its freedoms forever. A preferred practice among foresters and researchers, therefore, is not to advertise a leopard—or tiger presence—it avoids unnecessary panic, and keeps both people and cat safe.

Leopards are discreet, but the moment they break cover, the tamasha begins. People gather, become mobs, media adds to the throng and the cat is chased, cornered . . . panicking the predator, who will strike in sheer terror. A perfectly calm situation becomes a conflict zone.

❧

Interestingly, it is for this secretive nature, and remarkable ability to elude its hunters, that sportsmen labelled the leopard a 'bounder'. But the leopard, vouch those who live with it, is a gentleman. It is a peaceable creature, preferring to live, and let live. Left to itself, it will leave you alone too.

This fact has been verified by science. Wildlife biologist Vidya Athreya, has studied large carnivores including leopards in Maharashtra and other states for over a decade. Her research across rural and urban Maharashtra, and more recently in the popular hill station, Shimla (Himachal Pradesh), shows the close proximity in which leopards live with humans. She recalls asking a farmer watering his field if he had seen leopards, and got an unconcerned shrug in response. 'But I knew,' says she, 'that there was a leopard sitting just 20 m away!'

Vidya and her team recorded leopards eating their prey a few feet from a peopled thoroughfare, another raising her cubs next to a town school, and one frequenting the car park in an apartment complex. They knew of the cats' presence, as they were radio-collared, and the signals transmitted showed the leopard's movements, in real time, on computer screens, via satellites. Her study in the rural, human-dense landscape of Akole, Ahmednagar (Maharashtra), showed startling findings. The fields of Akole, with negligible forest cover had five leopards in 100 sq km of farmland, largely of sugar cane, earning them the sobriquet 'Sugar cane Leopards'. This 100-sq km mosaic of croplands, settlements and villages, also supports other carnivores like striped hyenas, jackals and jungle cats—and about 37,000 people!

Till the 1970s, Akole and its surrounds was a dry, scrubby region, with subsistence agriculture, and was possibly a stronghold of wolves. Massive irrigation schemes that flooded the region transformed it to lush green landscape dominated by extensive sugar cane plantations. Sugar cane boosted the local economy, and there was another, unexpected, beneficiary: the leopard. The tall, thick sugar cane grass offers excellent shelter, and little disturbance, with long intervals in between harvesting. While wild prey is deficient, there are plenty of dogs and livestock for the leopard to thrive on in this rural scape. Scat—polite for cat shit—analysis showed that domestic animals, mainly dogs—made for nearly 90 per cent of leopard food.

The leopards would lie low in the fields during the day, and patrol for food at night. When the research team scoured the area for leopard signs—pug marks, scrapes, scat they found them everywhere—in fields, near houses, bazaars, along paths. The cats were using the same paths as humans! Camera traps put across these paths revealed another startling find: The time lapse between leopard and people using these tracks was sometimes within minutes of each other.[14]

And there are no cases of fatal attacks in living memory, although there were a few aggressive encounters, when the feline and people accidentally bumped into each other.

Which brings me to the next puzzle: Why was there conflict in some areas, and not in others? And why did some leopards kill people?

Various explanations have been totted out: Corbett's theory was that old and injured predators were forced to kill humans for easier prey, while the Rudraprayag Man-Eater's lust for blood was fuelled by the easy scavenging of human corpses following an outbreak of influenza that killed many.

Destruction, degradation and fragmentation of forests by infrastructure and other projects is one major cause for human–wildlife conflict. In Uttarakhand, foresters point to severe depredation of natural prey, due to hunting for the pot, and grazing pressure from domestic livestock. They had another explanation—the alarmingly high levels of leopard poaching, averaging over 100 every year. Killing a leopard leaves a vacuum which is filled by another animal, who would be unfamiliar with the territory, stressed and therefore may bungle its way around, and resort to killing people.

Science established another factor. Ironically, studies pinned down the cause of the increasing conflict to the strategy deployed to tackle it: The practice to trap 'straying' leopards from people-dense areas and release them in a forest elsewhere.

As they did with the leopard that revealed itself in a camera trap in Delhi's Biodiversity Park in November 2016. The news of a wild leopard in the world's most polluted city was a sign of hope, and should have been welcomed with some optimism, a signal that the city was regaining its lost, withered ecology. But no, the leopard was persecuted, treated as a 'stray', an unwanted escapee. It was marked to be captured and taken to its 'rightful home', some forest faraway or a sanctuary somewhere. With the rare exception, media sensationalized the event, headlining a 'predator on the prowl', or 'leopard menace', fuelling fertile imaginations, and a non-existent conflict situation. The media, and forgive me for generalizing here, must stop imagining that the mere sighting of a wild animal is like a terrorist in the neighbourhood.

Local politicians make political capital out of such a situation, putting pressure on beleaguered forest departments to act, and trap the leopard. As it happened in Delhi, with its environment minister Imran Hussain indicating that the leopard be trapped for the 'safety of the animal'. So the Delhi government put up cages, violating the law and prescribed guidelines, which allow for trapping only if the animal has caused harm.[15] The Delhi leopard hadn't, its only crime was that it *existed*.

A study in Junnar, with a similar profile as its neighbour Akole, by Athreya et al. revealed that leopard attacks rose by an astounding 325 per cent between 2001–2003,[16] after translocations were resorted to in response to livestock attacks. Leopards were captured from human-dense areas from Junnar and also from other districts further away, and released in the natural forests surrounding the region. Over 100 such 'stray' leopards were shifted to these forests, and soon after, the attacks accelerated. Some of the trapped leopards were incarcerated. Those that were released had microchips inserted in them. A few were released in nearby forests, but they made their way back to their original territory. Some were taken about 400 km away north to Yawal Wildlife Sanctuary, which had its own population of leopards. The settlements around Yawal had never witnessed conflict, but soon after the new cats arrived, six attacks were reported. Trap cages were rolled out again, and two leopards caught. The microchips revealed they were the same animals brought in from Junnar . . . they had carried the conflict with them.

Translocation is a terrible ordeal for an animal. The leopard is trapped, surrounded by thousands of people—most of them curious, some feeling macho, what with being on the right side of the cage. They venture near, pose for pictures, poke the animal, to make it react, *snarl*. Media thrusts its cameras looking for an exclusive. The traumatized animal injures itself, banging its head against the cage, trying to break free. It is then transported some 100 km away, and left in an alien environment. It is not unlike parachuting a human without any resources into an unknown, hostile country, and being pushed back, and out by wary residents who do not want to share their space.

The leopard is clueless about the new place, hungry, stressed. As it attempts to negotiate its new environment, it is likely to be confronted by hostile residential leopards. Or habituated to livestock, it may consume more domestic prey, and encounter humans.

Ridding a place of leopards either by killing, or dumping them somewhere else doesn't solve a problem, it aggravates it. A place will never be cat free, a vacuum will be created, and other leopards will move in. Unfamiliarity triggers conflict. Young cubs go through schooling, with mothers acquainting them with the lay of the land—where the water is, secure places to conceal themselves. They teach the cubs how to avoid risks, and people, and to manoeuvre their way around their territory—all so essential to the young cat's survival. A leopard in a new territory is not equipped with such knowledge, and thrown into deep water, may act aggressively.

Translocated leopards will also try to make their way back home. Like most wild felids, leopards are territorial, and have amazing homing instincts. They will cover vast distances—a leopard in Africa is known to have travelled 400 km; or patiently bide their time to get back to their original territory. Sita (researchers named her after the goddess, for her calm demeanour) was pregnant when she was released 50 km from Nanashi, a village near Nashik where she had been trapped. Signals from her GPS collar showed her trying, repeatedly and unsuccessfully, to head back home. A month later she gave birth, and seemed to have settled down to raise her cubs. As soon as the cubs—about four months old—were capable of making the long trek, the family set off for home, reaching Nanashi a mere week later. Their trek was incident free; but such a journey, largely through unfamiliar, peopled terrain, is fraught with conflict potential.

Researching this story, meeting people who lived with and studied leopards, gave me an amazing insight and etched an animal so different than the one of my imaginations; leopards are shy, not aggressive; they are great travellers. They are not solitary beings— they recognize families, and care for them. Lakshai, a leopardess, and Jai Maharashtra, a young leopard were trapped in different locations. When released at the same site, they promptly gravitated towards the other. DNA tests later revealed them to be mother and son! When Lakshai littered, Jai, like any older sibling, would baby-sit, protecting the cubs, when the mother went hunting!

The secret life of leopards was revealed through radio-collaring, part of the 'Waghoba' project led by WCS-India's Vidya Athreya.

As astounding as this is, the most important message, particularly in terms of its conservation, and future is that: Man-eaters are *man-made*. The leopard strikes, not because it is innately ferocious, but because we have messed with it, hounded it, shuttled it around, imposing on it our man-made boundaries, and idea of wilderness.

The other important point is, a good portion of leopards live *outside* Protected Areas, thus calling for a strategy that considers the dynamics and vulnerability of species outside of Protected Areas. The need of the hour is a change in mindset, to accept that leopards in human habitation are not always strays, or transient cats from some forest around. In all likelihood they were the ghost residents, living among people in villages and towns.

And even in cities. Even in Mumbai.

❦

I thought I had seen, and heard it all. I knew to expect the unexpected from this wild cat. But that was before I met the leopard in India's financial and glamour capital: Mumbai.

I had arrived one bright morning in the metropolis, hopped off my flight, into a cab, inched my way through 'rush-hour traffic, past malls, multiplexes, multi-stories . . . to arrive at a Garden of Eden, otherwise known as the Sanjay Gandhi National Park (SGNP) in the midst of a delightful, chaotic madness called Mumbai.

Ten minutes inside the park, the jarring sounds of the city faded, to be taken over by the song of birds, and murmur of leaves swaying in the wind, my lungs expanded, my eyes took in the crystal clear stream snaking over moss, gushing between rocks, lapping the feet of trees. Within the next hour we—I was accompanied by wildlife biologist Nikit Surve, associated with WCS-India—had seen spotted deer, a pagoda ant nest, a chequered keelback snake, rat snake, grey hornbills and a giant of a moth appropriately called the atlas moth. I had also seen clusters of lush lavender flowers, the karvi, which blooms only once in eight years. I was assimilating this gallery of nature's wonders in the heart of India's most populated city, when I felt what I can only describe as 'eyes on my back', as though someone was looking at me. Intently. I turned, and the leopard knew it had been spotted as well! He—bless him—loped on to the road, just ahead of us and for the briefest moment I revelled in the sight of this gorgeous creature, his dappled coat pure gold under the light of the sun, before he vanished into his emerald forest. So graceful . . . his movements so fluid, it was like the flow of liquid gold.

I breathed again . . . and so did the forest; frenetic calls of langurs, drongos and peacocks now marked the leopard's trail, as they informed other denizens that the predator was on the prowl . . .

He ('L29', Male) was one of the thirty-five leopards, estimated in 2015 in SGNP and its surrounds, by the forest department, with which Nikit Surve collaborated. These leopards live in a city of over 20 million, and counting; packing in 20,000 people in 1 sq km. They survive, it might be better to say thrive, since this density of about twenty-two leopards per 100 sq km is amongst the highest in India. Mumbai is also the city with some of the most expensive real estate in the world. That a national park spanning 104 sq km exists, sitting in what is undoubtedly viewed as prime property, is not just astounding, it's a *miracle*.

Two minutes after spotting the cat, the city showed itself with tall apartments rising up to dominate the skyline, beyond the curtain of green.

Ten minutes later, I thought the leopard was a beautiful dream. I was caught in a terrible traffic jam, unable to hear myself think above the cacophony of impatient honks and loudspeakers alternately blaring bhajans and Bollywood numbers; the sweet smell of grass had been replaced by the stench of diesel fumes. Vehicles covered every inch of the road that skirted the park; the same road that was to take us to Aarey Colony, an old dairy establishment that still maintains green cover, and nine leopards.

Surreal doesn't begin to describe it. *How* did this animal survive here?

In the city, food is not an issue. Part of their diet is wild venison—cheetal, langur, wild pigs, peafowl. The city's garbage dumps feed stray dogs and feral pigs which in turn feed the leopards—most of whom work the unfenced boundaries of park and city, slipping into alleys and parking lots, gardens and garbage dumps, as darkness takes over.

It is, largely, a peaceful, edgy coexistence. It wasn't always so.

There has always been some level of conflict; between 1986 and 1996, fourteen people were killed.[17] The unpalatable fact is that here, in Mumbai (and in most of urban India), one is more likely to meet death by civilization, than by nature. Local trains that carry Mumbai's millions to work and back crush nine people to death, *every day*.[18] Yet, the trains were a lifeline, and a mere sighting of a leopard labelled it a menace and a man-eater. The leopard was the fear of the unknown, something out of your control, whose utility was suspect, not understood. And matters were to get worse.

Conflict peaked with twenty-four leopard attacks between 2002–4. Ten people were killed just in the month of June 2004.[19] Studies revealed the same pattern that was witnessed in Junnar; leopards had been brought in from outside of the park (SGNP), and farmlands skirting Mumbai, and consequently attacks peaked.

Forest officials responded fast. First, SGNP officials disallowed the park to be a dumping ground for leopards. In another almost revolutionary move for a government department, which is inherently opaque and inward, the forest personnel started engaging with the media and civil society. A unique state–citizen initiative called 'Mumbaikars for SGNP' was initiated. It had as its members wildlife biologists, conservationists and dedicated volunteers—many of whom were busy with other professions, but took pride in the leopard in their backyard. They visited apartment complexes where leopards were spotted, reacting to distress calls by societies panicking on sighting the big cat strolling down the alleyway. Media workshops were organized to ensure sensitive reporting that did not demonize the predator. The message promulgated was: Sighting a leopard does not constitute conflict. Quell the panic, do not crowd the cat.

There were other advisories: Kids were not to go out at night, post dusk it was safer to go out in groups, gibbering away. If alone, singing—however out of tune—kept the cat away. Tribals who have been living in the forest, and alongside the big cat, for generations, are well aware of precautions that need to be taken when living with wild animals. In fact, they worship 'Waghoba'—a large cat deity, a practice among many other such indigenous communities—and this veneration has led to a greater understanding of the animal and its acceptance within their geographies.

A 24x7 helpline was initiated, for a crack rescue team who would respond in case of a leopard in the neighbourhood.

Mumbai was also taught the significance of a wild cat in their midst. The leopard isn't just a beautiful wild creature; as an apex predator, it is the keeper of the forests. SGNP is a true wilderness, harbouring thirty-five mammal species, nearly 300 species of birds and a staggering 1,300 plant species; and is part of the Western Ghats, a biodiversity hotspot. It is Mumbai's green lungs, and a watershed of the lakes that meet a chunk of the city's water needs. The park is the last remnant of Mumbai as it once was, of its original landscape; it is our natural and cultural heritage.

It worked. Panic calls to take the leopard away have dwindled, people now call in to report sightings. In some apartments, there is a buzz around the leopard. In one such apartment complex I visited, leopards could occasionally be viewed from the bedroom window—on the wall across that borders the park. Some enthusiasts had equipped themselves with cameras, and have taken to policing the place to see the leopards were not disturbed, or crowded.

I was shown a photograph of a leopard sitting quietly atop a wall, under which a chaiwallah brewed tea. Have I used the word surreal too often?

Obviously, there are also ugly, discordant notes—like a posh society which would not allow any dialogue on the leopard issue as it gave unwarranted publicity, thus devaluing their property. Yet, these were the same luxury apartments that billed their properties as premium 'Park View' or advertised 'Living Close to Nature'. It is the great urban paradox.

That apart, Mumbai is undoubtedly a role model of how cities can coexist with predators like leopards, and indeed other wildlife. It's a model that can be adapted as urban areas grapple with this issue across the country, and a few places across the globe as well.

Los Angeles lives with cougars, London has its foxes, and bears are increasingly being sighted on golf courses and freeways in places across California.

Mumbai has found space in its crowded heart for leopards, but it's shrinking. The city is pressing down on the park. SGNP rests between Mumbai's northern suburb Borivali, and Thane which lies on its eastern tip. There are plans to build an 11-km tunnel through the park to cut commuter time by about an hour. Construction for a 'dedicated freight corridor' with frequent high-speed trains going on the tracks will soon be under way.[20] The railway line will slice through the SGNP's northern tip, and surrounding forests, with resident wildlife. There are plans to build a *car park* in Aarey Colony that abuts SGNP, harbouring resident leopards including cubs.

If the forest is shredded, Mumbai will lose its green lungs that it so desperately needs. And if the forest vanishes, so will the leopard . . .

Even when living with humans, leopards need a forest, or dense outcrops, rocky areas—some adequate cover for shelter and for rearing cubs. Sugar cane fields with their tall grasses and minimal disturbance provide ideal cover. Irrigated croplands are serving as a functional ecosystem for the leopard, but they cannot be a substitute for forests.

Leopards and people live together, but they make for uneasy partners. It's a fragile peace, with tensions simmering underneath, and one gets the uneasy feeling that a carnivore amongst people is potentially a time bomb waiting to explode. One tragedy can test the tolerance, rendering this coexistence tenuous. This is mainly because we are not doing the right things to avoid conflict. Conflict has largely been guided by knee-jerk reactions rather than a strategy towards its prevention.

Our strategy to conserve the leopard, and minimize the conflict, has to be multipronged. Conserving forests, and their much-neglected fringes and buffers must be a priority. Fragmenting and chipping away at existing habitats, for example SGNP, is a recipe for disaster.

Leopards thrive outside of boundaries of Protected Areas, and wildlife here is woefully neglected, unlike in a sanctuary where its conservation—at least on paper—is the primary goal. Wildlife outside of Protected Areas is of a lesser god, marked by a conspicuous absence of will to conserve it. There is a lack of strategy, focused policy and funds for its protection. Wildlife here is largely viewed as errant, which somehow must be stuffed back into the protected zone. But Protected Areas cover roughly 5 per cent of India, and a bulk of our wildlife lives outside, many in human-dense landscapes. A strategy for their protection, in a manner that the safety of the people is not compromised is the need of the hour.

Wild animals go out of their way to avoid humans, conflict occurs when they are provoked. Our approach to deal with conflict must be centred around people, focus on avoiding confrontations, making human lives safer. There needs to be greater understanding of leopard ecology so that decisions are knowledge-based. We must draw from the wealth of traditional knowledge as well. Since leopards live in close proximity with people, it is important to work with communities to ensure losses are minimal, so tolerance is not eroded.

Leopards have adapted to living with their most deadly predator, humans; but will we have the grace to accept the cat as our fellow resident. Or will the leopard become a victim of its own adaptability?

The River Guardian's Last Vigil

If a man fails to honour the rivers, he shall not gain the life from them.

—Anonymous

February 2016, Etawah, Chambal Wildlife Sanctuary, Uttar Pradesh

'*Bahut sharmila hain*,' the boatman warned us, '*bhag niklega*.' It's very shy, will vanish at our approach.

I found it difficult to equate the gharial, among the largest of the world's crocodiles (the male can grow up to a stupendous 22 ft), as a coy creature. Nonetheless, we let the engine die and moored our boat a good distance away from the reptiles, basking on a narrow strip of the river Chambal's sandy banks. Peering through my binoculars, I could spot five in a row: eyes shut, scaly skin gleaming in the sun, hind legs tucked under, long narrow jaws agape to reveal a row of razor-sharp teeth. As still as statues.

An hour passed by, but here time—and the gharials—appear equally unmoving.

We inched the boat forward, ever so slowly . . . but the alarmed gharials slithered away, into the water, till all that was visible was the lone male's bulbous *ghara* (pot)-like growth at the end of its snout that gave this crocodile its name.

The boatman, who has lived along the river, and its gharials, all his life, was right.

The gharial is one bashful beast.

It is also one of the rarest. The International Union for Conservation of Nature (IUCN) lists it as critically endangered—just a step away from extinction. Biologists call it a specialist, meaning unlike the more common mugger crocodile who can also muck about in stagnant ponds and swamps, the gharial dwells solely in swift, clear rivers, and thrives on an exclusive diet of fish. Such fussy habits have not served it well, restricting its historical aquatic habitat of over 20,000 sq km from Pakistan, through to India, Nepal, Bhutan, Bangladesh and Myanmar to currently limited river stretches in just two countries. Globally, only about 750–1,000 gharials survive, with 90 per cent in India, and the rest in Nepal. There are fewer than 250 wild adult, breeding gharials worldwide.

In 1885 William Hornaday, American zoologist, counted sixty-four gharials basking together on the banks of the river Yamuna in the space of a morning. Anyone who has seen the Yamuna today—especially in India's capital, Delhi—would find it hard to imagine that this filthy, stinky cesspool was once a river that flowed unfettered, its crystal clear water supporting unique, and diverse, life. The gharial also vanished from the Ganga, even as it carries the river in its name, *Gavialis gangeticus*.

Ironically, the gharial found sanctuary in a land notorious for its badass bandits and the river that flows through it—the Chambal, which hosts more than half the world's 'fish-eating crocodile'.

In Indian culture, where rivers are worshipped as mother deities, the Chambal is a rare exception, almost cacodemon in its repute. Legend has it that the Charmanvati—as it was originally known, flowed red and raw from the blood of thousands of holy cows sacrificed by the Aryan King Rantideva, and was thus sullied.

In the epic Mahabharata, the infamous game of dice whereby the Pandavas lost their kingdom, and their wife, Draupadi to the villainous Shakuni was played here. Humiliated at the attempt to disrobe her, the fiery Draupadi damned all who drank the waters of the Charmanvati, which flowed through Shakuni's kingdom.

Chambal's curse proved to be a blessing—no great cities or kingdoms flourished here, nor did it become a centre of piety, and therefore pollution, which was to sadly become the fate of the holy Ganga and India's other great rivers.

In contemporary times, protection also came from another unlikely source: bandits who flourished in the ravines that ran along its banks. These outlaws ruled the roost; the most (in)famous of them being 'Bandit Queen', the title of an award-winning biographical film on Phoolan Devi, who took to a life of crime to avenge those who had abused her, and went on to become one of the region's most notorious dacoits. Their terror and command in the region ensured that it remained untouched. Investors baulked at pouring funds into this hostile landscape, no industry dotted the banks belching its waste into the river. And so it flowed pristine, continuing to shelter aquatic life, long after other rivers, reduced to mere trickles and toxic soups, failed to offer refuge.

In the entire greater Gangetic basin, the Chambal remains the river with the highest conservation value. It hosts a significant population of the endangered Gangetic dolphin, and the Deccan mahseer—a large freshwater fish, eight species of turtles including the critically endangered red-crowned turtle, muggers, otters. It is one of two nesting sites of the Indian skimmer, which skims the surface of the water with—startlingly orange—beaks to catch fish and other aquatic creatures. During mating season the male courts the female by offering her the choicest bits.

And, of course, the Chambal harbours the largest population of gharial in the world!

Wildlife also finds shelter in the ravines, a unique geological formation, that flank the river. These steep and sandy mounds, with twisting valleys, and scrub and thorny vegetation, are excellent habitat for Indian wolf, desert fox, hyena, honey badger, star tortoise, jungle cat and the endangered caracal. Large communities of pastoralists graze their cattle here. The ravines also serve as natural barriers to flooding in the monsoon and bind the soil, preventing erosion. Yet, the government in its infinite wisdom, views the *bihad*, as they are called, as wastelands, and has a grand vision to flatten the ravines and let industry flourish here, instead.

The gharial's precarious situation was first noticed in the 1970s with biologist, S. Biswas of the Zoological Survey of India reporting that the reptile was extinct in the Kosi river. Following this, an extensive survey across the species range in India and Nepal was carried out by the Madras Crocodile Bank (aided by World Wildlife Fund-India). The results were alarming—the population had crashed to a mere 200 from the estimated 5,000 to 10,000 gharials in the 1940s.

Besides loss of aquatic habitat, another key reason was the gharial's hide—tough yet supple, and with a striking texture, it was in great demand for premium shoes, bags and other leather accessories. Hunters used bullets to fell the basking gharials, fishermen trapped the reptile in nets—the flesh was venison—and the skins sold, many making their way to the leather market in Kanpur (Uttar Pradesh). The long and fierce-looking gharials also made good trophy. There are stories—though unauthenticated of a former king who shot down 100 gharials in one day. This was in the 1940s in the river Mahanadi (Odisha).

The government of the day reacted swiftly to the catastrophe. Besides listing the gharial in the newly enacted Wildlife (Protection) Act in 1972, it launched Project Crocodile in 1975 and created six sanctuaries to give its aquatic habitat protective cover—a major one being the National Chambal Sanctuary unique in the fact that it transcended three states: Madhya Pradesh, Rajasthan and Uttar Pradesh. The sanctuary covers 601 km of the 960-km stretch of the Chambal river. An institute for crocodile researchers was also started in Hyderabad where top scientists in the field pioneered research and conservation, and trained young biologists.

A captive breeding programme was also initiated, under which eggs were collected from the wild and incubated in breeding centres. The young hatchlings—protected from predators and other threats—were released when they were about a metre long. Over the next decade, about 5,000 gharials were introduced into Ken Wildlife Sanctuary (Madhya Pradesh), Mahanadi Wildlife Sanctuary (Odisha), and in the Girwa at Katarniaghat Wildlife Sanctuary (Uttar Pradesh), but mainly—over 80 per cent—in Chambal. Gharial populations surged initially, and content that the gharial had been saved, an increasingly indifferent government withdrew funds from Project Crocodile in 1996.

This sense of complacency reflected in a 2006 survey: populations had collapsed again. There were now only 200 breeding adult wild gharials in the world (mainly concentrated in Chambal) confined to just about 250 sq km—in the past half-century they had vanished in 98 per cent of their habitat, prompting the IUCN to include it in the 'Critically Endangered Species' list.

The well-intended captive breeding or 'head starter' programme largely failed in its attempt to revive populations. The purpose of such a programme is to collect eggs, provide suitable conditions to hatch, rear for a couple of years before releasing them into the wild—thus giving the dwindling population a 'head start'. This was done in many zoos, and by various state forest departments.

Monitoring of released hatchlings was poor. Few survived, perhaps hand-fed crocs growing in still pools were not equipped to hunt, or were not robust enough to face turbulent rivers. When I visited the Mahanadi Sanctuary (Odisha) in 2010, forest authorities informed that the river system now had only two or three gharials, while over 700 hatchlings had been released here over a period of time.

Frankly, I am ambiguous about captive breeding or 'conservation breeding', as it is now called. I became even more sceptical when

I visited one such centre—in Deori, Morena (Madhya Pradesh) where the hatchlings were encased in *glass* walls—in temperatures that touch 48°C—no doubt aimed to facilitate trigger-happy tourists on the hunt for photographic trophies.

The Deori centre has over the years contributed to the pool of gharials that inhabit the Chambal today, but it made me wonder—and I am looking at the 'larger picture' here—why the welfare of animals rarely gains precedence, even in programmes meant for them?

I am aware of excellent conservation breeding programmes, and endorse that it provides a safety net for species on the brink, but if it is not backed by protection in the wild, the exercise is futile. The value of the gharial *is the river it is symbiotically linked to*. We need gharials in the wild, where they serve as indicators of clean, free-flowing waters. It's the apex aquatic predator and is a living symbol of the health of the river, as much as a tiger is of the forest. Its loss means the river is lost to us as well.

If we continue to destroy the habitat, leaving no wild for the species to live, and revive in, then frankly, a captive breeding programme is nothing more than a collection of a few sample species, caricatures of the wilderness they once represented, now behind bars lest we forget that they ever existed. And so we can feel good about not wiping them off the face of the planet. Captive breeding also demands disproportionately huge funding as compared to in situ protection, and takes away from the main focus of conserving habitats that wild species thrive in.

For the gharial, recovery looks difficult with threats to its habitat exacerbated: its domain has shrunk, dams and barrages have stilled and silted the rivers, pollution has defiled the waters, agriculture on the banks and sand mining robbed them of nesting sites. All these factors will be examined in detail later in the chapter. Another disaster hit the beleaguered creature in 2007–2008, with over 100 gharials perishing in a mystery die-off. The cause was never fully established though it was suspected to be a build-up of toxins. The epicentre of this catastrophe was in lower Chambal near Etawah, and not too far from Bareh, where it meets the Yamuna. Research by the Madras Crocodile Bank has documented gharials moving over 220 km. It is suspected that the gharials moved into the Yamuna, feeding on fish with toxic overload. Another possibility is a sudden surge of toxins in the river by, say, a truck carrying toxic material tumbling into the river from one of its many bridges, or a sudden influx of sludge or chemicals released by a factory pipeline.

Though the mass die-off has not reoccurred, the condition of the Chambal is on a steady decline, and the threat of another such disaster hangs like the proverbial Damoclean sword.

Meeting the Chambal in Bollywood

I first met the Chambal in cinema. In the early years—1970s and 1980s—it was B-grade potboilers with titles like *Chambal ki Rani, Chambal ki Kasam, Chambal ke Daku*, etc.[1] which were played occasionally in the travelling cinema, where projectors were brought into smaller towns to play films, or on VCRs. The films romanticized the brigands—big, brawny men, guns slung over shoulders, thundering through the ravines on horses more often than not with a hapless damsel flung across. They robbed the rich, helped the poor, and always got the heroines! Many years later, when I travelled to Etawah district through which the Chambal flows, and once the mainstay of many notorious dacoits, I was intrigued to find that in some ways the films had reflected shades of reality, if in a glamourized, over-the-top manner. The image of dacoits that endures here is akin to Robin Hood. Many of the locals I met—fishers, farmers, taxi drivers, dhaba wallahs and the wonderful Kamladevi who fed me an utterly delicious meal cooked over *goytha*-cow dung—remembered the dacoits with fond nostalgia. Sure, the outlaws ruled with an iron hand, their mere name invoking terror, yet there was some justice in their functioning, a code of honour, if you like: the rich were taxed, the old were not robbed, the women, honoured, rapists not spared. '*Ab sab chor hai, woh bhi soot-boot mein* (Now everyone is a thief, and they operate in the garb of "respectability"),' cackled Kamladevi, making an arch comment on the lawlessness and corruption that society was now steeped in.

There are layers and layers to this fascinating history, and I am curious to delve deeper . . . but another time. For now, the river awaited, and I had to heed its call.

Three months later, towards the end of May, I made my way to Chambal again. Rajeev Chauhan, conservationist, wildlife biologist and a walking, talking encyclopedia of this stretch of the river, had called to let me know that gharial hatchlings were expected, with the seventy-day incubation period nearing its end.

Gharials nest in high sandbanks, the females dig the nest holes, some three feet deep, at night scooping out the sand, with one hind leg, then another, just as we would with our hands. Once the eggs are laid, she flips sand over the nest and carefully binds it by pressing and thumping her body over it to disguise the nest. Jeffrey Lang, a scientist who has studied the gharials in Chambal for many years believes that through the incubation period, the female stays nearby, but not in the immediate vicinity, the strategy being not to attract unwarranted attention by hovering over the nests. When the babies are ready to come out, they call—quite plaintively—and the female gets to work, digging out the eggs, from which the little ones break through and instinctively make towards water. Throughout this ritual, the male hovers close by, at times accompanied by other gharials, just like an expectant dad, and other kin would hang around—anxious and excited—at the maternity ward of a hospital! The hatchlings usually stick close to the mother for several weeks, even months, and babysitting duties are shared among the females.

All this knowledge that I had gathered had not prepared me for the extraordinary sight that awaited me that last day of May.

We (I was accompanied by Rajeev and forest department staff) reached Kasua near Pinahat (Uttar Pradesh) having jeeped, biked and walked our way through the maze of ravines to arrive at a stunning vista of golden sand, craggy ravines and the beautiful river meandering through. We arrived just as dawn was breaking, the cool morning breeze refreshing in the hot and sultry May weather where temperatures soar to a searing 48°C. Along the bank, a concentrated assembly of some 300-odd hatchlings were lined close to the shore in shallow water. We halted a few metres away, sat still for a while, before sliding slowly down the bank to stop halfway. The hatchlings scattered, and moments later regrouped. We could spot a female, much further away, occasionally thrashing her tail to make her presence felt.

It was quiet, except for the gentle murmur of flowing water.

Then, from the depths of the river, a huge gharial—a male—arose. A buzzing, hissing sound—a 'buzz snort' whispers Rajeev—pierced the silence as the gharial breathed out forcefully. He was clearly agitated by our presence, sending us warning signals, and staying close to the little ones who then clambered on to his back . . . so much so that nothing except Daddy's—could he be 'dad' to so many?—'ghara' was visible! The kids piggybacked pretty much for the hour or so we were there, occasionally sliding off and scrambling back on.

It blew my mind. There are few species in which the male takes up parenting duty, but our Mr Gharial was clearly pulling his weight, and then some. To see a reptile, so feared and maligned, being a protective, attentive parent certainly tops any natural history moment I have been fortunate to witness.

The euphoria though was marred. Shadowing the sheer joy of watching a whole new generation of a critically endangered reptile was anxiety for their future. The sandbanks on which the gharials—as well as turtles and muggers—nest, and bask to regulate body temperatures, are the setting for a bloody battle over one of the most coveted natural resources of the twenty-first century: Sand.

Yes, 'lowly' sand on which our civilization is built, which is traded, legally, but mostly illegally, for billions of dollars and is a major driver of economies, globally.

Even though each one of us is a player in the lethal sand wars, few of us know they exist, even as they play out in our backyard.

'Forest guard Narendra Kumar Sharma was mowed down by illegal sand miners in Gwalior district (Madhya Pradesh), on 6th March, 2016. In a bid to stop the loaded tractor trolley from fleeing, Sharma jumped onto the vehicle. In the tussle that followed, he was kicked and pushed as the perpetrators tried to speed away, when the vehicle swerved, toppled, crushing him underneath.'[2]

Some of us may have read this news item sipping chai in the safety of our apartment. Most would have probably clucked sympathetically, without having the foggiest idea of the link between the brutal end of a forest guard, our glass of chai, our home, and one of the most endangered species in the world, the gharial.

Before I explain, some details of the tragedy of Narendra Kumar—and many others like him—who have been killed in the ongoing ruthless sand wars. The deceased, Narendra Kumar, was a 'star' member of the team cracking down on illegal sand mining from the Chambal sanctuary over the past fifteen months. Narendra's seniors say his courage was boundless. He knew the tricks to crack the trade and had the guts to take on the mafia. He was key to seizing dozens of trucks carrying sand.

And now he is gone, murdered by the mafia. He is not the first victim, and nor, unfortunately, will he be the last.

In April 2015, a truck carrying illegally mined sand mowed down police constable Dharmendra Chouhan in Morena district.[3]

Earlier in March 2012, a 2009 batch Indian Police Service officer Narendra Kumar was also crushed to death in the same district while leading a raid on illegal sand and stone mining.

The day the forest guard was killed I was about 50 km away in the Dholpur–Rajghat stretch of the river, with Rajasthan flanking one side, and Morena (Madhya Pradesh) on the other. We were headed toward Tighra–Rithora, a hot spot for both gharials—and mining. As we sailed down the river (sometimes bumping along, and literally pushing the boat through shallow waters) we watched a mugger grab an unsuspecting pond heron, turtles and gharials basking in the sun, a colony of skimmers on a tongue of sand, and just as we had given up hope, a rotund body flipped in, and out, of the water. This was the Gangetic dolphin, the other charismatic, endangered denizen of the Chambal.

Tell-tale signs of tractors criss-crossed the banks, and over the bridge that connected Dholpur to Morena, was the constant rumble of tractors and trucks carrying sand.

Later, we went and met the foresters at Deori chowki and Morena (district headquarters). They told us of the terror of the sand mafia, and the toll it's taking on the men trying to protect Chambal, and its gharials. The previous night, a forest ranger and his team had been attacked and shot as they attempted to stop dumpers ravaging the sandbanks. They were fortunate to have escaped alive. A few days before, another forest team along with soldiers of the Special Armed Force, deployed to crack the illegal extraction, were ruthlessly assaulted. Such assaults are routine; forest chowkis and vehicles have also been vandalized, even burnt in the process. Those on the frontline of the war live a tense life, their movements are stalked. When their vehicles leave for a raid, the miners *know*, and usually vacate the scene, or the raiding teams are intercepted and attacked. Most families in Morena district have a hand in the business as it is more lucrative than farming. For example, a truck full of sand can sell from anything between Rs 20,000 to Rs 30,000 depending on where it is sold: if it goes to say Agra or Gwalior the rates are low, if it reaches Delhi's National Capital Region, the rates spiral. Most locals own tractor trolleys and guns, and stand united in any attempt to stop the mining. They are a strong vote bank for politicians, so any serious attempt to thwart sand mining is blocked. And as mining escalates, the attacks are only getting more vicious.

Researchers working in the region say that there has been an explosive increase in sand mining, particularly over the past three to four years and stretches of relatively undisturbed sandbanks available for gharials to nest are shrinking alarmingly. Mining also destroys the habitat of benthic organisms, which are an important part of the aquatic food chain.

The impacts of sand mining go beyond destroying significant wildlife habitats. River sand is like a sponge, and the water it absorbs is slowly percolated into the ground. With the loss of sand, water rushes downstream. Riverbanks collapse and river plains are rendered vulnerable to flooding. Dredging riverbeds changes the very physical characteristics and the ecology of the river, which may alter its course, cause erosion, and allow for increasing salinity intrusion. It also destroys livelihoods, with agricultural losses due to dust, as well as declining water tables.

In Chambal, most of the sand mining is concentrated on the Madhya Pradesh side. There is more trouble brewing on this front, with reports that Madhya Pradesh is pushing to denotify parts of the National Chambal Sanctuary to allow for sand mining. The state believes that allowing limited mining will help stem the illegal trade, and provide relief in the ongoing 'sand wars', but it is a futile hope. In an earlier attempt to meet the 'local' demand for sand, a 10-km stretch of the sanctuary was denotified, but instead of halting the illegal mining, it only led to a spurt of mining sites across the sanctuary. The cover of the 'legal' denotified site was used to pass off the illegally gouged sand.[4]

The Uttar Pradesh stretch of the Chambal Sanctuary is relatively free from this scourge. A consistent crackdown by the forest department is one key reason, coupled with an active local network of forest guards who monitor the nesting sites, particularly, throughout the nesting season. Also, importantly, livelihood is predominantly linked to farming, and for farmers the mining spells disaster, with groundwater collapse and pollution. There have also been awareness programmes, and in this both Rajeev Chauhan and R.P. Singh, who hails from these parts and runs the Chambal Safari Lodge, have been very active.

Morena is not the only 'hotspot' for illegal sand mining. While mining inside a sanctuary such as Chambal is banned by the Wildlife (Protection) Act, there are rules, norms and guidelines that regulate sand mining outside Protected Areas as well, but they are openly flouted.

The sand mafia–political nexus ensures that the looting goes on unchecked. It has wrecked ecologies, farmlands, livelihoods and corrupted society.

In most states—be it Punjab or Uttar Pradesh in the north, Madhya Pradesh in Central India, Tamil Nadu in the south or the tiny coastal state of Goa in the west—sand mining is backed by powerful politicians. So much so that the influx of money is said to play a role in elections with parties using the ill-gotten gains to win over voters and for campaigning.

In the recent 2017 elections in Punjab, sand mining became an election issue. Mining was ruining villages and farms on the riverbanks. It is alleged that agricultural lands are grabbed by the mafia, and there are reports of the money gained financing the drug trade, which has ruined the youth and the once flourishing economy of Punjab. One contesting party alleged that the ruling party was getting kickbacks to the tune of Rs 3 crores daily from illegal sand and stone mining. While the numbers can be questioned, it does give an idea of the scale of the illegal trade. In Tamil Nadu it is estimated to have made about Rs 15,000 crores, while the government's annual revenue was Rs 188 crores (for 2012–2013). Clearly, the illegal trade resulted in huge losses of revenues to the states.[5]

The war rages across the country. No river is spared—from the holy Ganga to Periyar in India's southern tip, Narmada that flows west to Mahanadi in the east, Yamuna as it meanders through Haryana, Uttar Pradesh and India's National Capital Region. The mining is indiscriminate, on a massive scale, vociferous in its appetite. Riverbeds are gouged and stripped bare, and retaliation to those who enforce, regulate, expose or report is ruthless.

One prominent case was of an Indian Administrative Officer Durga Shakti Nagpal's suspension, which was linked to her taking on the sand mining mafia in Uttar Pradesh's Noida district. She had seized hundreds of vehicles, arrested people engaged in illegal mining.

Perhaps the most horrific incident is of Sandeep Kothari, a Madhya Pradesh-based journalist, who reported consistently on illegal sand mining. He was abducted, set ablaze, and his charred body discovered later. His murder was linked to the sand mining.

What is it about sand that has provoked such a deadly war?

At the root is the surge in demand for sand fuelled by rapid urbanization, industrialization and infrastructure growth.

Sand is the stuff that cities are made of. Concrete, the mainstay of construction, is essentially sand and gravel glued together by cement. India leads in the construction business, after China and the US. Historically, sand was never heavily exploited, but the scales tilted with the real estate development in the 1990s. The evidence is all around us: apartment and office complexes, malls, flyovers, multiplexes—and the roads and superhighways that connect them. As India continues to be concretized in its insatiable quest for growth, the demand for sand has skyrocketed. By some estimates the industry, mostly illegal, is growing at 10 per cent per year. The finer, smoother desert sand does not bind well, so river-banks and sea beaches are being pillaged to meet this demand, not just in India, but worldwide. Though construction is the main force behind this industry, sand is also an essential ingredient in the making of computer and silicon chips, cosmetics, glass, toothpastes and solar panels.

The impact of the surging demand for sand reverberates along India's dying rivers, its price paid by those who try to contain the destruction, and protect wildlife.

Will the gharials continue to bask and flourish on the Chambal's sandy shores?

The answer lies, at least in part, on whether people like us join the dots, and appreciate the real cost of rapidly expanding urbanization and growth. Few of us think of sand, know the essential part it plays in our lives, and the cost to obtain it. Truth of the matter is, the supply of sand is finite, but the demand is not. We have to think of alternatives, reuse, *conserve* . . . as we must do with all of our natural resources. There are alternatives that can supplement sand in construction, some of which include bottom ash (which forms about 15–20 per cent of the ash produced in power plants), quarry dust and foundry sand. Concrete and asphalt can be recycled. Most of these are accepted substitutes globally, and these need to be studied, explored and used in India, with the necessary standards and checks.

*

Sand mining is one major threat, the other equally fatal blow to the river is the diversion of its waters for industry and irrigation. The Chambal flowed unfettered till Independence. But the region is arid, with a pressing need for irrigation and electricity, more so, with Kota, on its bank, developing as Rajasthan's industrial hub. Its exploitation began in the 1960s, when the then prime minister, Jawaharlal Nehru, inaugurated the Chambal's first multipurpose dam, Gandhi Sagar; followed, over the next fifty years, by six major projects. Additionally, there are about 150 medium and small projects on the river currently, stilling the Chambal's natural flow, fracturing its ecosystem. Erratic water releases have inundated prime nesting sites of gharials and turtles.

In months following monsoons, and till the rains oblige again, the river remains parched, especially as the seasons enter summer.

The continuous harvesting of water from rivers for human use has rendered the river so shallow that it is reduced to virtual disjointed pools during the pinch period, restricting free movement of the gharials. Downstream of the Kota barrage, the river is not a *river*, it is devoid of *flow*, reduced to a mere trickle for about 18 km—a report by the premier Wildlife Institute of India (WII) bluntly says 'the flow is zero', rendering the river ecologically dead, till its tributary, Parbati, herself heavily harvested, infuses it with water at Pali.

Even so, fifty-two irrigation projects are under construction and 376 projects have been planned in the basin.[6] Also proposed is the Chambal, Parbati and Kalisindh link project, part of India's massive river-linking scheme. This will divert water from Parbati and Kalisindh, further starving the Chambal of water.

Alarmed at the situation, in 2011, the WII conducted a study[7] on the minimum water flow requirements of the Chambal river for its aquatic wildlife, particularly the gharial and Gangetic dolphin. The study also aimed to assess the cumulative impacts of various water harvesting projects proposed on the river. The WII report did not mince words, stating that the Chambal could not afford to lose any more water, if gharials and dolphins were to survive. Since the 1990s, the overall flow in the Chambal was showing an annual slide of 3.5 per cent. As flows still, the gharial loses more than half of its habitat between February and June. The dolphins fare worse, with waters necessary for their survival receding by 50 per cent by November till the monsoons. If a few of the proposed projects were taken into account, by April the gharial's range would shrink to lower than 1 per cent of its historical range. Reduced river flows would also destabilize the nesting sites, lower prey base, and reduce breeding success, especially given that lean periods coincide with nesting periods.

The gharial is doomed and dammed to death.

There is hope on the horizon, with good news coming in from the Gandak river in Bihar where a survey in March 2015 revealed a population of twenty-six adult gharials. Some of these may have come in from the Narayani—as the Gandak is known in Nepal. As it flows into India, it gets the protection of Valmiki Tiger Reserve, and then the Sohagi Barwa Wildlife Sanctuary, thus giving the crocodile a secure passage. These are now being supplemented by a restocking programme from captive-born population.

Even more exciting is the news that the gharial has returned to the Ganga. In February 2009, I watched as 131 little gharials—hatched in captivity—were gently steered into the river amid cries of *'Ganga Ma ki jai'* by a motley group of foresters, biologists, conservationists and local people. This was in the Hastinapur Sanctuary in Uttar Pradesh. It's been eight years now, and the gharials seem to have fared well. There are thirty subadult gharials now in this stretch of the river, some have ventured out. They are recolonizing the Ganga, with one gharial—released animals are tagged—found about 1,000 km away near Pratapgarh in the same state.[8]

Their long-term survival though is tinged with uncertainty. Along with the other plethora of threats, is the National Waterways Act, promulgated in March 2016, which will transform the Ganga, and over 100 of India's rivers, into a busy inland waterway to transport cargo. The rivers will require dredging to enable the traffic of ships, embankments and barrages for terminals, and their cargo will include everything from tourists to oil and coal—sewering the river, curtailing its flow, eroding its ecology, and entity.

The future of the gharial looks precarious, but save it we must, for its survival is linked to ours as well.

The gharials and dolphins need clean and clear waters—essentially uncontaminated, flowing river ecosystems, equally vital to the survival of *Homo sapiens*. Their presence symbolizes a healthy riverine ecosystem. No wonder ancients revered the gharial as the vehicle *(vahana)* of the goddess Ganga, and of Varuna, the god of water.

In 2010, a booklet by the ministry of environment and forests suggested for a re-evaluation of environmentally sensitive schemes of river-linking, and large irrigation hydel projects. Calling the gharial our 'river guardian', it called for a revival and rejuvenation of rivers.

❦

Stripped of its infamy and notoriety, the Chambal is tragically going the way of the other rivers. Most of India's mighty rivers have been reduced to filthy, toxic drains. Our rivers are dying. Forests that form its catchments and recharge rivers are being denuded and destroyed. Their flow is further throttled with back-to-back dams to slake our insatiable thirst. We treat the rivers no better than garbage dumps to sink our waste—from industrial effluent to defecation to cadavers. The water of many rivers is no longer potable, in fact, not even fit for bathing.

They cannot sustain life any more. Wildlife of the rivers— mammals, reptiles, amphibians, birds and fish—are the most endangered globally, their populations have plummeted by a staggering 81 per cent between 1970–2012, as per a World Wildlife Fund report.[9] In the span of my lifetime—I am a child of the '70s—we humans have wiped out over three-quarters of life that flourished in our rivers.

But rivers are our lifeline too. Civilizations have flourished by the rivers . . . and collapsed, deprived of water, stricken by drought.

Yet, we continue to spew our filth into rivers, choke their flows, killing the lifelines that sustain us.

Bird on a Free Fall

In pushing other species to extinction, humanity is busy sawing off the limb on which it perches.

—Paul R. Ehrlich

Circa 2003: An Ornithological Quest

My journey to know and understand one of the world's rarest birds began well over a decade ago. Like many of my quests, this one was inspired by the written word. While researching on India's 'Birdman', the famous ornithologist Sálim Ali for a story, I discovered that one among the many causes he had championed was of the beleaguered great Indian bustard, also known as the GIB. In a meeting of the Indian Board of Wildlife in the 1960s, he urged that the endemic and endangered bustard be chosen as India's national bird to 'focus interest and solicitude'. It wasn't; losing the title to the peacock, owing at least in part to the worry, that the great Indian *bustard* might be embarrassingly misspelt! Poor bird. Doomed by its name and otherwise as well. With fewer than 100 remaining, the GIB is the rarest of the rare, and is listed as Critically Endangered in the Red List of the International Union for Conservation of Nature (IUCN).

I was determined to meet the *Ardeotis nigriceps*. It was a disquieting prospect, like paying last respects to a chronically ailing relative, or I thought cynically, a journey to tick off one on the '100 Species to See before They Die' list?

I got an opportunity when I was on assignment in Rajasthan as an intrepid reporter with a brief to do a touristy piece on Jodhpur and Jaisalmer, sand dunes and camels, *ghoomar* (a traditional folk dance) and forts. I had other ideas, and rather than doing the rounds of kitschy bazaars, I found myself in the forest department office in the golden city of Jaisalmer, passionately putting my case forward for a permit to stay in the Desert National Park that lay some 60 km beyond the fortress city. The official-in-charge motioned me to sit, heard me out, offered some sweet tea and sage advice on the disadvantages of camping 'especially for a woman' in the remote region. '*Ek subah kaafi hai*. Go spend a morning, even the day. There is nothing to do there. It's desolate, and there are snakes,' he warned, little knowing that his words had a diametrically opposite effect than intended.

I was definitely going, and what's more, I intended to find my elusive quarry.

❧

The Desert National Park is spread over 3,162 sq km of the Thar, one of the most populous among all deserts of the planet. Extending over 2 lakh sq km, it straddles the border between India and Pakistan. It is mainly concentrated in Rajasthan (and to some extent in Kutch, Gujarat), parts of Haryana and Punjab and into the Sindh across the Pakistan border. Before I visited the Thar, I looked up a thesaurus. The synonyms attributed to desert listed a 'wasteland', or a 'barren' region. I didn't raise an eyebrow, this is the image I have grown up with, and this is what my Grade V geography book taught me. The time I spent in the desert was a revelation—and among many things, I learnt one is not to believe all that textbooks tell you!

Initially, to the untrained eye, the fable of the arid desert is perpetuated. It was high afternoon by the time I reached, and spread before me was a vast, desolate expanse of dry land, dotted with clumps of grass, shrubs and feathery trees. The sun was harsh, merciless—I found it impossible to equate it with the benign nurturer of life. A hot, fierce wind lashed my face, depositing brittle sand in my mouth, eyes, nose and every bit of exposed skin that it could find. Small balls of thorny fruits of *Cenchrus biflorus* locally known as *bhurat,* clung in impressive numbers to my salwar and duppata. I tried removing the bhurat, but they just shifted residence to my hands, instead.

Gradually, the secrets of the desert revealed themselves. Dotted across the sandy terrain were chinkara or the Indian gazelles, some solitary, others in small groups. From afar, they appeared like ripples in a landscape seared by the heat; when they ran, glided, into the horizon they were the waves in an ocean of sand. Up close, they were exquisite. Pointed, ringed horns, kohl-rimmed doe eyes, small, graceful body balanced on slim ballerina legs. Though the chinkara appears fragile, it is well-equipped for this hostile ecosystem. It has the ability to survive without water for days, quenching its thirst with moisture-laden flowers and leaves. There was a resident chinkara at the forest rest house. Rani had been found as a quivering and starving orphan by the forest staff, who nurtured her. She followed them around like a loyal little puppy, butting her head—pointy horns and all—in a rush of exuberant, if painful, affection.

A desert is usually equated with sand dunes, but dunes constitute just one feature of a desert. The greater part of the landscape is occupied by dry open grasslands. Vegetation in the desert is sparse with a few trees breaking the bleak landscape, of which the kair (*Capparis decidua*) is one. A squat, intense tree, its branches hang heavy with flowers and fleshy berries, inviting a number of birds, like the rosy pastor, a lovely pink- and black-coloured starling, who feed on the berries. There is also the khejri (*Prosopis cineraria*), deeply rooted in desert culture, and the tree that inspired India's first environment movement dating back to the seventeenth century! As the story goes, when the king's men marched into Khejarli village in Jodhpur district to cut the sacred khejarli trees to build a new palace, Amruta Devi along with her three daughters hugged the trees to save them. They were axed to death. This inspired 363 Bishnois—a tribe known for their reverence towards nature—to sacrifice their lives before the felling was stopped.

The desert hosts an incredible diversity of birds, especially raptors, as well as a number of lizards and snakes. I had an encounter with the latter. Well, almost. As darkness fell, I dragged the cot out to sleep under an open sky. This, alone, was well worth the visit. The sky was spectacular, illuminated by a zillion glittering stars, with the Milky Way blazing across. I pondered about the view from my window in Gurgaon, Delhi's dusty, glitzy suburb, maybe some 800 km away as the crow flies: Was it even the same sky? Or its poor cousin: painted a dull grey, the stars and their brilliance obliterated in the thick smog of pollution. Delhi currently ranks as the most polluted city in the world.

Next morning, prints on the sand showed that we were visited by a snake. I don't know which one, but the marks indicated a slim, scaly creature. Possibly the saw-scaled viper?

The GIB eluded me during this visit. While I did not see the creature itself, there was much that I learnt, not least being the patient persistence and the sacrifice of those protecting the bird— the frontline forest staff. It is all very well to visit the desert for a few days and be bewitched by its wonders, but it takes courage to live your life in a far-flung, forgotten corner in temperatures soaring past 50°C protecting a bird and an ecosystem few know or bother about, and against all odds.

Circa 2013: Last Chance to See

A decade later, I was at the Desert National Park again, and had spent the better part of two days traversing the landscape. I was accompanied by fellow conservationist Ramki Sreenivasan and G.S. Bhardwaj, the director of the park, keenly interested in wildlife, and leading a committed team determined to revive the bird. We had many wild encounters, including with the elusive desert cat, a fox with its young, a button cute hedgehog, a committee of critically endangered vultures, the rare cream-coloured courser, a pair of laggar falcons . . . but had still not met, in spite of every effort, our 'target species'—the great Indian bustard.

We had all but given up hope, and were back at our station— the forest rest house, when the walkie-talkie (used by the staff to communicate among themselves) cackled. One of the guards on duty had spotted four GIBs in the Sudasari enclosures in the park. Large areas in Sudasari were enclosed in the early 1980s as a strategy for intensive monitoring and protection.

Spurred by hope, we hastened—cautiously—towards the location. We spotted them as we approached . . . tiny, hazy dots that assumed the stately shape of one of the heaviest flying birds on earth. The bustard lacks the dramatic glamour of the tiger or the splendour of the peacock, yet is incredibly beautiful in an austere kind of way, perfectly in tune with the environment it thrives in. They were tall at nearly four feet, stocky, their ashy brown frame in sync with the desert environment. Like most males of the avian world, the GIB comes into its own during breeding time—strutting around with its pendulous gular pouch, making booming calls at regular intervals to advertise its presence to the ladies. No chance today of witnessing this spectacular display; what we had here was a bachelor party of nine male bustards. Most were busy pecking, while two circled each other, feathers fluffed in what appeared to be a territorial 'I am the boss' display.

We stationed our vehicle far, at a comfortable distance, so as not to disturb their peace—and spent a few precious hours watching these rare creatures. The experience was magical . . . if bittersweet. The GIBs before us represented about 10 per cent of its entire global population.

Were we, I thought, looking at a species without a future? How did this bird reach death's door?

*

Historically, widespread hunting, accelerated by vehicular access to hitherto remote areas, for sport and food precipitated the bustard's decline.

The bird made good eating. Mughal emperor Babur noted that, 'the flesh of every part of the *kharchal* is delicious'. The British considered the bustard a delicacy and it was among the top game birds. In fact, the story goes that the Queen of England had the bustard on her menu during her 1960 India visit—though this juicy titbit is unconfirmed.

What made the GIB even more attractive for so-called 'sportsmen' was its large size as well as the fact that it offered surprisingly close access by vehicle; the bird, apparently, had no fear of vehicles. The female and young birds, with their tender flesh are a preferred bag. Like most mothers, the GIB female is fiercely protective of her young, rarely leaving the nest, usually a carefully concealed spot on the ground. Poachers and trappers would corner the female bustards by setting the areas surrounding the nest on fire, making her an easy target.

Shikar records show that the GIB was formerly abundant in the dry bush and grassland of the Indian subcontinent, ranging from Pakistan through to Punjab and Odisha in the east, extending southwards to Tamil Nadu—spanning eleven states in India. Its strongholds were in the Thar desert and the grasslands of the Deccan plateau, and even the United Provinces as per the records of one F. Wilson, who writes of spotting a flock of sixteen in 1881 in *Stray Feathers*, a journal edited by Allan Octavian Hume, ornithologist, British civil servant and one of the founders of the Indian National Congress. Old records show the GIB was plentiful in Rajasthan—Hume writes in 1890 of 100 bustard eggs collected in Bikaner. The abundance—and the scale of the hunt—is indicated by records in *The Oriental Sports Magazine* of one Robert Mansfield who bagged no less than 961 GIBs between 1809 and 1829 in Ahmednagar district, where even the ghost of the bird is lost now, erased even from human memory.

Over the next century, the bustard's fortunes plummeted, its numbers and range, dipping steadily and alarmingly.

The decline did not go altogether unnoticed. In 1952, nature's most ardent spokesperson, writer and conservationist M. Krishnan warned that the 'bustard is going, going, though not quite gone'. He believed that in a dying race, the reproduction urge is exceptionally strong, as the survival instinct kicks in. But a bird as persecuted as the GIB had little chance. Krishnan appealed to the government for action, urging 'that unless sufficient living space, food and protection are provided, a last minute resurgence will not save the species'.[1]

In its first meeting in the same year, the Indian Board of Wildlife included the GIB among the thirteen rare animals to be protected. This protection remained largely on paper, matched with little action on the ground, and the GIB continued to decline rapidly. In 1969 Dharmakumarsinhji, former prince of the Bhavnagar state and a keen hunter-naturalist, conducted, with the support of the World Wildlife Fund (WWF), the first survey of the GIB estimating about 1,260 birds, which further dwindled to 750 in 1978.[2]

Then, in the same year the bird got a reprieve, curiously by an incident on a royal hunt—of another species of bustard. The houbara bustard is a winter migrant to the subcontinent, and running the bird down with falcons especially trained for the purpose is a popular 'sport' among Arab royalty, and the arid grasslands of Pakistan, a preferred haunt. During the mid-1970s, the Arabs extended their hunting grounds to India, reportedly at the invitation of the Indian government. Interestingly, at the time Atal Bihari Vajpayee[3] was the foreign minister. The hunt was illegal, against the Wildlife Protection Act, 1972, but the law was a mere blip, in view of the 'petro dollars' the Arabs brought in—especially at a time when India was reeling under a foreign currency crisis.

'We were shocked at the hunting of protected species and realised we had to do something and next year, when the Arabs and their falcons turned up, "we were prepared",' writes Harsh Vardhan, a veteran conservationist in the journal *Cheetal*. He led a silent March in Jaipur in 1978 to protest the hunt, having worked over the past few years to galvanize support. What started as a murmur by a few concerned people grew into an unprecedented public outcry across the country against 'government supported poaching'. The media took up the issue—this was unusual news, with an exciting mix of rare birds, royal hunts, external affairs—and this inflamed the issue. Ultimately, the matter was taken to court, which stayed the illegal falconry, and the Arabs were requested to leave.

Support for the bird gained momentum with an international symposium on the great Indian bustard, held in Jaipur the following year and organized by the Tourism and Wildlife Society of India. A GIB postal stamp was released, the then prime minister, Indira Gandhi put her weight behind the effort, and 'Bustard States' came forward to establish eight sanctuaries to protect it. Rajasthan declared the GIB its state bird in 1982, and the Bombay Natural History Society launched a 'Study on the Great Indian Bustard' to advocate its protection, and research.[4]

This reprieve, which even saw a marginal rise in GIBs in a few areas, turned out to be temporary, a brief season of hope, before the downward spiral continued. By 2008 there were fewer than 300 birds left. The bird's population had plummeted by 75 per cent within three generations. India's ministry of environment and forests, not given to alarmist tendencies, warned that the GIB could probably go extinct within the next three generations.[5]

It has been wiped out of most of its original range, even in sanctuaries created for its protection. For instance, thirty-five bustards were counted in Karera or Son Chiriya (as the GIB is called locally) and Ghatigaon Bustard Sanctuaries in Madhya Pradesh in the 1980s when they were created. There is not a single one left now. Equally bereft is Gaga-Bhatiya Bustard Sanctuary in Gujarat, Sorsan and Sonkhaliya in Rajasthan, Rollapadu in Andhra Pradesh and Rannibenur in Karnataka.[6]

What went wrong?

❦

There are many ways to kill a bird. Hunting is the obvious culprit, and was the initial cause of the massive decline. It continues to be a threat, more so in Pakistan, which supports a tiny population of the bustard, though no extensive surveys have been conducted. A paper published in *Current Science*,[7] in 2008 notes that of the sixty-three birds sighted in four years (2001–4), forty-nine were poached. Were they ours, or 'Pakistani bustards'; did they belong to any country at all? The sky knows no boundaries, and birds, unlike us, fly free across borders. A colleague fretted, 'Will they (in Pakistan) want to save a bird which carries the prefix "great Indian"?' he pondered, his tone hysterical, and suggested a change in nomenclature!

Then in 2013, I received in my inbox images of bustards in flight in the Cholistan desert along the Indo-Pak border. Cholistan runs contiguous to the Thar desert in India. Even more promising was a conversation I had with one of the naturalists involved, 'Neither country can save the bustard alone. Can we not have a collaborative initiative to protect the bustard? A joint task force, even a trans-boundary Peace Park for the GIB.' Music to my ears, but his despondency echoed mine, 'Will it ever happen?' Will this critically endangered bird be considered insignificant, perhaps even trivial, in the larger issues that dominate Indo-Pak relations? Will we condemn the bustard by our politics, inaction and apathy? If only it could be a symbol of peace between our nations . . .

While India may not have the same levels of hunting, it does occur across the birds' range. Even in its best stronghold, the Desert

National Park. In December 2012, a GIB was gunned down by hunters in broad daylight—at noon, just a few yards from the Sudasari enclosure.

Hunting is just part of the story. The key cause of the GIB decline is the steady annihilation of its habitat—the bird now survives in barely 3 per cent of their original range.

To understand the bustard's unfortunate predicament, we need to know the nature of the beast.

The GIB is an awkward sort of species. Large bodied hence sluggish on the wing, the bustard is also a slow reproducer, mostly laying only one egg at a time. This is when the bird is most vulnerable. The biggest threat is from livestock which may trample over the egg. As in most bird species, frequent disturbance during the incubation period may dim the chance of successful hatching.

The other problem is the lack of local support. The GIB is a wide-ranging bird, flying as far as 100 km. A considerable portion of its diet intake is crops for which it visits the fields around. Farmers don't really have so much of a problem with the bustard as the damage it causes is nominal.

The main source of antagonism is the Protected Area itself, which the farmers feel has alienated them from their own land, and denied them some basic facilities like irrigation and connectivity by way of roads and telecommunication. This can be traced to the fact that delineation of sanctuaries was not done wisely, the boundaries drawn inappropriately, including within their ambit a number of villages. For instance, 95 per cent of land in Maharashtra's GIB sanctuary spread over 8,500 sq km was private, over which the forest department had no control, and even included the Solapur town with a population of nearly a million people! There is no bustard left in this sanctuary today, and a large chunk of it has been denotified.

This is a no-win situation for all. For instance, the Desert National Park has within it a cluster of seventy-three villages. The people were resentful as they could not avail bank loans with their land as mortgage or develop or sell it, as Indian legislation governing Protected Areas severely restricts land use. The park authorities have control over just about 4 per cent of the park, leaving the rest beyond the scope of management as this land is not under the control of the forest department. As for the bustards, they are in a 'sanctuary' overrun with people and cattle and no undisturbed haven to call their own.

This is the pattern in all GIB sanctuaries which deteriorated under insipid management. Even the breeding sites are not secure, and heavily disturbed with unrestricted movement of people. Former director of the Bombay Natural History Society, Asad Rahmani, cites the example of Karera Wildlife Sanctuary (Madhya Pradesh) where they had repeatedly advised for securing a mere 10 sq km of area that was identified as nesting sites of the bird. Even this miniscule area was not secured, and populations thinned with no new young. But the GIB was kept alive on paper; and false increases were reported.[8] Today, it is yet another of the sanctuaries from where the GIB has vanished.

The main cause of the bustard decline, however, is to do with the habitat it prefers. Bustards are the pulse of grasslands—which are the most endangered, ill-managed, misunderstood and undervalued ecosystems in the country. Strange, for grasslands are the most pervasive and vibrant ecosystems—supporting a large mass of wildlife, as well as *Homo sapiens*. We derive nearly 75 per cent of our diet from grasses. Most of our cereals—wheat, rice, corn, barley, millets, and other foods like sugar cane are derived from grass that has been selectively bred, developed and cultivated over thousands of years.

Little surprise then, that India's Planning Commission–appointed Task Force for Grasslands and Deserts says Protected Areas of grasslands are 'gene banks—an important genetic resource in the form of grass and shrub species crucial for ecological and food security of the country'.

Grasslands also support some of India's rarest wildlife—the pygmy hog, the wild buffalo, the Nilgiri tahr, wolf, caracal, swamp deer, hog deer, to name a few. The other bustard species, the Bengal florican and the lesser florican, are also grassland dependent, and in dire straits.

Indeed, the only big mammal to go extinct in India in the twentieth century was the cheetah, who thrive in dry, open grassland where they can pick up speed—they are the fastest animal on earth—to hunt prey.

But they were outpaced by man. The last record of cheetahs in India is of three males shot dead in 1947 in the principality of Koriya in present-day Chhattisgarh.

Yet, there has been no attempt to document the value of grasslands, much less conserve them. According to reports of the Wildlife Institute of India (WII) less than 1 per cent of the grasslands come under the Protected Area network.

On the contrary, grasslands are considered 'wastelands'. About 70 per cent of this—the Thar belt—region is considered 'unproductive', and as part of its policy, the forest department diligently converts them to woodlands in well-funded afforestation drives. Native species, kair, kejri, jaal, bordi—life support systems in a harsh desert—have largely been ignored, while exotic trees were planted over the years. Most prominent among these was the *Prosopis juliflora*, colloquially referred to as the *gando baval*, or 'the mad tree' for its propensity to spread madly, and colonize the landscape.

The GIB is part of a programme of the Union environment ministry to revive endangered species. Rajasthan has made it its emblem, as the state bird. Yet, the same government has a systematic programme that obliterates the habitat of the GIB by such plantation drives. Bustards are *grassland* birds, needing wide open spaces, and scrub, to nest, to breed, and to fly. Even as I write—and this is somewhere in mid-2016—the madness continues. There are reports of ongoing massive plantation of exotic trees in Mokla–Parevar, one of the largest and finest grasslands in the area.

If the trees wreaked havoc, even more damaging to the Thar was the Indira Gandhi Canal Project with its grandiose vision to pull water from Punjab rivers to green over 4,000 sq km of the arid desert. Well, this wet dream was a grand failure, and a disaster for the native ecology. The canal caused drastic hydraulic changes. Excessive irrigation, seepage and increased salinity waterlogged the areas where the canal brought water, submerging land and the native grasses that sustained both cattle and wildlife.

The availability of water drew in people who had little understanding of the desert, and land was cleared to take advantage of the irrigation system. Farming practices changed and more land was cultivated intensively and throughout the year, whereas earlier it was one crop during the monsoon, leaving it fallow for wildlife—bustard, chinkaras, desert cats, foxes—to use for the rest of the year.

It also attracted graziers, increasing livestock pressures—all of it resulting in heavy destruction of the *sevan* grasslands, which are crucial bustard habitats.

They have become '*wastelands*' now, those areas we sought to de-desert. Oh, the irony of it.

There were other excesses. Wasteland is a convenient term, lending the land to easy exploitation. So, over the years, grasslands were degraded, diverted, destroyed for real estate, industry, roads, mining, canals, agriculture. Oil wells were dug in, gypsum dug out, and the productive outer layer of the Thar stripped to mine limestone. The mines brought in ancillary disturbances—trucks to cart the minerals and factories to produce the cement.

Over the past few years, another insidious threat hit the grasslands from unexpected quarters—harnessing the wind and the sun for energy. Wind and solar farms have taken over swathes of prime bustard habitat in both Thar and Kutch, further crunching its nesting areas, and isolating the small fragmented grasslands, favoured by the birds.

The Mokla grasslands in Thar were lost to the bustard following the installation of wind turbines and high-tension transmission lines between Salkhan and Mokla area. Large numbers of wind turbines also came up just north of the Sam-Sudasiri area, further shrinking prime bustard habitat. More than twenty-four GIBs were sighted in just two hours by Desert National Park director G.S. Bhardwaj in 2013 before the installation of wind turbines in the Salkhan landscape. There is little trace of bustards here since then, with only the very occasional sighting. It's the same situation in Gujarat, which has the second 'largest' population of GIBs—a grand twenty[9]—after Rajasthan. Yet, prime bustard habitats between Naliya and Bitta in Kutch have been allocated for renewable energy projects.[10]

The world over, the lethal power of turbines is well established, with a US-based study estimating that somewhere between 1,40,000 and 3,28,000 birds die each year globally from collisions with wind turbines. In fact, some wind farms employ cleaners to bury the corpses as the birds and the bats—another casualty of the turbines—fall.

It is not the killing, however gory, that's worrying as much as the direct loss of natural habitats.

The footprint of an individual wind turbine might be small, but collectively wind power stations require associated infrastructure development. To install and maintain such 'farms'—though I prefer not to be Orwellian and say it like it is—a Wind Power Station—roads are constructed to lug turbines, earth movers and JCBs rip the grasslands leading to immense disturbance and its eventual destruction.

India has a renewable energy generation target of 175 GW by 2022, of which 160 MW is expected to be met by solar and wind energy, requiring massive amounts of land and much of it will be in the 'wastelands' aka deserts and prime bustard habitats. Other favoured sites are equally sensitive ecologically—for example, the plateaus of the Western Ghats, a global biodiversity hotspot. Wind farms have been set up in prime tiger habitats, and proposed even inside sanctuaries.

Renewable energy is critical in an era of climate change, but its placement must undergo scrutiny for biodiversity impacts. Its status of being clean energy gives it a halo, an assumption of being less disruptive, but we cannot turn a blind eye to its huge ecological costs. How can a clean source of energy be called 'green' if it destroys the ecosystems and the wildlife that thrives in them? And in this case, contributes to the extinction of a species.

🖋

On 15 September 2015, I got a cryptic message announcing the death of Alpha. This was devastating news—Alpha was one among the three GIBs in Nannaj Wildlife Sanctuary in Maharashtra (besides the rare transient ones). As his name suggests, he was the dominant male—productive—and had successfully mated this April. 'It gave all of us at the sanctuary so much hope. It was after six years that we were recording summer mating of the GIB,' wrote Vaijayanti Vijayaraghavan, a biologist working in the area,[11] in a note. The other male is younger, and imaginatively called Chottu (usually an affectionate moniker for a younger child)! Both had been tagged by wildlife researchers, to understand the mystery that surrounds the birds. The solar-powered GPS[12] yielded some crucial information like the fact that they travelled long distances, and like all wild creatures they avoided humans. The bustards would spend the night foraging in the fields; and as the day dawned and people streamed in, they would take off to the tall grasses close by or wing it to the adjacent Nannaj Sanctuary. It was on one such morning that Alpha crashed into an electricity transmission line inside Nannaj. He died a painful death—as he lay injured and bleeding, feral dogs ripped him to death.

With the loss of Alpha, only two GIBs remain in Maharashtra.

With such critically low numbers, the loss of every bird is catastrophic—pushing the species closer to the brink.

The maze of power lines in GIB habitats are a major hazard for the bird. GIBs fly at low heights, and coupled with their relatively small binocular field vision, they are more prone to such collisions. In the past decade, six GIBs have died as a consequence of collision or electrocution. Alpha is the seventh.

So, will this iconic bird vanish in our watch? There is no genteel way to say this: It is our appalling apathy and inaction that have brought the GIB to death's door. We continue to annihilate its habitat in full knowledge of its imminent extinction. We are allowing the bird to die out.

We need to recognize this, if we want to save the bustard.

What we cannot do is give up on hope, and on the great Indian bustard.

The time to act was yesterday. But, we can still push back its extinction, possibly revive the species, if we take *urgent*, focused action. There is an immediate need to designate well-protected core breeding areas, with a landscape conservation strategy where any activity factors in the bustards' ecological needs. Within Protected Areas, and even outside in bustard landscapes, a network of large and well-maintained Sudasiri-like enclosures must be maintained and protected as core breeding areas for the bird. These must be inviolate, with no disturbance whatsoever.

The GIB is a landscape species, flying great distances, feeding from traditional farmlands. The GIB needs people, particularly those it shares space with, on its side. An antagonistic local population will doom the bird. The need of the hour is community-based conservation programmes that aim at resolving empowerment and livelihood issues, and take up decentralized, low-footprint eco-tourism, joint monitoring of the bird, etc.

Degraded habitats need to be restored. Maharashtra did a remarkable job in Nannaj, by uprooting exotic trees, and restoring prime bustard habitat.

Detrimental infrastructure projects must be curtailed in priority areas and changes made in favour of bustard-friendly grazing and cropping policies. High and medium voltage power lines can be taken underground, immediately, around core areas used by bustards. Equally important are programmes to control free-ranging dog populations around areas—particularly breeding sites—used by the bird.

There are other issues, bustard sanctuaries are low on the priority radar, and are meagrely funded and staffed; which must be urgently addressed.

Rajasthan is the last battleground for the long-term survival of the species, and there have been some positive steps here as well. The state announced the 'Great Indian Bustard Project' allocating funds for its protection in 2012. The park has a committed team, who is determined to give the GIB a fighting chance. Even though the political party changed in the next elections, 'Project Bustard' was honoured—political will across parties is crucial—and the current state chief minister Vasundhara Raje promised her support. In a meeting of the State Board for Wildlife held in May 2015, she said her, 'government was serious about saving its state bird— the great Indian bustard—from extinction and no stone would be left unturned.' She enabled NGOs, conservationists and scientists, involved them in the effort and availed of their expertise.

Scientific surveys were carried out in a collaborative effort of the WII and the state forest department to understand the distribution of the GIB in the Thar Desert, to enable targeted conservation efforts.

In Sudasari, field staff enforced the exclusion of cattle, the fencing was strengthened, monitoring and protection stepped up. Better anti-poaching mechanisms are in place. The efforts have paid off, a poacher was arrested in 2013 for allegedly killing, and cooking,

Rajasthan's state bird in 2013. This was a first and sent a message: You could end up in jail for roasting a *godawan,* as it is called locally.

The grasslands in Sudasari are reviving. Other such enclosures have also come up. A colleague sent me a photograph—actually on the day 2017 dawned—of five GIBs foraging in lush grasslands. When I had visited this area—Gazai—in 2013 it was heavily degraded, with more cattle, and little sign of any wild creatures and certainly no bustard.

Today, there are better community networks, and wider outreach. And a visible collective effort, with NGOs, scientists, local experts and groups coming together, and supporting the forest department to revive the GIB. There have been renewed efforts to involve local people. NGOs like the Bombay Natural History Society, which has been at the forefront of the battle to save the GIB, continue to play an active role.

A remarkable initiative is by Pramod Patil, a doctor by profession, and with a passion for the GIB. He works with local herders and farmers to enlist their support. Pramod draws on his medical skills to build a rapport with the villagers. He offers basic medical care and counselling, periodic health camps, and in return they offer their commitment to the GIB. They report sightings, have helped identify new breeding sites and restore pasturelands.

The idea is to build a relationship with the local people, connect community benefits with GIB conservation so that they are *for* the bustard.

What is worth noting here is that, anyone can contribute to conservation, contribute their skills, time . . . and make a difference. It's an oft-repeated adage, but it's true—if there is a will, there is a way.

Landmark steps have been taken. The Rajasthan government decided not to set up any more windmills or wind power projects in the areas which have GIB presence. The National Green Tribunal in September 2016 banned installation of windmills near Desert National Park—though there are news reports that work continues despite the ban.[13] In fact, experts assert that windmills on the flight path of the bustard must be uninstalled.

Another commendable initiative by the park management has been to work with the army, as many parts of the Thar are under army control due to it being a strategic border. This effort has made significant strides and the army has come forward to support a joint survey, and protect the bird within its domain.

India has also announced a captive breeding programme, and allocated some initial funds for the purpose, but some experts warn that the foundation population is too small and strict protection of the GIBs (and their nests) in situ, will be far more effective.

For the bustard it may be a case of too little, too late. Yet as long as the last bustard lives . . . so does hope.

As I reflect on the grim fate of this bird, I am reminded of a book I read, *Witness to Extinction*. It's about the *baiji,* the Yangtze river dolphin, a species as old as 25 million years, and revered as the 'Goddess of the Yangtze' in China. The dolphin was declared extinct in 2007. Writes the author Samuel Turvey, 'All that's left on stage are the commemorative baiji statues. As for the baiji itself . . . it looks like it is the only thing not made in China anymore. Poor old baiji. You deserved better.'

The great Indian bustard deserves better too.

The Last Voyage

The sea, the great unifier, is man's only hope. Now, as never before, the old phrase has a literal meaning: we are all in the same boat.

—Jacques Cousteau

29 February 2012: Nature's Maternity Ward

It's twilight, in a remote beach in Ganjam district, Odisha, where the river Rushikulya pours its waters into the sea. The sky was ablaze with stars, outshining the pale hue of a curved moon. The beach was barren; the air, pregnant with expectation. We are awaiting the *arribada*, or 'the arrival', as the mass nesting of the olive ridley turtles is known. I had rushed here the day before in response to a call from an excited 'Turtle Rabi'—more on this remarkable man later—who urged me to get here *stat*, if I wanted to see the turtles congregate.

Oh, yes. *Yes*.

Science has not yet pinned down what exactly decides when the arribada will occur. Local lore has its own indicators—a brisk wind that blows in from the south, a half-moon night, a trickle of turtles landing ashore.

The night I arrive, so do the turtles: Thousands and thousands surged on to the beach, their heart-shaped, olive-hued shells luminous in the pale moonlight. Using their flippers, they hauled themselves up the sandy slope and, once on the flat beach, they marched, possessed in their frenzy to find suitable nesting sites. It is only the females who have arrived ashore, to lay their eggs; the males never hit land after they leave the beach as hatchlings.

Turtles have blanketed the beach—scurrying, skirting, bumping, climbing over each other, in their frantic bid to find a patch to nest. It was futile to try and count: the next day, newspapers herald the arrival of well over a hundred thousand turtles. Any empty space is promptly occupied. On a busy night like this, real estate is a tough find . . . and I noticed, more than once, a turtle digging up—unintended—the nest of another, eggs flying out with the sand.

The ridleys seemed to be in a stupor, focusing on their task with grim intent. Once the nesting site is zeroed in, they laboriously scooped out sand using their flippers. Ever so often, I would see one pause, as if to take a breather and gather strength before continuing its arduous task. I peered closely at one, and found she was teary. The heart believes it is emotion and exertion—but the turtles are only shedding excess salt from glands located close to their eyes!

Once the funnel-like hole—as deep as a bathing bucket—was ready, they dropped the eggs, soft and white like ping-pong balls—and filled the nest with sand. This done, the turtles raised themselves on top of the nest and started thumping their bodies—rhythmically rocking up and down to seal, and secure, the eggs. With a multitude of turtles employed in the task, the air thrummed with an earthy drumming sound . . .

You know what was even more extraordinary than this spectacular event for me? The fact that I was right in the midst of it, amongst the turtles, occasionally, absently, bumped by one. This was *nice*. Heart-warming. A lifetime spent in the forest has taught me that wild animals—from a mongoose to an elephant—are wary of humans (but obviously!), and usually vanish at our approach.

And here I was, sitting with the turtles—and they were supremely indifferent to my presence!

What an *honour*.

I was fortunate. An earlier attempt to see the arribada, nearly a decade ago (2008) at the Gahirmatha rookery, also on the Odisha coast, was a tragic affair. I did not witness mass nesting, or sporadic nesting. In fact we did not see even one live turtle. What we saw, instead, was a coast littered with rotting carcasses of adult olive ridleys. Accompanied by Aditya Panda, an Odisha-based conservationist, I walked the coast, trying to count the dead. We gave up after the first 100. I shut my eyes, covered my nose, but the sight and the stench of death refused to go away.

We couldn't close our eyes to reality.

It couldn't be wished away.

This was not a one-off tragedy. It's a carnage that occurs with sickening regularity annually with thousands of turtles killed—the 'accidental', fatal, by-catch of the industrial-scale fishing in our seas.

Here's their story.

Before conservation was law, ridleys—like all other turtles—were killed for their meat in great numbers. Their blood was sold as 'medicine'. Zai Whitaker, author and director of the Madras Crocodile Bank, records the grisly trade in the Tamil Nadu town of Tuticorin in her book,[1] 'When the turtles were cut up the blood drinkers would queue up—mostly old people hoping to revive their waning powers through the elixir for one rupee a glass.' Apparently, when the Wildlife (Protection) Act came into force in 1972 banning the trade, the 'Sea Turtle Blood Drinkers Association of Tuticorin' wrote to the state government to be allowed to continue their traditional activities!

The main hub, though, was Odisha. Ridley eggs were consumed and traded. In fact, before Independence the local zamindaars would extract an *anda kar*—a tax on boatloads of eggs. Till the early 1970s, the state issued permits for egg harvesting, and it was during this period that trade in turtles—now illegal—from Odisha shot up, propelled by demand in West Bengal. Helpless nesting turtles were hauled in, trussed up and transported to meat markets. It took one gutsy woman to document the trade. India's first woman herpetologist, J. Vijaya, or Viji as she was known, scoured the fish markets of Kolkata and Howrah and exposed the horrific massacre. Her account of the slaughter with grisly black and white photographs appeared in the news magazine *India Today* in 1982[2] and shook the public. It caught the attention of the then prime minister, Indira Gandhi, who promptly took action. She asked all coastal states—especially Odisha, to be more vigilant, also directing the coastguard to 'prevent the hunting of turtles and collection of their eggs'. In a response to a letter from Archie Carr, chairman of the Marine Turtle Specialist Group, she assured, 'We are well aware of the importance of endangered species to ecosystems, and all measures would be taken to ensure turtles are looked after.'

The trade dwindled to almost negligible, but it was only a temporary reprieve.

The ridley now faced new dangers. The construction of massive infrastructure along the coast, polluted seas and industrial trawlers have rendered its habitat hostile and its passage unsafe. Marine fishing was rapidly changing. India's approximate 7,500-km coastline, traditionally dominated by small, artisanal fishermen, had morphed into a massive industrialized operation catering to a hungry international market. The same story played out in Odisha. Traditional fisherfolk in their small boats and nets did not present a threat to the turtles. The advent of mechanized trawlers began in the 1980s, and the 'industry' grew exponentially. Controlled by powerful businesses, trawlers crowded the coast, without any heed to carrying capacity, ecological impact or laws that governed marine fishing. Nor was there any significant enforcement.

For the turtles, the trawlers are lethal.

Fishing trawlers drag an enormous, weighted bag-like net across the sea floor that scrapes the seabed, scooping up everything in its path—eggs, fry, fish, coral, molluscs, sharks, dolphins, turtles. Over 90 per cent of the catch in such nets is wasted. Marine ecologist Aaron Lobo likens it to a marine equivalent of clear felling rainforests, killing everything in its way.[3] Turtles are such 'accidental' by-catch in the fishing industry. Turtles (and dolphins) are air breathers, surfacing every few minutes to breathe—they suffocate to death when entangled in nets. Survivors are usually clubbed to death, so that they can be easily pulled from the net, and thrown back into the sea. Yet, these survivors have a chance. When caught in nets, some turtles become comatose with shock, and can be revived. But of course, no trawler makes the effort, nor is there any initiative from the authorities concerned to initiate and encourage the practice.

Another method of fishing, gill nets, is even more lethal. These are long, flimsy nets spread across oceans—a single net can extend up to a few thousand metres. Turtles—and other creatures—get entangled in this wall of death, and meet an agonizing end. If they survive, their flippers are chopped off to save the nets and then tossed back to sea. Bivash Pandav, a Wildlife Institute of India (WII) scientist who has worked extensively on the ridley, recalls the horror of watching a gill net collapse under the weight of entangled turtles off the Gahirmatha coast. It was the nesting season of 1999. Bivash dragged the loaded net ashore—it took him five hours—and counted the dead, 'There were 193 turtles.' The potential scale of it terrified him. 'There are hundreds of such death traps spread across turtle hotspots, we simply do not know how many die . . . We can only speculate, and it is not a pretty picture.'

Peak fishing season coincides with turtle mating season, leading to large-scale slaughter. Only a small percentage of the carcasses land ashore, most sink in the seas. Biswajit Mohanty, the force behind 'Operation Kachhapa' (*kachhapa* is the Odia word for turtle), launched in 1998 to conserve turtles, reckons that, at least 10,000 turtles are killed by trawlers and nets every year. He also points out that the state has failed to deploy high-speed patrolling boats at the congregation zones, so turtles continue to be needlessly slaughtered every season due to lack of effective patrolling.[4]

There are solutions. Trawler nets can be equipped with Turtle Excluder Devices (TEDs), which have flap doors that allow dolphins and turtles an escape route. But they are not being employed: not one trawler uses the TED, claimed a researcher working in Rushikulya, a statement corroborated by some of the fisherfolk we spoke with. Trawl operators fear that with the turtles, the catch will escape too, though studies establish that only 2 to 8 per cent of the catch escapes.[5] Yet, after an initial enthusiastic push by governments and NGOs, serious attempts to adopt this technique have fizzled out. Not a single licence of a trawler has been cancelled for non-use of TED, which is mandatory.

TEDs don't work for gill nets, but there is an effective way to avoid the massacre. Turtles do not spread at random in the sea, but assemble in large patches, termed by scientists as 'reproductive patches' off shore of nesting sites.[6] All that is required is to keep trawlers and nets off these sites during the mating and nesting period. These crucial patches represent a mere fraction of fishing area in the sea, mainly within 5 km from the coast. Yet, even as this information has been available for well over fifteen years, it is not yet part of marine fishing policy, and practice.

Do we even *want* to save the turtles?

The state seems indifferent to its plight, shrugging off its responsibility to this unique natural heritage. Odisha is, after all, the only mass nesting site for olive ridleys on the Indian coast.

And as destructive as industrial fishing is, it's just one among the deadly cocktail of threats that the ridleys face.

To understand this, let's travel back to the beginning of the voyage of the world's smallest and most enigmatic of all marine turtles.

Marine turtles are also called living fossils, as they date back to the late Jurassic era—they have been on this earth for about 150 million years, living out most of their lives in the sea. Ridleys are one among two marine turtle species (and the only one in India) that converge to nest in huge numbers in a synchronized manner. Some fifty-odd days after the arribada, the matchbox-sized hatchlings crack open the eggs and make a mad dash towards the sea, evading rapacious predators both on land and in water: Raptors, gulls, jackals, crabs, fish. The current carries the young hatchlings, and so they swim, sometimes across entire oceans; we don't know the journeys they make. What we do know is that the journeys are perilous, and getting more so by the day. They must navigate an increasingly crowded, inhospitable sea, which is getting more acidic, warmer due to pollutants and global warming.[7] Its waters roil with effluents, sewage, trash, plastic. Most of the plastic we use, from cling film to wrap our food to disposable cutlery to fibre from synthetic clothes, is dumped into the sea. By 2050, says the World Economic Forum, there will be more plastic rubbish than fish in the oceans!

The plastic usually breaks down, and the tiny, confetti-like pieces are mistaken by turtles, and other marine life for fish (for instance, the wispy, translucent jellyfish). Plastic clogs their digestive tract, leading to a slow painful death.

Very few hatchlings survive: Of every 1,000 sea turtles, *one* will reach sexual maturity, which takes about a decade and a half. As adults they traverse back, and the female returns to her natal beach to give birth, likely guided, aver scientists, by a biological compass and by sensing the earth's magnetic fields. It is believed that each coast has a unique magnetic signature.

And so this cycle has gone on for millions of years—the olive ridleys are older than dinosaurs. But could *potentially die out within our lifetime.*

On the face of it, it appears improbable. After all, lakhs reach Indian shores annually. For instance, in 2015, about three hundred thousand turtles nested in Rushikulya. Surely such copious numbers can withstand the loss of a few thousand? Indeed, this apparent abundance of ridleys has led to downlisting of the species from the 'endangered' category to 'vulnerable' in the Red List of the International Union for Conservation of Nature (IUCN) in 1997. The shenanigans behind the move are another story; suffice for now to know that a weakened status renders its conservation harder. The message it sends: Turtles are thriving. But the reality is bleak. It is a fallacy to be fooled by the numbers game, to be lulled into thinking there are 'enough'. The natural mortality of ridleys is colossal, so a critical number has to be maintained to sustain the population. Precipitous declines have been recorded in the western Atlantic ridley population. By some estimates, global populations have fallen by 30 per cent from historic levels before the era of mass exploitation.

The success of the olive ridley lies in the phenomenon of the arribada, nesting in huge numbers so as to cushion the extremely high mortality. And with nesting sites eroding, collapsing, the future of this ancient mariner is grim.

In India, the countdown has begun.

About half of the world's ridleys come to India (they inhabit the tropical waters of the Pacific, Indian and Atlantic oceans, and also mass-nest in Mexico and Costa Rica), and of these over 90 per cent reach Odisha's coast. While sporadic, sparse nesting occurs all along the country's mainland coast, and islands, the arribada is limited to three beaches in Odisha: Rushikulya, Gahirmatha and Devi, all located near river mouths. We do not know, conclusively, why the turtles home in on these nesting beaches, but it is likely a combination of favourable factors: the type of sand, an ideal temperature, a productive coast that was, till recently, remote, pristine and undisturbed. The flush of sweet water from rivers, creeks and estuaries pouring into the sea provides the turtles with a rich, diverse diet of fish, crustaceans and molluscs.

The rookery at Gahirmatha Wildlife Sanctuary was the finest in the world, welcoming the highest number of ridleys. The earliest documentation of such mass nesting dates back to the accounts of Captain Alexander Hamilton in the early seventeenth century, who writes of 'prodigious amounts of sea tortoises laying their eggs in a sandy bay near the river mouth of Ballafore (Ballasore)'.[8] For centuries, the ritual continued; in 1991 Gahirmatha recorded about 6 lakh nesting turtles.

When the arribada in Gahirmatha beach was first discovered in 1975, nesting spanned the 10-km stretch of the beach near the Maipura river mouth, from Ekakula to Habalikhati. The 1989 cyclonic storm—and subsequent upheavals—ripped apart Gahirmatha beach into two, limiting the mass nesting to a 3–4 km beach, now called the Ekakula Nasi rookery. These sections further splintered, partly due to a super cyclone in 1998, the situation aggravated by the massive dredging taking place along the coastline with construction of jetties, ports and other development. The nesting site has fragmented into smaller islands; and the rookery, Nasi II, shrunk to a mere 800 m.[9]

Beaches are not stagnant, they are dynamic, and have been called 'rivers of sand', for the continuing ebb and flow of sand carried by waves and currents. Erosion is a natural process, but the wind and the waves that take away the sand deposit it elsewhere, augmenting or creating another beach, usually in its immediate environs. So beaches shift—one may erode, while another may arise, around the same area; a process that turtles are attuned to.

Construction, mining, dredging and other such development along the coast has altered this equation, accelerating erosion and hindering the reformation.

For the ridley, the first fatal blow was a missile testing range set up by the Defence Research and Development Organisation (DRDO) on Wheeler Island adjoining the nesting beach of Nasi.

The Wheeler Island, renamed Abdul Kalam Island after the late former President of India, is where most of India's missiles are tested. DRDO armoured its beach to prevent sand loss, and secure its island and investments. The boulders literally drew a line of concrete, locking up sand that would otherwise be deposited on an eroded beach. Plus, the crashing of waves against artificial walls increases its force, accelerating beach erosion alongside—in this case, the turtle's nesting site.

Turtle moms are fussy about their nests. Their nesting spots have to be just so—not too near high tide lines, as the waves would swallow up the nests. Not too far, else their little hatchlings would not be able to make it to the sea. With a shrunken beach, such ideal spots are scarce, and only about a third of the turtles can nest successfully. Barely 25 per cent of eggs hatch—the rest are inundated by waves, are eaten, or become accidental victims of turtles digging up older nests to make way for their own. In 1999, more than 90 per cent of the eggs laid in the rookery Nasi II were lost due to inundation.

There is another problem with the missile range, ports and other development and inhabitation rapidly expanding along the coast: light pollution. Turtles navigate by visual cues. Nesting sea turtles get disturbed by artificial lights on the horizon, and may not make it to the beach. For the hatchlings lights can be a matter of life, or death. They make their way towards the sea guided by the bright glow on water that reflects a dark sky illuminated by moon and stars. Lights from ports, industries, aquaculture units and towns have changed the night skyline of these once-desolate beaches. The glare of artificial light befuddles little turtles who then turn towards this brighter source of light, away from water. They fall easy prey to predators, get crushed on roads, shrivel to death in the heat of the sun as they struggle to find their way back to the sea, or simply die of exhaustion in the process.

One study found that 80 per cent of hatchlings headed in the wrong direction, responding to light from a single industry.

A study by wildlife biologist Divya Karnad indicated that, in Rushikulya, even the lights from nearby villages outshine the soft glow of reflected moonlight, pulling more than 60 per cent of turtles towards it.[10]

A

Another development which hit the turtle hard was the Dhamra Port, constructed about 13 km from the Nasi group of islands and Gahirmatha Marine Sanctuary, and just 5 km from Bhitarkanika National Park, one of the most diverse mangrove forests in the world.

The port endangered both the Protected Areas and the turtles. Environmentalists had opposed the port ever since it was proposed in the late 1990s, notably Greenpeace India, which led a spirited, high-profile and controversial campaign.

Dhamra requires an annual dredging of almost five million cubic metres to maintain the channels to allow the passage of ships. Biswajit Mohanty of Operation Kachhapa explains that the dredging area is very close to the congregation site of the breeding turtles. They had noticed heavy erosion of the Nasi island after the dredging work was carried out some years ago, leading to a decreased nesting area for the turtles.[11] It also alters the benthic flora and fauna which the turtles feed on. Fearing that the Dhamra Port will seriously impact Gahirmatha's nesting turtles and could lead to the beach being abandoned by the marine creatures, the Supreme Court's Central Empowered Committee categorically asked for an alternative site for the port.

There *are* alternative sites where a port can be constructed, but there are no alternatives for the turtles.

The state, however, bent over backwards to accommodate the port. In what proved to be fortuitous for the port, but not for the turtles, reduction in Protected Areas ran parallel to the development of the port. The 1988 draft notification for the Bhitarkanika National Park had the present Dhamra Port site within its 367 sq km, but when it was finally notified a decade later in September 1998, it had been reduced to a mere 145 sq km. The national park now excluded the port site. In 1998, the Odisha government had entered into a contract with International Sea Port Pvt. Ltd[12] for the expansion and development of Dhamra Port. Similarly, the draft maps of the Gahirmatha Marine Wildlife Sanctuary measured 65 km in length and extended 10 km seawards, taking in its fold Wheeler Island where the DRDO facility was developed, as well as the proposed site of Dhamra. Both these sites were excluded when the forest department demarcated the sanctuary following a request from the government in 1997.[13]

The Dhamra Port was granted environmental clearance not by the ministry of environment and forests (MoEF), but by the ministry of surface transport (MoST). This bizarre manner of doing things was due to a 1997 amendment in the Coastal Regulation Zone (CRZ) notification where the MoEF handed over powers of clearances of port projects to the ministry responsible for their execution—MoST.

When I met the CEO of Dhamra Port Pvt. Ltd at a press conference in Mumbai, he dismissed wildlife concerns with a perplexing, 'If you asked the turtles, they would want the port too,' to a defensive, 'The port would not harm turtles,' to a flippant, 'So what if a few were to die? There are plenty more turtles in the sea; a few mortalities here and there did not really matter.'[14]

The port had also violated forest laws. A series of documents made available—including a letter—to the MoEF by its regional office in Bhubaneswar revealed that the port was being constructed on Protected Forest land, for which no permission was sought under the Forest (Conservation) Act, 1980, as was legally required. Yet, one month later, the MoEF at Delhi, under the leadership of Jairam Ramesh, filed an affidavit before the Supreme Court's Central Empowered Committee stating that the port was not on forest land—a complete contradiction of its own regional office report.

The ministry was endorsing a gross violation of forest laws, even as its document co-authored by the WII on 'Turtle Friendly Development' advises no ports, harbours and jetties within a range of 25 km of any important nesting and congregating site.

Regardless, the port is set to grow. Currently with 25 MTPA, Dhamra[15] is set to expand to 100 MTPA. Like all ports, this one is linked to ancillary industries and infrastructure: Offices, residential colonies, railways to transport cargo, Special Economic Zones, thermal power plants—with their own sets of problems, including pollution, waste disposal, oil leakage and spillage, hazardous material emissions. Ships plying here carry cargos of cooking coal, thermal coal, limestone, iron ore; now there are plans to attract petrochemical cargo and refining capacities. Any oil or chemical spill here would not only devastate the offshore waters—turtle mating sites—it could also spread into the labyrinthine Bhitarkanika mangrove forests, making any cleanup impossible.

There are other problems. Some, seemingly far away, like the plunder of sand from the river Mahanadi, many miles away. During the monsoon, the Mahanadi washes down sediments which is critical to the beach-building process in the marine sanctuary, but the massive mining means less sand is carried over to the nesting beaches, shrinking them further. Equally destructive are apparently benign activities like tree plantations. The Odisha coast is hit by frequent storms. In a futile bid to stem the damage, the state, flush with funds for 'afforestation' covered the entire Odisha coast, including turtle nesting sites—with exotic casuarina trees. When the 1999 super cyclone hit, the casuarinas collapsed like matchsticks.[16] The plantations mutated the open sandy topography to a woody one—ruining the beaches, rendering them useless for turtles.

This collective onslaught is crumbling Gahirmatha, and the finest of turtle nesting sites is dying a slow death. Turtles still nest, lulling us into believing all is well: in 2010, over 3 lakh landed ashore. But the fact is, their world is shrinking, becoming uncertain.

Arribada at Gahirmatha was a continuous, regular event till 1987. It is now increasingly becoming erratic and occasional, the key reason being changes in the beach profile.[17] In 2013, about four lakh turtles nested, but they failed to turn up the following year. While 2015 was a good year, reportedly, the numbers in 2016 had declined drastically.

The future of the Gahirmatha rookery, the finest ridley nesting beach in the world, is uncertain.

We have already lost Devi; there has been no documentation of mass nesting here for over a decade. With thousands of corpses washed ashore, it is more a site for mass burial now. The annual slaughter by trawlers and gill nets has been highest on this stretch. And far from reviving this haven for turtles, the state has reportedly gone on an overdrive to plant casuarinas, laying the beach to ruins.

By all accounts, the ridley's best prospect in India is the Rushikulya beach, which the turtles seem to increasingly favour, as others are rendered inhospitable.

❧

Turtle Rabi—his given name is a dignified Rabindra Nath Sahu—can't pinpoint when he met the marine reptile he has prefixed his name with. He hails from Purnabandha, a fishing village on the edge of Rushikulya beach where the turtles nest. They were annual fixtures of the landscape, as far as his memory goes, and few paid heed to the thousands that crowded their backyard each season. What Rabi clearly recalls, if with some distaste, are the eggs. He, along with other schoolkids, would dig the eggs out for food, mainly to be fed to the goats. They smelt bad, were not high on taste, but they were free, as against chicken eggs which cost 50 paise a piece.

Then, in 1994, a 'sahariya' (city boy) arrived at their village. The sahariya was Bivash Pandav, a researcher studying turtles: he observed, tracked, tagged turtles, on the coast, and into the sea.

The villagers were initially amused at this inordinate, inexplicable interest in the reptiles. Rabi, then thirteen, viewed it as a fortuitous escape from the daily grind, and started tagging along with Pandav. He attended school by day, and helped 'Bivash Sir' track turtles at night. One such night, they counted over 30,000 nesting turtles. Rabi pauses when he tells me this, as though trying to stress the import of that night, '*Ajeeb raat thi, jaise doosri duniya se* (The experience was other-worldly).' It changed him. It dawned on him that their village was the custodian of something extraordinary and unique. And so he became 'Turtle Rabi'. He learnt all he could to understand the reptile—to read the wind and the weather, track mating pairs, count nests, monitor mortality. His friends mocked him, his family despaired of his wastrel ways. But Rabi had discovered an exciting new way of life, he now had a purpose. He started dissuading his people from taking the eggs. 'I explained that the turtles are guests who have chosen *our* beach over so many others. They come to us when they are most vulnerable, laying their eggs in our trust,' he says.

In 1998, with the help of Bivash, Rabi and other local youth set up the Rushikulya Sea Turtle Protection Committee. Rabi and his gang of volunteers started patrolling the beach during the nesting and hatching. Gradually, the egg collection stopped. As the rookery gained fame and a place on the world natural history map, it drew more ecologists, scientists and journalists. One day, TV cameras came to their village, and Rabi was on Doordarshan, India's national channel, talking turtles! 'It made my village sit up and look at me with some respect!'

The committee is very active today: they keep the beach clean, monitor the arrival of turtles, protect eggs, help baby turtles disoriented by light back on track, hold awareness drives with locals and schoolchildren—all of which has helped them gain support for the turtle.

Such ownership, and support, from the locals is vital for conserving turtles, but the issues are complex. Fisherfolk resent the fact that the presence of turtles has led to a ban on fishing with mechanized boats and trawlers (there is no ban on traditional boats) during the turtle season. But more than the turtles, say some of the fishermen gathered at Purnabandha, it is industrial fishing that has edged them out.

The large trawlers are not just killing the turtles, they have destroyed artisanal fishers. They must now fish for longer hours, risking their lives in traditional boats in deeper waters for tiny quantities of fish. Even the composition of catch has changed—more commercially lucrative species have simply been fished out. The sea is jammed with 'trawl traffic' and the trawlers come closer to shore—though the shallows are reserved for artisanal fisherfolk—sweeping the sea, sucking its creatures, indiscriminately, not unlike giant vacuum cleaners.

Such industrial-scale plunder is emptying the oceans, pushing many fish species, and marine life, to extinction. The sea is being emptied of life. Worldwide, populations of marine species have *halved* since 1970.

Cornered, many artisanal fishermen have been forced to work as labourers with the very industry that has forced them out.

There is little scope for alternative livelihoods, and while turtle tourism is being explored as an option, there are genuine concerns about the impact of unregulated tourism on one of the last arribada beaches. Tourism could be a golden opportunity, providing local livelihoods, giving the local communities a sense of 'ownership' of the turtle. At the same time, it would help generate awareness, gain support. If people watch this spectacular natural event, surely they would become a champion for the turtles? Problem is, can we achieve the fine balance of livelihood benefits while maintaining a light footprint? Experience shows this is unlikely. What would hordes of selfie-obsessed tourists driving down in buses and cars armed with cameras, mineral water bottles, plastic bags, power torches et al. do to an eco-fragile area, and a creature that can be killed by *light*?

And if the turtles are promoted as a 'tourist attraction', mega tourism infrastructure will rapidly come up along the beach.

There is also the question as to who would be the real beneficiaries—the locals, or powerful outsiders, as is usually the case.

🐚

There is another dire foe, common to both the turtle and the artisanal fisherfolk: reckless exploitation of the coastline. Over time, the path of industrial development is drastically changing the land use along the coast, and hence natural coastal ecosystems and associated livelihoods. Mangroves have been felled, creeks filled, swamps reclaimed, and in their place have emerged ports, industries, power plants, real estate projects and tourism resorts. A sparsely built natural coastline is our best insurance against an increasingly turbulent, stormy sea.

The Sagarmala, 'Necklace of the Ocean', project, announced in March 2015, is set to accelerate the process with port-led industrial development, and infrastructure development along the coast. Calling coasts the new 'engines of growth', Prime Minister Narendra Modi announced that India is set to double its port capacity by 2025, with targeted investment of Rs 1 lakh crore.[18]

There is a logic that drives this growth. For instance, power plants use resources such as seawater in large quantities, and use imported coal for which they have captive jetties, and hence are cost-effective.

The socio-ecological costs, however, are discounted. By some estimates, India has a port every 28 km. India also has a fishing hamlet every 2 km.[19] Neither these, nor the turtles, seem to feature in India's plan to develop its coast.

The construction, dredging, mining and reclamation that such development requires is eroding beaches, wreaking mangroves and estuaries, heating and poisoning the oceans, endangering marine life, plummeting fish populations. It threatens livelihoods of over three million fisherfolk residing along India's vast coastline. The impacts of construction and other related activities completely change the morphology of the coastline as land gets eroded, and disappears. Forty-five per cent of India's coastline is facing erosion—erasing beaches, swallowing villages, displacing people.[20]

Also being eroded to facilitate varying scales of coastal land grab is the regulatory regime to protect the coastline. The CRZ Notification was introduced in 1991, and again reintroduced in 2011. The interim period saw the original notification amended some twenty-four times, each time to permit a new construction activity within the eco-fragile 500 m of coastline—home to fishers and other coastal communities. Throughout its history, fishing communities and environmental groups have fought for and demanded greater participation in the implementation of this law. With all its flaws, the current notification has elements that can protect the environment.

Unfortunately, five years later, the notification was again reviewed, and amendments introduced in a remarkably opaque process and with fewer public consultations. Decision-making bodies of the CRZ[21] remain paper authorities with little capacity to function and violations of the coast continue unabated.[22]

Back at Rushikulya, Rabi is gearing up for more battles. He is worried about the upcoming infrastructure along the turtle coast. Ports are planned all along the Odisha coast, including close to the mass nesting sites. Rabi says seven ports are proposed to the north of Rushikulya. The Gopalpur Port, some 15 km from the nesting beach, is already under construction. Rabi asserts it has accelerated erosion. He is right, the impact area of a port is considered to be at least 20 km beyond the actual land it occupies. Rabi walks me about a kilometre (from the nesting beach) as the crow flies, or the turtle swims. We are standing on a narrow strip of sand, but Rabi says it was a beach not five years ago. A parking bay, actually, where fisherfolk moored their boats, but the sand tongue is too narrow now, and has left the fisherfolk in a quandary. 'If all the ports come through, Rushikulya won't survive. We are developing the coast to death.' He pauses, adding, 'And its people. And turtles.'

The Sounds of Silence

The world is full of magic things, patiently waiting for our senses to grow sharper.

—W.B. Yeats

Poverty of Our Present

There are many ways to gauge the rapid ecological changes taking place on Planet Earth—the scientific monitoring of temperatures as they rise, tracking weather as it gets more unpredictable, erratic, counting the pace of extinctions: Yearly. Monthly. Daily.

There are other indicators . . . all around us, but usually, they pass us by.

It's as if there is something missing from our lives, but we can't quite place our finger on what. My diagnosis of this unidentified malady had two eureka moments. One was over a decade ago, the summer of 2002. I was curled up in my favourite chair, reading, the dog at my feet, when I realized that the ceiling fan was on—in fact, it had whirled the summer through, a luxury not seen for many summers. Here's why. When I was growing up, in the 1970s through to the 1990s, sparrows were aplenty. They were so ubiquitous, we almost didn't notice them, but for the ceiling fans. A number of sparrows had made our home, theirs—nesting in the crevice behind the painting, in the upside-down lampshade, in that little nook under the curtain rod, and such like. They would fly back and forth, beaks stuffed with straw, grass, leaves, twigs and such other construction material for the perfect sparrow home. The problem was the heat—temperatures hovered around 40— and if the birds were in, the fan was out. The spinning blades could brutally chop these diminutive birds. It happened once . . . one tiny little being flying exuberantly across the room to meet its mate was slashed into two. It was grisly—blood spattered on the floor and across the wall. Worse, its bewildered mate circled over the still body, chirping plaintively.

Post this tragedy, the family duly passed the Sparrow (and Other Home-Dwelling Birds) Protection Act. The principal clause was that fans were not to be switched on under any circumstances, whatever the provocation, no matter how high the mercury shot up. We bore the heat stoically and the sparrows were given right of way, albeit amidst much grumbling. I do not know when they disappeared, till the year the fans ran from spring through to the summer, the floor sparkled unlittered with bits of grasses and other more messy, icky stuff, and the air devoid of cheery bird calls, felt silent and lonely.

It hit home: the sparrows had dwindled, if not vanished. I realized later that the sparrow had not just vanished from my turf, a global concern had been raised for its decline. In Britain, for instance, their decline was said to be some 60 per cent in urban areas.

My second discovery was more profound, and recent. I was reading John Vidal's piece in the *Guardian*[1] on *The Great Animal Orchestra*[2] by Bernie Krause. The book recounts the author's lifelong quest to record natural sounds in wild habitats across the globe. Krause has recorded the sounds of over 15,000 species. Quotes Vidal from the book, 'A great silence is spreading over the natural world even as the sound of man is becoming deafening. Little by little the vast orchestra of life, the chorus of the natural world, is in the process of being quietened.'

Later when I got to reading it, the book stunned me, and I am not even talking about 'the silencing'. Here was a completely different perspective of relating to nature, identifying species and their vast diversity, and the ecological changes around us through their auditory expression. I lived in an aural universe I was pathetically unaware of.

When did we get so removed from nature that we failed to perceive its ebb from our lives?

If we are to go a step further, how do you miss something which you perhaps have never encountered? Like my little niece (on her first visit to a village) who stared in wonder at the sky hanging heavy with stars, a sight her eyes had never met in a densely populated and polluted Mumbai.

Our lives are boxed in concrete, we drift between temperature-controlled spaces, even our leisure is aided, if not controlled, by technology. IPads, IPods, smart phones dominate the auditory world; Fitbit and co. measure the steps taken (if we take them at all). Our senses have been dulled: How do eyes penetrate the darkness, when they have for generations been aided with artificial glows? How do you 'hear' the sounds of nature above the deafening din of civilization?

Well, the book set me thinking about the 'biophony'—as the author Bernie Krause calls the sound of all living organisms (except *Homo sapiens*)—that surrounded my childhood, and how the sounds are now barely a whisper . . .

A Silent Spring

During my childhood, as the sun set, and the din of the urban jungle dropped to an occasional sound, a different set of acoustics gradually set in, increasing in crescendo as darkness engulfed the city. It usually started with a metallic '*tchak tchak charrk*'. I would peer, warily, above the bed, and there it would be, glued to the roof (defying the law of gravity) in the neighbourhood of the bulb—a house gecko. Small, slim, bulging eyes and a tail that had a life of its own *even when cut off from the body*. It was a ploy to distract a predator, and in this endeavour the tail would do a little jig, wriggle around, while our friend simply grew another one!

My mum, who had a philosophy of 'live and let live', dismissed my fears and pronounced the creature harmless, and useful, as it ate (ugh!) flies, mosquitoes, termites and the like. So, I lived with it in peace, as long as it kept to its space, and did not invade mine—especially falling, *platt* on my face, during the night, as had happened far too often for my liking.

There were other sounds—the most pervading of which was the crickets. I hated it, seriously, truly hated its insistent, ear-piercing screech, till I discovered that even this decidedly ugly insect (it's quite difficult to see this insect, the first time I 'met' it was in a lithograph) was quite an interesting creature. Only the male—thank god for small mercies—is blessed with speech, and manufactures its music by rubbing its wings mainly to attract a mate. It changes its tune to claim its territory, and ward off other males vying for favours.

Love and land (territory) pretty much sum up the motivation for birdsong too. Though ornithologists will argue, and rightly so, on this terse dismissal of what is surely the most beautiful, vibrant repertoire of melodies. I agree with them, birdsong is the *only* music I am addicted to; nothing, not the finest opera compares to the avian symphony.

I recall the varied ditties that accompanied the day: the raucous call of the peafowl at dawn (and their vibrant dance in the monsoons), and as the sun climbed, the koel's soulful cry would waft in through the window. Sparrows chirruped, babblers argued, and the magpie robin, attired in a dapper black and white suit, sang its heart out. Cawing, cooing, cheeping, tweeting (I mean it the old-fashioned, bird sort of way). Wonderful.

Insects fluttered, bees buzzed, squirrels chattered . . . and then there were the strong, silent types like snails encased in their shells ponderously making their journey across the garden floor.

Monsoons brought alive another orchestra—the guttural chorus of frogs as they serenaded their mates in the pools formed by the first showers. The croaks, while not high on the melody scale, were so very welcome. For, along with the song of the pied crested cuckoo,[3] they heralded the monsoon. Years later, I read noted author, the late Khushwant Singh's note on this, 'For me the chief importance of June is the arrival of the monsoon bird. It is nature's messenger, appropriately named the megha papeeha or "the song-bird of the clouds". I record its advent in my diary as soon as I hear its distinct wailing cry. This has varied from the 1st to the 15th of June, almost a month after they are sighted on the Malabar Coast.'[4]

What moved me the most, though, were those memorable nights when the jackals howled, the eerie yowl piercing the soul. It was primitive . . . it was the cry of wilderness in a bleak and concrete jungle. I marvelled at this ghost of the darkness, which I only heard, rarely saw: Where did it live? Who was it calling? How did it survive in this hostile, peopled world?

I can't pinpoint when nature went silent . . . but it has. The magnificent symphony has dropped to a soft, apologetic murmur. Birds still sing, but the tremendous orchestra that drowned all other manner of sounds is an increasingly rare pleasure. I hear the occasional parakeet screech, welcome the odd squirrel into my garden, sparrows visit, attracted by birdseed and water I put out. Dawn breaks, silently, and dusk still falls, but minus the soft hoot of the owl, or the insistent 'did-you-do-it' call of the lapwing.

No wonder, there are fewer trees for owls to tuck themselves in, no messy, undisturbed corners for the ground nesting lapwing to hatch its eggs. The lawns are manicured, lined with uniform, ornamental trees and sprayed with pesticides that does no insect, bird, or us any good. Old trees with canopies and deep roots are not favoured, as they mess with overhanging wires, and their roots interfere with underground pipes and cabling.

Over the years architecture and the kind of buildings that dominated urban areas has changed drastically. Old bungalows with their nooks and crannies—prime real estate for birds—have been replaced with high-rises and apartment complexes which offer little room for nesting. But it wasn't just the physical spaces that were demolished, what also shrunk was that space in the human heart for fellow beings. I recall a time when most households would spread out grain, rice every morning for the birds and sugar for ants; families made chapattis for the neighbourhood dogs by rota, and would even light small fires outside for warmth in bitter winters. Returning home late one night, I found the dogs missing, but a couple of jackals curled cosily by the still-glowing embers!

As we sanitized our lives, spraying pesticides and poison on any creature we deemed as pests, our world diminished, and perhaps yet unknown to us, got lonelier.

Bee hives in the odd tree that finds space amidst concrete towers rarely survive. In gated colonies like mine, the hives are simply sprayed with pesticides, killing the bees in one efficient stroke. I have not heard the papeeha for years, and it is TV which informs me that roads are clogged, thus announcing the arrival of the monsoon.

As for the jackals . . . I can't recall when I heard them last, and if truth be told, I miss them the most. Forget the edges of urban India, you can't even hear them in some forests where they were once abundant. I particularly recall the famous bird sanctuary, Bharatpur in Rajasthan. You couldn't sleep, as jackals howled the night through, mainly in winters. And if you stepped out, you could also listen to the quiet foraging of the occasional porcupine. Last time I went, the nights were silent, interrupted only by the occasional howl. But there is no peace in the quiet, only a deep sense of loss.

This silence is seeping across landscapes, as forests, fields, wetlands, lakes, gardens are cleared, paved over with concrete. As jungles shrink, and thin, animals are on the retreat. Many moons ago, I was in Dachigam National Park, in the beautiful valley of Kashmir, which harbours the hangul, a beautiful rare red deer endemic to this region. An old soldier of the forest, the late Qasim Wani recalled how when he was a child the golden valleys of the forest boomed and echoed with the rutting call of the hangul. Now, with barely about 150–200 of these deer remaining, only the odd rut pierces the air.

There are many such examples, where within one lifetime, natural sounds have muted. Not just in the terrestrial landscape, the mighty oceans and vibrant coral reefs suffer the same fate. Whales are musical, with an amazing range of songs. The songs of the humpback whale are especially haunting, complex and can last for hours. Different humpback populations may have their own 'anthems'—with populations in different ocean basins having their distinct songs. Their music is not static, it evolves . . . and travels far, reaching across oceans.

They are not the only marine creatures who make music—fish, crustaceans, shrimps, puffers—all 'talk' as well by varied means— gnash their teeth, swing their tails, exhale, grunt, belch. The Gangetic dolphin, a creature of the river is near-blind, and to it sound is *everything*. It speaks—even though we can't hear its call— through echolocation. It sends out sound waves that echo back so it can sense things out. That's how it finds mates, and averts risks.

The repertory is shrinking, and the desolate sounds of extinction are making waves here too.

As wild creatures retreat and extinctions occur—the earth has lost half of its wildlife in the past forty years—a silent spring dawns on our natural world.

We are all witness to it, but we have chosen to close our eyes and ears to it.

What's also deepening the silence of nature is the cacophony of humans. What are the sounds that surround you? Well, if you live in a typical city, it is likely that your aural universe is a deafening mix of honking, motor engine sounds, construction ruckus, clanging of passing trains, the piercing noise of aeroplanes should your house be unlucky enough to be placed on a flight path . . . and so forth.

Noise is so much a part of our lives that many don't even think of it as noise *pollution*. It was one of the reasons I shifted out of Mumbai. I found I couldn't escape the constant, deafening noise of traffic and local trains that ply the city, performing the vital function of an easy commute for its citizens. My nerves were on edge, and coupled with the diesel fumes, my headaches became all too frequent, impairing my regular functioning.

I had the luxury to move, and I did, albeit to a city that is now the world's pollution capital—Delhi (and am now preoccupied with seeking an escape route)! There is nothing out of the ordinary about my affliction, noise pollution is linked to many ailments like heart disease, hypertension, and can lead to debilitating hearing loss.

Our world is getting noisier. The increase in noise follows the graph of human populations, only it grows faster, the decibels doubling every thirty years, by some estimates. The space for 'quiet' is shrinking . . . new technology, brings new noise— vacuum cleaners, car alarms, loud, and louder, stereo systems, mobile phones. What can I say, my cell phone trills out a birdsong, every time someone thinks of me, telephonically speaking.

Day at Night

What I also acutely miss are the nights, which are no longer 'nights'. The darkness has gone out of our lives—and I mean it literally— by pervasive light pollution, a constant glare from excessive, unshielded night lighting. Have you seen the satellite images of our planet during the hours of darkness? It looks beautiful, a ball of black marble aglow with light, with only a few dark spots—a telling image of the earth that is alight 24x7. Surely that is desirable. Safer. Aesthetically pleasing? It is difficult for most of us to imagine light as pollution. Many of us fear the dark . . . But life on earth has evolved under natural cycles of light—night and day. Animals have a biological clock that regulates periods of rest and activity, guides in their functioning of navigating, foraging for food, etc. Nocturnal animals sleep during the day, and are active at night. Marine turtles use the glow of moon and stars on water to guide them from land to the sea, dung beetles navigate with the help of the Milky Way.

Radically altering the light levels and rhythms these animals are adapted to is one of the most drastic changes that humans have made to their environment.

Personally, the light has robbed me of the magical nights of my childhood. As a child, one of my greatest pleasures was watching fireflies. I can never ever forget the first time I saw this miniscule pinpoint of light flitting around in mid-air. It was difficult to grasp it was a *living* being . . . how does it stay alive when on fire? Full of curiosity, I chased it, trying to capture that flame. But soon more such little lights flew by, coming in thick and fast, in swarms, setting the night aflame with a brilliant, flowing gold. They flew zigzag, they lit up paths, they settled on trees. I remember our young neem tree dotted with what appeared to be a million fireflies. They seemed to be blinking their lights in some sort of rhythm. I was to read later that sometimes fireflies synchronize their flashing, apparently to help female fireflies recognize potential mates. Don't ask me how.

It was magic, though scientifically speaking it's bioluminescence, and occurs in a number of life forms, even in the open sea. It happened in Mumbai's Juhu beach recently—November 2016—with the sea shimmering a bright shade of blue. It was the bioluminescent phytoplankton—small microbes that produce their own food like green plants; that lit up the waters at night.

For fireflies, it's a mating thing, that light flashing off their tiny bum is a come-hither signal that the male beetle (yeah, the firefly is a beetle) flashes to attract a mate. If the female approves, she flashes back, guiding the male to her. There are about 2,000 species, they don't all glow, but each that does has a unique flashing pattern.

It was a rare enough event in my childhood that appears to have fizzled out, at least, from the urban landscape. Need I add that as always, the problem is us, humans. And our usual list of suspect activities—mainly our sprawl, rapid urbanization, light pollution, pesticides, and a warmer climate which is bringing in invasive species.

How do we let such enchantment vanish from our lives? How do we fail to recognize the poverty of our present?

'A Great Thinning'

A few monsoons ago, another vacuum hit me in the gut—a loss of abundance. This epiphany occurred when I found that the rains arrived, but did not bring with them their menagerie of insects and frogs that I always equated with the downpour. After the first rains hit, wetting the parched earth, the surrounds would suddenly be flooded with an avalanche of insects. Doors and windows would be hurriedly shut as they would rush to the light and flock around it, obscuring the angry yellow glare of the bulb. I don't know what they were, how many kinds. I remember luminescent glassy insects flitting about—masses of them like tiny little fairies. I thought the rains had hatched them, but was amazed to see them emerging from the soil. I discovered that they were termites, and some take wing with the rains. The next day they were gone . . . leaving the floor littered with silvery glassy wings.

Yet another loss.

Naturalist and author Michael McCarthy calls this 'vanishing of abundance in the natural world'. An image he evoked is of 'driving through snowstorms of moths, so thick that at the end of the journey you had to wash the windscreen? Now the windscreens are clean.'[5] I remember this well—when our beloved, cranky old car was rolled out on rare occasions, it would, inexplicably, attract hordes of insects on balmy nights.

The abundant have become extinct. The most famous is the passenger pigeon, which was described in 1833 as the most numerous bird on the continent by American ornithologist and painter John James Audubon. He illustrated this by describing 'a mile-wide flock of migrating pigeons that passed over his head and blocked the sun for three straight days!'[6] By the early twentieth century they were extinct, the last known passenger pigeon, Martha, died in 1914 in captivity at the Cincinnati Zoo.

I will bring you another such tragedy of the commons from closer home. At one time, the vultures soaring in the Indian skies were so numerous, they couldn't really be enumerated. Some estimates suggest there were over 40 million vultures in the Indian skies around the late 1980s, early '90s. I remember seeing the skies darken with a profusion of vultures as we lay on our charpoys in the courtyard, and have witnessed them—hundreds hunched over a carcass and stripping it to bone in twenty minutes. They would thus dispose of millions of road kills and cattle carcasses—performing the vital, dirty job of cleaning up after death.

Almost overnight, the skies emptied, with populations crashing an astounding 97–99 per cent in a matter of years. The main cause was a veterinary anti-inflammatory drug, Diclofenac routinely and disproportionately used as a painkiller for cattle. It's toxic to vultures, who perished on consuming cattle carcasses on a steady diet of Diclofenac. The drug has since been partially banned in India.

Like with most creatures, we have a schizophrenic relationship with vultures. It is worshipped as Jatayu, the vulture god of the epic Ramayana who died protecting Goddess Sita from the demon king Ravana. We also tend to think of this bird with some distaste, and morbidity, as harbingers of death. In common lexicon, a 'vulture' has negative connotations, used as a metaphor to describe one who preys on the weak or who benefits from the misfortune of others.

And so, few mourned its passing. But we had it wrong. The bird plays a valuable role in the ecosystem as a scavenger—its loss has affected the health of people.

The dramatic decline of a scavenger created a vacuum, and millions of carcasses were left rotting, increasing the possibility of the spread of zoonotic diseases such as anthrax.[7] Other scavengers such as rats and feral dogs moved in, but they lack the efficiency of vultures, whose metabolism is a true 'dead-end' for pathogens. Dogs and rats, instead, become carriers of the pathogens spreading disease.

A marked increase in the dog population—an estimated seven million—coincided with the period of vulture declines. A study on the wider implication of the vulture die-off indicated that this sudden increase in dogs, is thought to have at least partially caused the rabies outbreak estimated to have killed 48,000 people from 1992–2006 in India.[8]

The loss of one bird has led to nothing short of a health crisis. A conservation catastrophe had caused a human tragedy. This brings in a sombre note, but it tells about the value of a vulture, and the hidden impacts of biodiversity loss. Extinctions have wider ramifications, some of which are beyond our scope of understanding. Extinctions slowly unravel the web of which we are all a part.

The absence of nature is making life intolerable. Our cities are heating up. We know of this anecdotally. I have heard many times over of how fans were not needed in Dehradun, in the lovely Doon Valley of Uttarakhand, or the garden city of Bangalore some thirty to forty summers ago, but now people install air conditioners in their homes. Environment researcher Max Martin says that Indian cities are turning into 'heat islands'. In an article for *IndiaSpend*[9] he explains that trees, shrubs, waterbodies, grass and soil absorb heat and cool the land. But these are being cleared. 'What's left is concrete and asphalt, which soak in and intensify the day's heat, staying hot for many hours at night.'

What is the future of nature in Indian cities, especially as India embarks on the ambitious 'Smart City'[10] programme? At best it seems uncertain. The development of the Smart City programme is viewed through the technological lens, but it needs to factor in the ecological element as well, if smart is to be sustainable.

It doesn't take a scientist to tell us that green cities are healthier cities; wetlands are efficient water treatment plants, cleaning up water contaminated with sewage and pollutants; trees absorb the polluted air—lowering asthma and pollution-related diseases. A study in Tampa, Florida, worked out the worth of a tree and found that trees save the city nearly US$35 million a year in reduced costs for public health, storm water management, preventing soil erosion and other services.

Trees also make us happy, relieve stress, heal us . . . We don't really need science to tell us this, though there are enough studies to support the healing powers of nature.

Reviving the Magic

While I deeply mourn the loss of such abundance, I have strived to get some of the magic, and the wild back, in my life. Sometimes, the magic comes to me. Like it did while I was stuck in a traffic jam barely a mile away from my home in Gurugram—for *hours*—with a throbbing headache, cursing life. I looked up idly, and saw that the sky was obscured by swarms of black that whirled around like huge ribbons swaying in the skies. Curiosity piqued, I looked again, intently. It was not a black cloud in my horizon, quite the contrary. It was a murmuration of rosy pastors, swirling, swooping, flying, putting up a spectacular aeronautical display. It was awe-inspiring—thousands of birds flying as one single being en masse. Nature's extravaganza thrilled, right here in a crowded, concretized city! Rosy pastors are migrants from Central Asia that pass through northern India around August to reach the south by the winter.

My heart lifted, and suddenly, the world wasn't such a fraught place after all.

India is fortunate in its diversity of wildlife, so much of which lives amongst us in our villages and cities. Delhi the most polluted city in the world—is also one of the richest in birdlife, with well over 400 species. That's a little under a third of the number of bird species found in India. Most cities support an amazing avian life. You can go birding, scouting for butterflies and other life forms, in green spaces—parks, small wetlands, open areas of shrubby grasslands or woods. Or invite them home, like I did.

I don't possess a green thumb so I go by the thumb rule of letting the garden grow wild, and put the pruner away. On the wall, and behind a curtain of riotous creepers and a few assorted plants and young trees (the easy to grow kind, manageable even in large pots), I put up birdhouses, mainly small earthen pots attached firmly with their mouths facing the wall, and small openings for the birds to enter. To lure the birds, food—an assortment of grains and bits of fruits—was supplied morning and evening. I also kept sand in a flattish bowl for the birds to bathe in. It's a wellness thing—dust smothers skin and feather parasites. There is a watering hole nearby for a drink by way of a shallow earthen pot that also doubles up as a swimming pool, with many a winged creature plunging in for a cool dip. I improvised, putting in some pebbles and twigs in the water bowl, thus giving wasps some 'leg' to stand on. This brought in other guests. Dragonflies flew in, perched on the twigs, and soon there were so many of them that additional water sources had to be provided for. I am fascinated by these tiny drone-like insects, so dainty with their glittery, glassy wings. I recently read that dragonflies are one of the greatest migrants of the planet—the 'global skimmer' dragonfly, no bigger than an inch and a half, flies non-stop for thousands of miles across oceans. Scientists have logged dragonflies crossing the Indian Ocean to eastern Africa!

Nature never ceases to surprise.

I have now listed more than twenty bird species in my miniscule, half-a-handkerchief size garden from the tiny sunbird to the occasionally visiting peahen. They have turned gardeners and I now have a few plants which they have bestowed via pollination! Two snake species have been spotted as well, though I keep such sightings to myself, the neighbours don't look too kindly on the much-maligned reptiles. Along with a few friends, we have become their champions, with occasional awareness campaigns on how snakes are largely harmless, and useful to the ecosystem.

This is what all of us can do . . . get the wild back in our lives. Become its champion. Most important of all is to shed our fear and prejudices, open our minds and hearts. Don't subdue the garden, let it run riot, let the children play in the mud, don't look upon the bees only as insects that sting and producers of honey, but as tiny little pollinators that some say plant a majority of the world's food! If you don't have a garden, green your balcony, or try wilding a shared community garden. Citizens are coming together to wage battles to protect the remaining green areas, and regenerate what has been lost. Bangalore fought to protect hundreds of trees being cut for a new road.

In the city where I live, Gurugram, Delhi's southwestern edge, a citizen's initiative led by the group 'iamgurgaon' transformed a barren, scarred landscape—parts of it was mined—into a lush forest with over 400 species of indigenous plants, 200 species of birds, 100 kinds of butterflies. The Aravalli Biodiversity Park now is a forest in the making showcasing the endangered flora of the northern Aravalli.[11] In Bangalore, a collaborative network of local residents worked with researchers and the local government and restored Kaikondrahalli lake at the southeastern periphery of the city. Till 2000, writes Harini Nagendra,[12] 'The lake was filled with fresh water, surrounded by groves of fruiting trees, and frequented by birds, foxes, and snakes.' But over the next few years Kaikondrahalli had been reduced to a parched, polluted sewer. After a massive effort that started in 2009, the lake has been restored, is flush with water and birdlife, its islands and surrounds support over 1,000 native trees, invites migrant waterfowl and is a thriving recreational spot for many.[13]

I learnt about other amazing stuff happening across the world: New York in 2015 announced it would shut off non-essential lights to help migrating birds navigate routes in spring and autumn. Birds rely on stars for directions, and get disoriented by lights, millions die when they collide into buildings in the confusion. The world is waking up to the noise pollution in the oceans, and there is a movement to give whales and other marine life some peace and quiet from the constant din of oil and gas drilling, sonar, ships and submarines.

There is still an incredible array of wildlife in our city. The other day I spotted an endearing family of mongoose—a pair with two tiny ones, scurrying across the road. In many avenues—like parts of Lutyens' Delhi, large fruit-eating bats nest in old trees. Small pockets of Bangalore still harbour the slender loris, a tiny nocturnal primate, essentially a creature of the forests of southern India and Sri Lanka. Madhya Pradesh's capital Bhopal has tigers on its fringes. As you saw elsewhere in the book, the leopard is a Mumbaikar, as much of the city as its people, thriving in the Sanjay Gandhi National Park, and other green spaces around. Unfortunately, when a leopard was spotted in Delhi's Yamuna Biodiversity Park—a space envisaged as a conservation project to restore the region's native forest and biodiversity—it was trapped, and sent packing.

But animals going wild in the city is such welcome news, an indication that its fractured ecosystems are reviving.

Admittedly having large wild animals in cities may seem unsettling, but there can be peace. Wild animals are shy, and adapt to people's activity patterns, emerging only in seclusion. The presence of such species in our cities challenges the way we imagine both the urban, and the wild. It calls on us to reappraise our cities, and how we define them. The animals are adapting to an urban environment, and we need to be good neighbours and share our spaces with them.

There *is* room for us and the wild in an increasingly crowded world.

Deceptions of Development

In every deliberation, we must consider the impact on the seventh generation.

—Constitution of the Iroquois, a historically powerful
and important Native American confederacy[1]

In 2010, I was appointed to the standing committee of the National Board for Wildlife (NBWL),[2] and spent the next three years working with six other non-official independent expert members on policy and other issues concerning conservation. One of our tasks was to evaluate and regulate proposed development of any kind within Protected Areas and their Eco-Sensitive Zones (ESZ)—10-km transition zones where land use is regulated, thus acting as shock absorbers for parks.[3]

At one meeting, we were asked to consider the construction of a viscose yarn factory in the immediate vicinity of the Karnala Bird Sanctuary on the outskirts of Mumbai in Maharashtra. Most independent members of the committee objected: the fibre factory had a captive power plant; chemicals, fly ash and toxic effluents would pollute the sanctuary and seep into the river it formed the catchment of. Surely a yarn factory could be built in another, less sensitive location?

But the project, we were told, was, apparently, in the 'national interest': it would contribute to the growth and development of the nation, the implication being that it should be green-lit.

I remember asking if this, therefore, also meant that protection of a sanctuary, and its rare wildlife, was *not* in the national interest.

It is a question that rages in my mind as project after project is permitted within crucial wildlife habitats. What 'development' is it when it threatens to wipe out even the last refuge of an endangered species? How is it 'progress' when copious amounts of water are drained from an overexploited, rapidly drying river for a thermal power plant when other less environmentally harmful options are available? Especially when that river slakes the thirst of millions, waters fields, and harbours the planet's last gharials—the only surviving species from an ancient lineage of crocodilians dating to the pre-dinosaur era.

I question the sensibility which considers rare wildlife and the habitats they live in dispensable within the development matrix. Those forests, wetlands, mangroves and other natural habitats provide crucial ecosystem services. Forests are our buffers against a warming world, soaking up nearly nine billion tonnes of greenhouse gas.[4] Together with the oceans, they allow us to breathe; between them they produce nearly all the oxygen we need.

Mangroves provide a shield against flooding from devastating tsunamis and storms. In the 2004 tsunami that battered peninsular India, areas buffered by mangroves suffered far less damage than those without such vegetation. Villages with mangrove cover saw less destruction, and death, while those without were almost completely destroyed. These coastal forests also shelter a spectrum of wild creatures—water monitors, king cobras, kingfishers, tigers—and are the breeding grounds for many species of commercially valuable fish, crab, shrimp, etc. They sustain communities. Over the past century, India has lost over 35 per cent of its mangroves, and continues to hack the swamp forests for hotels, waterfront homes, aquaculture, ports, etc.

Do we factor in these costs when we rip such habitats apart?

My issue with an ideology that puts a yarn factory over a wildlife sanctuary is part of a larger concern about what we deem as 'development'—which has become one of India's holy cows. Questioning its efficacy or laying bare its hollow claims or social and environmental consequences can make your patriotism suspect, and even put a question mark on your love and fealty for the nation.

India's growth fetish is hurting its ecology in an insidious manner, with environmental regulations being viewed as a straitjacket on economic growth—and civil society and environmental activist groups as a threat, accused of negatively impacting economic development. Increasingly, their voices are being muzzled. A 2014 report by India's Intelligence Bureau (IB) claimed that a few foreign-funded NGOs were taking down India's developmental projects. It noted that NGOs protesting against extractive industries, nuclear and coal-fired power plants, uranium mines, genetically modified organisms (GMOs), mega industrial projects and hydel projects, threatened to slow down economic development by a staggering 2–3 per cent.[5] The maths of how 2–3 per cent of possible gross domestic product (GDP) growth is lost is not adequately explained.

The report again raised the bogey of the 'foreign hand'. The phrase had entered the political lexicon during the 1970s when Prime Minister Indira Gandhi raised the spectre of dark foreign forces trying to destabilize the country—and used it to suspend civil liberties. In the Congress-led United Progressive Alliance (UPA) regime, Prime Minister Manmohan Singh followed suit when in a 2012 interview to *Science* he indicated that foreign-funded NGOs were fuelling protests and opposition to nuclear power plants and commercialized GMO crops.[6]

The government has cracked down on NGOs, cancelling licenses, crippling fund flows. One such high-profile case was that of Greenpeace India, an environment advocacy group which was accused of trying to 'take down India's coal-fired plants and coal mining activity'.[7] The organization had authored a report[8] which detailed how coal mining is destroying prime tiger habitats in Central India. It also took up a campaign to halt open cast coal mining in the Mahan coalfield in Singrauli in the state of Madhya Pradesh, supporting the villagers who were opposed to the mine. The mine would be exhausted in fourteen years, after destroying over 1,000 hectares of what is one of Asia's oldest sal forests. Mahan is close to the Sanjay Dubri Tiger Reserve and sees the occasional tiger and elephant, besides other wildlife like leopards, sloth bears, pangolin, etc. It is also the catchment of the perennial rivers, Rampa and Mahan; and the livelihood of over fifty villages is linked to these forests.

The case hit headlines when in 2015 a Greenpeace campaigner, Priya Pillai, was offloaded from a flight to London. She was to address a British parliamentary group[9] on the London-registered company Essar Energy's plans to build a coal mine in the Mahan forests, and its potential environmental and social impacts. She was offloaded on orders of the central government, which argued that her testimony could harm India's 'national interest'.

Fortunately, Mahan's forests have been saved, and will not be auctioned for coal mining.[10] But Mahan is the rare case, and just one of the hundreds of coal mines slated in forested India.

Greenpeace is an international organization and its campaigns are flamboyant, designed to catch the public eye. Many such organizations, and individuals taking up cudgels for the environment, or for their livelihood, face similar intimidation.

The state, across governments, has increasingly adopted an approach of crushing dissent. As finance minister in the UPA, P. Chidambaram, was to say that the Government of India is 'willing to tolerate debate, and perhaps even dissent, as long as it does not come in the way of 8 per cent growth'.[11]

The hostility to such democratic freedoms has become even more acute. Accountability and transparency in the NGO sector is essential, but it is alleged that suspending registrations, permissions and discrediting civil society groups is more a tool of retribution.

Such persecution of green groups—by governments and corporate actors—is a global phenomenon. As problems of deforestation, pollution and habitat destruction escalate, environmental groups have stepped up their efforts to highlight these and get governments to act. The *Guardian* points out that no less than sixty countries have passed or drafted laws under which civil society organizations, international aid groups and their local partners are vilified, harassed, closed down and sometimes expelled.[12] There are high stakes involved in this war over scarce natural resources, and environment defenders, or those who report on it, are being ruthlessly attacked. The year 2015 was particularly deadly with 185 environmental activists murdered worldwide.[13] Environment journalists reporting on land and natural resources conflicts work in an increasingly hostile climate as well—ten have been killed between 2010–15, most from South Asia, including India.[14] Says the Pulitzer Center on crisis reporting, 'In many parts of the world, environmental reporting is no longer a branch of science writing: it's war correspondence.'

But India is the world's largest, most vibrant democracy, priding itself on diversity, plurality, and freedom of expression and belief.

So, why is dissent not only being silenced, but viewed as unpatriotic, if not criminal?

Surely there can be differing views, and opposition to the viability, and wisdom, of a project, and the juggernaut of development that has swept across the country? Is it against the nation's interests to fight for your land and livelihood, or to challenge projects that poison a river or destroy habitats of India's rare wildlife, including its national animal?

Isn't it imperative, and infinitely more productive, to understand the concerns of the people—India's citizens—and why such projects are being opposed, to find a way forward? Aren't public discourse, debate and dissent intrinsic to a healthy democracy?

Up until the 1990s, India prided itself on its economic independence. The slogan I recall was 'Be Indian, Buy Indian'. During that period, the flaunting of wealth drew disdain. At the start of the decade, India took a dramatic shift from a borderline socialist and welfare state to a neo-liberal one, opening up its economy and ushering in a free market. The momentum of growth and foreign investments raced. The 1990s transformed Indian society—and fundamentally changed the Indian consumer. With a swelling middle class with greater disposable income, private spending spiked. From thrifty consumers with limited choices, Indians now had at their doors an array of goods and services previously unimaginable. India is now poised to be the world's biggest consumer market by 2025, and an economic superpower.

But all is not well within the citadels of progress.

Before I proceed, I would like to clarify that this is not meant to be a diatribe on development, nor is it a call to go back in time. I do not wish to romanticize the past, pre-1990s, pre-liberalization, or the pre-industrialization era. My concern is the environmental consequences of our current dharma of 'development without breaks'. The advantages of India's liberalized, globalized economy have been much discussed and applauded, and there is little doubt that the reforms process accelerated growth, ushering in an astounding variety of goods and services, and benefits such as raised literacy levels, lower infant mortality, etc.

There is, however, little accompanying commentary on the ecological wounds that the process has inflicted, and this is what I attempt to highlight.

A major problem is that India's development is narrowly defined by the GDP. As a sole indicator for economic health and well-being, the GDP model is riddled with problems. It counts the sum value of monetary transactions within an economy, uncaring of what it's spent on. At one end of the spectrum, the GDP does not measure inequalities; at the other, it welcomes misfortune, accidents and disasters—anything that makes money flow for insurance, hospital bills, reconstruction and repairs.

India's booming middle class today enjoys unprecedented levels of comfort and a lifestyle comparable to the developed world, though only a fraction of its people can shop in glitzy malls, visit multiplexes for entertainment, or download services from apps on their smart phones. A significant part of its population struggles to fulfil its basic needs. At 15 per cent, India's malnutrition rate is worse than our neighbours Nepal and Bangladesh;[15] and one in three of our children have stunted growth;[16] 20 per cent of communicable diseases are related to unsafe drinking water; and though significant strides have been made in improving literacy, India has the largest number of illiterate adults in the world.[17]

These are the beleaguered citizens of the 'Other India' who have been assured—every election cycle—that the GDP benefits will trickle down and lift everyone up. Eventually.

But India shines only for a few: 1 per cent of its richest people control 45 per cent of the wealth, while the bottom half gets a mere 2.1 per cent, making India one of the most unequal countries in the world.[18] India's growth is not only lopsided, it's jobless. The lack of employment generation has been termed as the one issue that economic reforms have failed to address,[19] giving rise to 'jobless growth'. In over twenty-two years of unprecedented economic growth (1991–2013), less than half the Indians who sought jobs got them—140 million of 300 million, as per a report by the United Nations Development Programme.[20]

Economist Amit Bhaduri argues that the current model of development is not merely inequitable, 'Its reality is far worse. It threatens the poor with a kind of brutal violence in the name of development—a sort of "developmental terrorism" by the state primarily in the interest of a corporate aristocracy, and a self-serving political class.'[21] Bhaduri refers to the wholesale corporate takeover of lands for industrialization and infrastructure, more often than not 'aided and abetted by land acquisition policies of governments'. Development can turn perverse if it destroys livelihoods in the name of industrialization, or by way of construction of mega-dams that submerge fertile lands and forests.

So is this what development really amounts to: the gifting away of scant natural resources—forests, water, minerals—to a select, favoured few? But natural resources are no one's property. They are for the benefit of *all* citizens—rather all denizens—a common heritage, held in trust by, not belonging to, governments.

Across the country, projects which have displaced people have rarely brought prosperity for those whose lands they now occupy. There is no institutional mechanism to assess and monitor claims of jobs generated or to count the jobs and value of livelihoods that development projects destroy.

Even as urban India grows, despair and rage have engulfed India's hinterlands. There are mutinies everywhere. It would not be a fallacy to say that a majority of mega industrial projects and infrastructure projects are under fire from local communities who protest the loss of their land and resources—wetlands, rivers, forests—to which their livelihoods are tied.

Be it on the fringes of India's capital, Delhi, where farmers opposed the takeover of their fields for a highway; or farmers in Raigarh (Chhattisgarh) whose fecund orchards were laid waste overnight by debris dumped from coal mines and power plants; or Monpa Buddhists in Arunachal Pradesh resisting a hydropower project which would drown the habitat of the rare black-necked crane, revered as the embodiment of the Dalai Lama. A report to the Parliament in December 2013 found that India has the shameful distinction of having the highest number of citizens uprooted for development projects in any nation in the world, with 60 to 65 million people displaced since Independence. That's around one million people every year. Development is the single largest cause of displacement within the country.[22]

India's people are challenging the paradigm of development as we understand it today. A common refrain I heard when visiting sites of such resistance was, 'Whose development?'

Many of us living in urban India are insulated from the reality of such projects, the consequences of development. Such desperate struggles of the rural poor are very distant; we barely hear their voices, let alone allow them to stir the conscience.

The problem with such a development strategy is that while it might create more output or GDP, it destroys the natural economy that provides livelihoods and sustenance to a vast majority and fails to provide adequate alternative livelihoods.

Growth is a means of achieving economic development, not an end in itself. Whether growth gains 'trickle down' will also depend on whether greater public revenues accrued are spent on public health, education and other such social sectors.

*

It is the same 'development terrorism' that stalks India's remnant wildlife habitats. Evidence of the ecological catastrophe is all around us. Urban India is drowning under its garbage. Life-giving rivers have been reduced to sewers. Air pollution is the country's fifth biggest killer; in the capital, Delhi, the air is apocalyptic, shearing years and lung power from its children. Thirteen of the world's twenty most polluted cities are in India. Climate change is not a distant, vague threat; it is upon us. Scorching heatwaves took a toll of about 1,500 people in the summer of 2015, shrinking glaciers are reducing stream flows in Himalayan states like Kashmir. Extreme weather events—like the flash floods of Kashmir (2014) or a sudden hailstorm in drought-stricken Maharashtra—have become routine, causing humongous damage and destruction. India's ancient forests are being cleared, its wetlands and open spaces are being built over and encroached. Many of its rare creatures, including snow leopards, wild buffaloes, bustards, and brow-antlered deer, aquatic wildlife like freshwater dolphins and gharials, and marine mammals including dugongs (or the sea cow as it is popularly called), are on the brink of extinction.

The GDP cares nought. It doesn't account for or reflect natural capital loss, or the depletion of natural resources to increase growth. On the contrary, the GDP surges, with depletion and destruction of nature. In GDP terms, a standing, living forest that shelters biodiversity, sucks in—and stores—carbon, provides a watershed for rivers, binds and nourishes soils, has *no value*; even if it is priceless. The GDP starts climbing when the trees are felled and sold as timber, when the land is mined to gouge out minerals.

It will factor in air pollution, and the diseases it causes—which means hospital visits and bills and hiked insurance premiums. Sickness makes money move.

As the then US presidential candidate Robert Kennedy said in 1968, 'It [GNP][23] counts air pollution and cigarette advertising, and ambulances to clear our highways of carnage. It counts the destruction of the redwood and the loss of our natural wonder in chaotic sprawl. It measures everything in short, except that which makes life worthwhile.'[24]

The prevalent and strong view is that for the sake of its development, India should ignore environmental costs. As a young, aspiring country with pressing poverty, growth is an imperative; and the attitude is that 'the environment will be taken care of later'. At the start of the economic reforms in 1991, the finance minister at the time, Manmohan Singh, had said that India needed reforms and a high rate of economic growth to generate money for environmental conservation.[25] This 'pollute first, clean up later' belief system rests on the environmental Kuznets curve, which suggests that economic development initially leads to a deteriorating environment but after achieving a certain level of growth, increased incomes and improved technology will help reduce the degradation.

This reasoning is flawed, and this model has been widely contested.

Environment issues such as pollution can be tackled to some extent—not totally—with technology and adequate safeguards, but they cannot fix loss of forests and wildlife. We lose sight of the fact that environment damage and the plunder of nature are often irrevocable. Old-growth forests take hundreds, often thousands of years to evolve, and monoculture plantations are no replacement. Flattened mountains will not stand again, and our inefficiency in cleaning poisoned rivers, even the holiest of them all, Ganga, is legendary.

And, extinction is forever.

India hankers to become the next China, with its galloping, unbridled growth, even as it is an environment disaster. China is a living example of the consequences of unregulated growth, with small communities living near polluting industry becoming 'cancer villages' because of heavy chemical exposure.[26] Its soil is so polluted that a fifth of the farmland is unfit for use.[27] A study found air pollution responsible for the deaths of about 4,400 people in China *every single day.*[28]

A number of China's wild species are now extinct: the Yellow river has reportedly lost nearly a third of its fish species,[29] and it has fewer than fifty tigers in the wild. Another tragedy is the loss of its iconic *baiji*, the Yangtze river dolphin, which breathed its last in 2007, though it survived in thousands till the 1950s. Industrialization and dams reduced the mighty Yangtze into a trafficked, crowded, toxic artery of mass shipping. The river could not sustain life. China's exponential growth rate has not been able to clean its air, or rivers, and no amount of yuan will bring the baiji back from the dead.

A January 2013 article in *Fortune* magazine termed China's environment an 'economic death sentence', and said that 'unless it can muster the political will to avert an ecological calamity, it will almost certainly spell the end of the Chinese economic miracle'.[30] China's people are questioning economic growth at all cost, and have taken to the streets on environment issues. It's a common grievance that has united both the working and middle classes, and astoundingly for a country where crackdown on dissent is legendary, environment inspires some 1.8 lakh protests in a year, and they are becoming difficult to ignore, pushing the government to respond and to act.[31]

India is as much an environment basket case as China.

Air pollution causes the early death of 1.1 million Indians, that's—reportedly—two Indians a minute.[32] In fact, India is choking faster than China, since 1990, early deaths due to PM2.5 have shot up by a whopping 48 per cent, as compared to China's 17.22 per cent.

It is Also Costing Our Economy

A July 2013 report from the World Bank, a strong proponent of economic growth as a pillar of development, tears India's celebrated growth story to shreds. It stated that environmental damage costs India 5.7 per cent of GDP each year.[33] The gains of economic growth are being negated by environmental damage caused, or ignored, by this growth. Given the precipitous state of the environment, in the long run, poor conservation policies will result in both failed economics and even politics.

Unfortunately, in India, mainly urban India, we largely still have our blinkers on, refusing to acknowledge the environment crisis.

As a conservationist, I have often been confronted by those who believe that all that I stand for—*conserving wildlife*—is obstructionist; India needs to develop, the mines must happen, the forests must go, and coal power—even if it clogs air with soot—is imperative to scale growth.

But when I help my young niece don her pollution mask as she steps out into Delhi's toxic air, or when my nephew's eyes light up as he watches elephant calves gambol in a waterhole, 'just like me and my friends in a pool', I know that development cannot be at the cost of environment. We deprive our children of a glorious future when we destroy nature, make it less secure; a future diminished of abundance and opportunity and wonder.

The current path of growth-at-all-costs is not just unsustainable, it's suicidal. It is undermining the future, laying waste the natural ecosystems that have sustained India for millennia, the lands, the forests, rivers, mountains, wetlands and seas. Natural resources are *finite*, and they are running out. In the past three decades, one-third of the planet's natural resource base has been consumed.[34]

As per a report by Global Footprint Network, we need 'two Indias' to provide for its consumption and absorb its waste. Interestingly, this report published in 2008 was co-authored by the Confederation of Indian Industry. The chairman of its Green Business Centre, Jamshyd N. Godrej, was to say, 'India is depleting its ecological assets in support of its current economic boom and the growth of its population.'[35] We are drawing on the principal now, depleting our capital assets.

It gets further complicated with an ostrich-like mentality to our demographic karma: India is set to be the most populous country in the world in another five years,[36] with 1.7 billion people by 2050. Unlike many other countries, India's population is getting younger. While economists wax eloquent about 'demographic dividend', with the majority of its population of working age by 2030, where are the jobs to absorb this mammoth workforce? And what natural resources will we bequeath to our children, given its unsustainable consumption? Seems to me that we are looking at a demographic disaster, especially since we have swept the issue of an exploding population—a political hot potato—under the carpet.

The deceptions of development cannot be allowed to continue. The 'Progress Project' must be probed, its myths, busted. Who gains from development, and at what cost? Whose lives are crushed? What are the ecological costs, say, of the loss of groundwater when a wetland is built over? What does it mean economically and socially for households dependent on that wetland? Who will measure the poignant loss of a species from this earth? Shouldn't development be inclusive, not just of the have-nots, but also of future generations, and those who have no voice or vote—the country's wild denizens?

India cannot afford such environmental plunder, nor can it afford to ignore the environment. It's a matter of livelihood for our farmers, fisherfolk and tribals, those who depend on the land and the sea for their occupation. It is their concerns that are now increasingly in conflict with economic objectives that the country has set. India is particularly vulnerable to climate change with coasts supporting almost 30 per cent of its human population and farmers who depend on monsoon rains to nourish their crops. India faces an acid test: How does it balance current needs without selling out its future? It has to meet the needs and aspirations of its 1.3 billion people, without compromising those of the next generation. And do we obliterate the wild creatures who called India their home before any of us did?

There is no magic bullet to resolve this dilemma, but a start would be to *redefine* development, and rethink the overemphasis on growth. While no country has given up the GDP, other models have been adapted to complement it as a more holistic indicator. The Organization for Economic Co-operation and Development, or the OECD, ranks its member countries using the Better Life Index.[37] It uses eleven indicators that include health, education, environment, jobs, civil engagement, life satisfaction, and work-life balance. The OECD website urges that 'there is more to life than cold numbers!' India had taken a step in this direction by introducing the 'Green GDP' in 2009, which would parallel the current index. The Green GDP, explained the architect of the concept and environment minister at the time, Jairam Ramesh, 'would measure economic performance after being adjusted for environmental factors'.[38] But with his exit in 2011, the concept had been given a burial.

Conservation cannot and should not be considered inimical to development. It *secures* natural resources and ecosystems, which perform a wide range of services, including sequestering and storing carbon, their loss will further exacerbate global warming.

India's prime minister, Narendra Modi, referred to this when speaking at a conference on 12 April 2016, saying, 'We need to define conservation as a means to achieve development, rather than considering it to be anti-growth. This calls for factoring in the value of the ecosystem in the economic arithmetic of development and growth.'[39] Coming from the prime minister, this was a powerful statement.

Unfortunately, the statement has yet to rise above rhetoric. One is yet to see any substantial initiative from the government which internalizes conservation concerns in its development model.

✤

My colleagues and I have been at the centre of the battle as development projects are planned in ecologically fragile places—new roads in flamingo breeding grounds, shopping malls laid over wetlands, thermal power plants constructed in close proximity to spectacular coral reefs, and so on. I have travelled to many such places to understand the issues better. I chose to take you to a place most people are familiar with, and love: Goa, the tiny state tucked between the Arabian Sea and the gloriously rich forests of the Western Ghats.

Like so many others, I turn to Goa to soothe my weary soul. I would vanish into its less-visited interiors, trek its forests, kill time in sleepy villages, stroll beaches more visited by turtles than humans. Over the years, I found this beautiful, laid-back Goa of old slowly fading. It now bristles with tensions over mining, tourism, real estate development and industrial projects which are wrecking the state's pristine landscape and the community's social fabric. Claude Alvares, a long-time soldier fighting to protect Goa's beleaguered environment, says with horrifying matter-of-factness, 'Goa is being gang-raped.'

Over the years, I have seen the ravages: Beaches and villages covered in rotting trash, mountains flattened, forests stripped bare and replaced by mounds of red dust of mined ore, green fields, ponds and wetlands razed for hotels and gated colonies, turtle-nesting beaches overrun by resorts, shacks, cafes, bazaars.

My last Goa visit was to a site where a project to develop a new airport will devastate wildlife, and has the locals up in arms.

Circa 10 July 2016, Barazan, Goa

We were at the Barazan plateau on the northern tip of Goa, more famous as the site of Mopa, the state's upcoming airport, peering with delight at a lumpy mound of faeces not unlike the *gobar* of the venerated cow. Yes, *delight*, because that particular turd came from the largest bovine in the world, the gaur, or the Indian bison. A herd of gaur had trampled the verdant grassland just before our arrival.

The gaur is listed as a Schedule I species—it has the same level of protection as the tiger under the Wildlife (Protection) Act of 1972. Ordinarily its presence could possibly prevent construction of an airport, but there are ways around such hiccups. In a separate move, the state had sought to declare the gaur a 'nuisance animal' for the damage it causes to farmers' crops,[40] even though it had not actually assessed and quantified the loss. Goa conveniently forgot that the animal it announced as a pest was its state animal.

Also in our line of vision was a peacock, jauntily swaying its vibrant plumes, as the monsoon clouds rolled over the green plateau. This was another creature dismissed as vermin, though the state had to retract that statement when reminded that the peacock was the national bird! The move to recast endangered animals as pests, ostensibly to help farmers—and allow their selective elimination across the country—has been taken up by various states, with support from the central government. Crop depredation by wildlife does cause losses, at times colossal, and is a genuine issue that needs to be addressed. But such stand-alone measures that lack a sustainable, comprehensive strategy have failed to halt crop damage.

There is another likely agenda: to ensure that rare animals are not hindrances to build airports, infrastructure and other mega projects in wildlife-rich landscapes.

It bears thinking what the state would do about Vithal Kambli, a farmer, who is as much of this land as the gaur and the peacock. Kambli says his land was acquired after it was declared as public purpose for acquisition.[41] Kambli had no say in the matter: he protested by refusing to sign the notification, and has not accepted any compensation. Nothing, he says, can compensate what the land gives: paddy, millet, pulses, turmeric, sweet peas, okra, pepper, potatoes, jackfruit, cashew, papaya, tamarind, and much more. The land has fed and sheltered his family, educated his children. Vithal Kambli is part of Mopa Vimantall Piditt Xetkari Samiti,[42] an initiative spearheaded by Sandip Kambli, which has moved the Supreme Court against the land acquisition. The airport will require a staggering 90 lakh sq m or 2,271 acres.[43]

Like all airports, Mopa is being promoted as an engine of growth that will have a catalytic impact on regional development in Goa's 'backward' region, and of course fly in tourists. But the state's sagging infrastructure and fragile ecology can ill-afford more tourists—at about four million they are already double Goa's resident population.

The site of the airport, the Barazan plateau, is a place of ecological and cultural significance. During my whirlwind visit, besides seeing signs of gaur, I caught a glimpse of barking deer, saw a Malabar giant squirrel leap from tree to tree, and watched a great Indian hornbill take wing, one of the fifty-odd bird species we met. A systematic survey of the plateau by scientists yielded direct sightings and found the presence of leopards, gaurs, otters, giant squirrels, sambar and the Indian pangolin.

Barazan also hosts the occasional tiger. Signs of breeding tigresses have been recorded in the adjoining forests of Tillari–Dodamarg–Chandgad, part of a region recognized as an important habitat and Eco-Sensitive Area by the Bombay High Court. This region is part of the larger Radhanagari–Sawantwadi–Dodamarg–Mhadei–Bhimgad–Kali tiger landscape spread across three states, including Maharashtra and Karnataka, and forming an important contiguous wildlife area. The Maharashtra government is considering declaring the evergreen forests and grassy plateaus of Tillari a wildlife sanctuary. But the Tillari forests are too small, and to sustain them the health of abutting forests is crucial.

A development of the scale of the airport will splinter the landscape, dooming the tiger and other wide-ranging large mammals.

Tigers, however, do not find a mention in Mopa's Environmental Impact Assessment (EIA) report, on the basis of which the project got its environment clearance. The EIA states that there are 'no major wild animals in the study area of 10 km radius',[44] and corroborates its claim by listing the mammals recorded as 'domestic dogs and cats, cattle, and common house mice and rats' among a few others like mongoose and jackals. The impact study also ignores the region's endemic plants, and is constrained by the fact that it was conducted only during one season, thus failing to reflect seasonal changes in plant and animal diversity.[45]

According to the report, there are no sites of cultural importance—omitting mention of an ancient Buddhist-era cave and sacred groves that are protected zealously by the local people. I went to one of these—Barazan, from which the plateau gets its name—and was administered a stern admonishment for walking in wearing shoes. The grove is a living temple, venerated for generations, a site that is now counting its days as it stands on the runway of the proposed airport.

But the biggest flaw in this report is that it fails to consider that the construction could be fatal to the water security of Goa. The rocky plateaus of the region, locally called *sadas,* are the region's water reservoirs. The porous laterite rocks and grass soak up monsoon rains, which seep into the ground and are released slowly into springs. No fewer than forty perennial streams flow from Barazan, feeding the people and fields downstream. As per a hydrological study,[46] the plateau plays a pivotal role in the local hydrology of the area and recharges an estimated 2.2 million litres of water every year. The massive construction will choke the streams with sediment; the runway itself will be built on three streams, wreaking havoc on the state's hydrological system.

Regardless, the project received environment clearance in October 2015. It was subsequently challenged in court by the National Green Tribunal; the land acquisition case is being heard by the Supreme Court.

Ecological and social impact aside, detractors have questioned the airport's economic viability. Another airport, Chipi, is being built just 80 km away and Goa is already serviced by Dabolim, a civilian airport within a navy enclave. The limitations of operating a civilian airport in a defence regime, and the consequent conditions it imposes, are among the reasons cited for a new airport. Though this has also been challenged by experts who say that with the expansion and integration of the Dabolim airport in 2013, it can take an additional load to cater to Goa's needs for a decade.[47]

Safety concerns were also raised by the executive director of the Airports Authority of India of the time, R.C. Khurana, who chaired the site selection committee for Mopa. He categorically stated that, 'Mopa is unsafe and inadequate as a location in Goa's future interest from an aviation point of view.'[48] In an interview with the newspaper, *Goan,* in February 2013, he explained that three sides of the plateau had sharp drops, making it unsafe for landing aircraft—even if the runway was adequate. He also noted that the site would not allow for future expansion.

What then fuels this 'development' of Mopa? I don't have answers but it is certainly a question that demands to be asked.

It has long been alleged that the real reason is real estate development, with political and business interests hoping to reap substantial profits on cheaply bought land investments. A quick Google search reveals that the real estate market in the region is hot, with a number of exclusive gated communities and vacation homes on the anvil, with proximity to the upcoming airport cited as a prime attraction.

But tourists and second homers—and I am one among them—escaping to Goa for their share of paradise may find that it is already lost.

Prime Minister Modi laid the foundation stone of the Mopa Greenfield Airport in November 2016. The foundation stone was laid remotely, from a stadium in Goa's capital Panjim,[49] safely away from the actual site and uncomfortable issues. He did not see the lush landscape, its natural wonders or fecund fields that the airport will decimate. Vithal Kambli and other aggrieved farmers never got a chance to ask their prime minister: 'Are we hurdles to development as well?'[50]

In laying that stone, the prime minister endorsed not just a shoddy and inept EIA but also sent a message that wildlife, environment and people's concerns are of little consequence in the trajectory of India's economic growth.

As I left Goa, I pondered over the fact that in a few years, my flight may land at the snazzy Mopa terminal, likely an edifice of glass and mortar, built over the ashes of sacred trees and wild creatures I'd met not so long ago. I wondered if I would abstain from flying into Goa as a mark of protest and respect for those wild creatures, and the brave, embattled farmers who would have become mere statistics among India's displaced millions. Or if I would succumb to the apathy, and be seduced by convenience as is the case with most of us, not just about one airport in Goa, but on the larger issue of the *real* costs of 'progress', as we are led by the Pied Pipers of 'development' into a holocaust of our environment.

❦

For many, the truth is too inconvenient; it pulls us out of our cosy cocoons. It demands that we make tough choices and changes in the way we live. I am not talking about having bucket baths or using CFC bulbs and carrying your own shopping bag instead of using throwaway polythene—though those steps matter and you might do that as well.

Instead, this moment in history calls for fundamental changes in our high consumer lifestyles, as individuals and as a society.

We need to understand the *real* cost of our consumption beyond the MRP:[51] Is the electricity that lights up your home powered from coal in an elephant forest, or from a hydel project in the North-east that has submerged forests, displaced people? Did we ever imagine that our mobile phones connect us not just to our family and colleagues, but to the fate of endangered gorillas? Most electronic devices we use, like tablets and laptops, use 'coltan', a mineral sourced mainly from the Democratic Republic of Congo in the forest home of the eastern lowland gorilla. Mining activities are decimating gorilla populations through habitat loss.

It calls for questioning and deviating from the comfortable, existing systems that are at the root of the crisis, systems founded on an endless cycle of extraction, production, consumption and waste that fatten the GDP. It means we need to reconsider and change the way economies function, creating new systems that are truly sustainable. Throughout history—barring recent history!—humans have used foresight in the spending of natural resources. A basic example is that hunting, or fishing, was not practised during the mating and breeding season. There was no law that called for this, it was innate wisdom and foresight to ensure that the resource remained renewable, lasting generations. This may seem simplistic—but it is the fundamental rule that we need to apply to ensure intergenerational equity of resources.

It might be blasphemous to say this in the current political climate, but it is time that we accept that there are limits to growth. It will mean making tough choices. For example, should India mine coal on the edge of the Tadoba Tiger Reserve (Maharashtra), knowing it will compromise the tiger? Should one build a port that threatens the Pulicat Bird Sanctuary[52] and the second largest brackish water ecosystem in India, which hosts thousands of migratory waterfowl each year and supports over forty villages? Or should we choose the path of a slower growth rate that is less destructive, protects species and livelihoods, and can be sustained in the longer term?

One of the toughest challenges we face is the energy conundrum. How do we provide electricity to the 250 million people who currently lack access? Given the pace of economic growth, demand for power is expected to double in the next twenty-five years. Over 60 per cent of our power needs are met from thermal power; the target of Coal India is to produce 1 billion tonnes by the end of this decade.[53] But most of the country's coal reserves lie in rich forest areas, including prime tiger and elephant habitats. Coal is dirty energy, spewing out half of India's greenhouse gases; plus, deforestation will mean the loss of a valuable carbon sink. Hydropower has an approximate 22 per cent share in the energy pie, and comes with formidable ecological and social consequences, submerging forests, endangering species, interrupting and altering river flows and leading to large-scale displacement of people.

India has taken up renewable energy in a big way, with projections that 57 per cent of total electricity capacity will come from non-fossil fuel sources by 2027.[54] This is important to lower our carbon footprint, but here's the problem: Clean energy is not necessarily green and must come with its checks and balances. Renewable energy, especially wind and solar, is a very land-intensive industry, and with its associated infrastructure has led to the destruction of pristine wildlife habitat. The scales of renewable energy could trash the earth. For example, a key ingredient in solar panels is silicon which is mined, while windmills require a range of minerals—bauxite, iron ore, molybdenum and rare earth minerals as well.

While being a strong proponent for renewable energy, India's leading green think tank, the Centre for Science and Environment, advocates greater environment scrutiny and regulations for this sector. It has pressed for 'no-go' areas for this sector.[55]

Again, there are no easy answers here, but the choices we make have to strive for both India's energy as well as ecological security.

The share of renewable energy in our energy basket must be significant, but the way forward is decentralized renewable energy—sunlight falls everywhere, and the wind blows everywhere as well. Energy should be harnessed by small-scale electricity generators which may be households, businesses or mini-grids. We need solar panels on rooftops, instead of the heavily polluting diesel generators that most gated colonies and corporate houses rely on. A chunk of urban and rural needs can be met by such localized units.

The other way is energy efficiency, first, by way of minimizing the power losses. India loses about 23 per cent in transmission and distribution,[56] and while the country invests heavily in new power projects, there is a huge investment shortfall in plugging these losses.

Use of energy-efficient appliances also helps lighten the power footprint—for instance, Maharashtra is saving 93 MW of power daily during peak hours by shifting to LED bulbs.[57]

Such demand-side management, efficient use of energy is crucial, and a much-neglected aspect of our energy policy. We also need to face the inconvenient question: Is the current consumption of energy sustainable?

But will we take that small step, and a giant leap, forward?

If nothing else, doesn't the fact that our children are breathing in poison, so much so that schools were shut down, and children advised to stay indoors, tell us that it is time to act? The air pollution crisis is nothing short of an emergency that demands priority, and lasting solutions. Yet, we continue to raze forests, build over wetlands and mangroves, concretize urban forests and open green spaces, which are key to improving air quality. How is it that we define forests as the 'lungs' of our planet, yet we destroy them with impunity?

The way forward is difficult, but I believe we will be the change. That we will speak up, like Vithal Kambli and his neighbours in Goa. Or the farmers in Raigarh, the tribals in Mahan, or the many other earth warriors who fight for their lives and livelihoods, and speak for those who don't have a voice: wildlife. We may think the battles are not 'ours', or that 'saving the tiger' is the job of the conservationist. But the health of the environment is everyone's cause. It doesn't make distinctions between the rich and poor. We all breathe the same air; polluted groundwater and toxins in the soil will cripple our bodies indiscriminately. And we all have a yen for crisp air, free-flowing rivers, green valleys . . .

Which is why I have hope that we will be willing to make the changes needed to bequeth a living planet for our children. Hope that we will shake our governments into acknowledging and addressing the crisis: the onus is not just on lawmakers to protect the environment, it's on, 'we, the people'. We live in a democracy, and the government will continue on this reckless 'developmental terrorism' path unless the electorate questions its claims—and the model where 'progress' at any cost is the holy grail.

Afterword

March is drawing to an end as I sit to pen the afterword in 2017, putting this book to rest . . . even though my mind is anything but restful. It's baking hot as temperatures soar—every year they reach greater heights, break new records. It has inched past 40°C in a time of the year I remember fondly as crisp clear spring. Even so I am fortunate, in some parts of India—from Lucknow to Nagpur—it's nearing 50°C. In Maharashtra, five people have already succumbed to the heat,[1] even though summer is yet to *really* arrive.

It's a season of discontent.

In Tamil Nadu, water levels in major reservoirs have dropped to less than 10 per cent of their capacity,[2] and wet, lush Kerala is withering, facing its worst drought in over a century. In the foothills of the Nilgiris, in Tamil Nadu, newspapers report that four elephants—including a six-month-old calf—have died, presumably due to starvation and a paucity of fodder.[3] Lack of water has also escalated conflict, as the elephants blunder about in human-dense areas—desperate to slake their thirst and hunger. Two people have been killed (in Kerala) in the chaos that ensued.[4]

The land is parched. We are facing a future sans water as India suffers the worst-ever crisis in generations—rivers, lakes, wetlands are drying; crops, grasses, trees withering; and an immense heat wave engulfs us all.[5]

The sceptre of an ecological catastrophe is upon us, not in some distant, unseeable future.

India's wildlife crisis has only deepened.

We have touched new lows. We crushed our national animal, literally, and in other ways.

On 17 March 2017, a tiger was crushed by a bulldozer close to the Corbett Tiger Reserve. Yes, you read me right. The big cat had reportedly killed two people—and the rapidly gathering mob demanded 'justice'. He had already been tranquilized when bulldozers were brought in to 'control' the staggering tiger and pin him down. The tiger was rammed repeatedly, quashed by the excavator, with the mob egging the perpetrators with: 'dabao, dabao' (press, press him down). He was injured, and died enroute to the Nainital Zoo.

Tiger protectors also met the same fate. In the following week, a forest department watcher was crushed under a tractor in the Corbett landscape[6] when he tried to prevent the illegal loot of sand and boulders from the Kosi riverbed—used extensively by tigers, elephants, bears, sambar deer and other wildlife.

New roads are tearing up pristine areas: a national highway would be constructed through the core of the Corbett Tiger Reserve. And much as I try to keep emotions at bay—conservation derides emotion—this hits hard. As though the road would cleave, and carve, through my heart. Corbett is where I took my baby steps in wildlife. Where I first met elephants, and saw the flight of the great Indian hornbill. It's the holiest of the holy. Corbett is where Project Tiger was launched in April 1973, where India committed to protect this great cat. We kept our word, against all odds, reviving the tiger, leading the world in its conservation.

If we fragment and cut Corbett, move in men and machinery, pave it with roads . . . where will we stop?

Even the stories of hope seem ephemeral. Remember Nagarjunasagar–Srisailam, the tiger reserve, back on its feet, and thriving, after a decade of insurgency? Part of it, now called the

Amrabad Tiger Reserve, will be surveyed for uranium.[7] I wouldn't place any bets that the presence of our national animal will stop us from gouging out uranium if the surveys yield the mineral ore.

The wildlife scenario is grim.

Even so, I see promise. I see a future. There is an increasing awareness—especially among the young, and I find there is a growing tribe disenchanted by the current economic systems and way of life, going back to their roots, seeking succour in nature, and within this bleak landscape, there are stories of hope.

Let me start with a remarkable event in March 2017 in Kashmir's Dachigam National Park. The state government, after dawdling for over two decades, ousted the sheep farm that illegally occupied prime habitat of the hangul deer. This was the culmination of years of struggle and efforts of conservationists, forest officials and staff, biologists, NGOs and a number of determined citizens. A committed team of officials is now partnering with experts to restore the area for hangul. The deer's future continues to be precarious, it still faces a plethora of threats. Dachigam is increasingly islanded by a growing city and mines—but this is a strong signal that indicates that Kashmir is standing by its state emblem, the hangul, and has taken a tough political decision to revive it.

Battles to protect wildlife habitats is being fought in court. Sometimes, wildlife gets a reprieve. In April 2016, India's National Green Tribunal suspended the environment clearance of a hydro power plant to save the nesting and wintering grounds of the black-necked crane in the Pangchen valley in Arunachal Pradesh's Tawang district. At the forefront of this battle are the Monpas, an indigenous tribe, who consider the crane an incarnation of the sixth Dalai Lama.[8]

Religious communities and groups are coming forward to conserve wildlife. Lhagyala, among the oldest monasteries in Arunachal Pradesh, officially declared about 85 sq km of forest which they own as a Community Conservation Area for the preservation of the endangered red panda.[9]

I see a change in mindset. The Uttarakhand High Court declared rivers Ganga and Yamuna 'legal and living entities'—legal persons with all corresponding rights and duties. Oh, I am cynical—after all the divinity of Ganga did not prevent it from being one of the most polluted rivers in the world. I wouldn't undermine the import of this judgment though, unprecedented in India, in granting a living entity status to non-humans. It grants the rivers a protective shield. It demands that we relook, and halt, the rampant loot of sand and water, the construction of dams, changing their directions and flows, morphing them into a busy riverine national highway.

Concerned citizens are also speaking up for a clean environment and the brightest star on the horizon is a little girl of nine, Ridhima Pandey, who has filed a petition in the National Green Tribunal against the Indian government for failing to act on climate change, and calls on the government 'to take effective, science-based action to reduce and minimize the adverse impacts of climate change'.[10]

There are other voices, rising collectively for the right to a clean environment. As the book goes to press, citizens of Goa are speaking out against the plan to recast this exquisite coastal paradise as a coal hub by expanding the capacity of a port and building highways to transport millions of tons of coal through the villages, rivers and forests of Goa.

Yes, there is hope. But my optimism is cautious, muted, threatened by despair. Such voices are few and far between. The ecological crisis is glaringly missing in public discourse. In February 2017 five states went to poll. Three of them—Punjab, Uttar Pradesh and Uttarakhand—have nine of the most polluted cities in the world—yet tackling pollution was not a decisive factor in elections. In fact, it had no place in the electoral debates, dialogues and campaigns.

Not surprisingly then, governments are dismissive of the problem. Somewhat like US President Donald Trump calling climate change a Chinese hoax, India's environment minister Anil Madhav Dave chose to downplay the evidence linking early death to air pollution, saying that 'there is no conclusive data to establish direct correlationship of death exclusively with air pollution'.[11]

The solutions that we seek are part of the problem. Instead of taking governments to task and working to resolve the pollution crisis, we have equipped our homes with air purifiers. Trendy pollution masks by fashion designers have hit the market. But these are private, knee-jerk responses that are largely ineffective; indeed they only accentuate the fact that we have accepted toxic air as a way of life. We don't strive for clean air—it's easier to indulge in a new gadget.

This silence and inaction is perplexing.

I found my answer in Amitav Ghosh's *The Great Derangement*, an erudite and unflinching take on, arguably, the greatest catastrophe to hit mankind, climate change. When questioned in an interview in *Hindustan Times*, on how difficult it is to create a dialogue around the issue, Ghosh said, 'Thinking about climate change is like thinking about death. Nobody wants to think about it, but it does exist.'[12]

That's the problem with the wildlife crisis today. It exists, the scale of the problem is enormous, dwarfing us with its harsh reality. And burying our head in the sand only means we dig ourselves in deeper. The environment movement is growing, but it's slow, yet to seize the imagination of the country, to become a mass movement . . . and the time frame in which we must act is narrow.

Individual choices and actions—even well-meant ones, like lowering your own carbon footprint—are good, but what is needed is institutional change, and collective action, a rethink of priorities and direction where ecology is at the core of economic decisions, if not the driving force.

Our vision is tunnelled. We view 'nature' within a limited framework, confine it to a neat compartment that is the domain of the conservationists. It is not, however, a narrow issue of activists or scientists or even the concerned government departments. Conservation has to be a mainstream political and economical issue. It needs to be part of all disciplines—health, agriculture, engineering, mining, construction, hydrology, the works. Fact is, nature is linked to our health, livelihoods, economy—indeed, all of it is dependent on a healthy environment and a robust biodiversity. Drawing these links is crucial.

The ecological ignorance that we are mired in is our collective failure—we have disdained, and are eroding traditional knowledge. Nor is it ingrained in our educational system. Nature studies and ecology must be taught in every educational institution.

Conservation is everyone's task simply because its impacts are truly democratic, affecting each and every one of us.

Religious groups and leaders can play a greater role because of their enormous following and sway on the human race. I do not study religion, but from within my limited knowledge all religions revere the earth, support all forms of life, and can involve themselves in conservation. India has an enormous advantage here—our culture venerates all forms of life, and nature. It is part of our ethos.

On another level, India needs to up its ante on Protected Areas, increase its cover. As I mention in the book, Protected Areas cover a mere 5 per cent of the country—less than most of our neighbouring countries. Globally, 15.4 per cent of the world's terrestrial areas, and 3.4 per cent of the seas is protected.[13] There is a grand—many have termed it audacious—vision globally espoused by the great evolutionary biologist E.O. Wilson to protect 'half-earth': to set aside half the planet for wildlife. This could potentially save 80 per cent of the species alive today. Audacious? Yes. But then, writes Wilson, 'The only hope for the species still living is a human effort commensurate with the magnitude of the problem.'[14]

I have another thought I would like to share. What we also need to shed is our hubris, our anthropocentric view of nature, of the world: 'Conquering' mountains, 'taming' rivers, 'exploiting' land. It requires a change in our thinking, and in our lexicon. Nature is not a *resource*. Rivers are not a *resource* which must be tamed, harvested, dredged, linked—exploited to its full potential, and any drop unused for human consumption considered a 'waste'. Wild animals are not a *menace*, they are co-inhabitants of this planet. Animals are not 'beastly', *intentionally* cruel, or have beastly morals—they function as evolution ordained.

Biodiversity ensures a healthy planet, decreases the risk of environmental collapse. It may not need us, but our sustenance depends on a healthy, robust biodiversity.

India's development model must be truly inclusive and sustainable, finding solutions not only in mega-projects, but also in the micro and local. Its people must urge their government to factor in conservation in development agenda. They must drive the change.

And the time to act is now.

As each day passes more forests are destroyed, rivers dry up, species are lost. The losses are irrevocable—if Ken river is linked to Betwa, the forests of Panna will be destroyed forever. Our children won't be able to see the beauty of the flamingos if its only nesting ground is destroyed by construction of a road, and other activities. Nothing, *nothing* will bring the great Indian bustard back to planet Earth, if we lose the last hundred-odd birds.

The choice is ours to make: Will we stand by silent and watch the slaughter? Watch the forests fall? Watch, as wild creatures fall off the map of India? Do we want an India that is silenced of the roar of the tiger? Do we want to live in a country where forests are barren, its land infertile? Or will we stand up and fight?

Explanations

The International Union for Conservation of Nature defines Protected Area (PA) as 'a clearly defined geographical space, recognised, dedicated and managed, through legal or other effective means, to achieve the long-term conservation of nature with associated ecosystem services and cultural values'.

PAs may include National Parks (which are accorded the highest level of protection), Wildlife Sanctuaries and Conservation Reserves. Tiger Reserves may encompass national parks, wildlife sanctuaries and even reserve forests, particularly in their buffer areas. All tiger reserves are required to have a core critical tiger habitat which is surrounded by a buffer to cushion the impact of human populations. I have taken the liberty to use the terms parks, reserves, sanctuaries interchangeably, unless I am referring to a specific area.

I use the term 'ministry of environment and forests' (MoEF), but any reference to it post May 2014—when the name was changed—it's 'ministry of environment, forests and climate change' (MoEFCC). I refer to it at times as the 'environment ministry'.

I use lakhs and crores, as per the numbering system used in India. According to this: One lakh (1,00,000) equals one hundred thousand (100,000). One million equals ten lakhs. While one crore is ten million. One billion is 100 crores.

Two different terms are used in the book: 'Eco-Sensitive Zones' (ESZ) and 'Eco-Sensitive Areas' (ESA). While the underlying principle of graded protection and wise-land use is the same, they have a basic difference. ESZs are areas, extending upto 10 km, notified around PAs. An ESZ is site-specific, and the idea is for it to be a shock-absorber for the PA, by regulating activities within the zone, before it spills into an industrial, urban area with severe anthropogenic pressures. They also act as transition zones from areas of high protection to one shorn of protective cover. An ESA, on the other hand, is larger, aimed at landscape-level conservation. Its prime objective is to safeguard ecologically fragile areas through land use planning against pressures of aggressive development, pollution and other damaging activities. Some such areas include Matheran, Doon Valley, Mount Abu, the Aravallis, Murud-Janjira. Both are notified under the Environment (Protection) Act.

There may be a few repetitions and overlaps across chapters, inevitable in a book like this. Say, the explanation of what the National Board for Wildlife is about, or I may talk about the same issue, like the establishment of a yarn factory near Karnala Wildlife Sanctuary—in different chapters, the context will be different. Also, my idea is that each chapter should stand alone, as much as possible, to give the reader the chance to pick chapters to read. I also find that the enormity of the crisis takes a while to assimilate, sink in, and so . . . a chapter at a time.

I am loath to refer to animals (or for that matter rivers and mountains) as 'it', but in most places I have. But once I 'meet' an animal, for instance, the tigress who crossed my path in Kanha, or the elephant matriarch 'Lakshmi' who I observed for hours, or even the recently killed hyena whose still-warm body I carefully moved away from the road, and other speeding vehicles, I refer to them as she or he as the case may be. I *know* the animal then, and I find it disrespectful.

While the book essentially highlights the wildlife crisis, you will find that the last chapter touches on the social consequences of the 'development without breaks' model; it also talks a lot about the environmental impacts, notably air pollution. As I try to explain in the book, the wildlife crisis is not isolated—what is driving species extinct has detrimental consequences on us as well. When rivers are linked, it is not just the loss of tiger forests, or the loss of aquatic wildlife like dolphins, it means loss of livelihood for fishers and farmers. When we use pesticides that kill bees, it harms our health as well. When we talk of ill-planned, reckless development, its impacts are not just on wildlife, but equally have environmental, social, cultural consequences—and these are the threads that I try and link.

I may also, occasionally, use nature, wildlife, ecology, environment interchangeably though each is differently defined, and environment, for instance, encompasses greater disciplines than wildlife. Similarly, ecological crisis also has a broad context to include air, water, soil, noise pollution, soil erosion, ozone layer depletion, climate change, species extinction.

The Central Empowered Committee (CEC) was constituted vide notification File No.1-1/CEC/SC/2002 by the ministry of environment and forests under sub-section (3) of Section 3 of the Environment (Protection) Act, 1986. It was constituted primarily to deal with the large number of cases pending with the Supreme Court of India on matters related to the Wildlife (Protection) Act, forest and other environmental laws. Since 2007, the CEC is functioning as a Supreme Court appointed committee on matters related to forests and wildlife.

The Forest Advisory Committee (FAC) is a statutory body of the MoEFCC formed under the Forest (Conservation) Act. When the Act was constituted in 1980, 'Forests and Wildlife' was under the preview of the ministry of agriculture. The ministry of environment, forests and wildlife was established in 1986, and the FAC under the Forest (Conservation) Act was formed then.

The subject of wildlife crisis is vast, complex, nuanced. I can't claim to have covered it all, nor even attempted to. My effort here is to try and give an idea of certain aspects of the crisis. I have also largely stuck to the crisis in the current context (while providing a brief history), covering the past few years, taking off from the 1990s when India saw a great shift in its political, economic, social and ecological environment.

Acknowledgements

My life's mantra is 'Animals First', so I'll begin by expressing my deepest gratitude to the denizens of the forest for the infinite happiness and wonder (and heartache!) they have brought into my life.

I am deeply grateful to the publisher Penguin Random House India, and to my editors Premanka Goswami and Paloma Dutta, who believed in the book—and are blessed with infinite patience and a soft spot for the wilds. Thanks for steering the book to the finishing line, into publication. I am in awe of Eleanor Crow's talent who has beautifully illustrated the cover . . . thank you.

This book has been read, reread—and reread (till the editors pretty much snatched it away. Thanks, I think!)—to check for facts. If there are any mistakes at all (God, please *no*), the blame is all mine. I will be grateful if the reader can draw my attention to any errors, and also will be happy to get additional information, perspectives, insights that would enrich my understanding of the subject further.

I would like to acknowledge the publishers of www.dailyo.in where parts of 'Drowning a Tiger Forest', 'Sounds of Silence', 'Lines of Blood' and 'Deceptions of Development' were first published. I acknowledge Fountain Ink where part of 'Failing Our Gods' was first published as 'The Elephant Men of Odisha'. Acknowledgements are due to *India Today*, *Sanctuary Asia* and *Pioneer*, where small parts of some of the chapters have been published over time.

I owe it to a lot of people for making this book happen and were I to name them all, it might require a tome in itself, but there are a few I simply must bow to for helping me over the years, shaping my life as a conservationist and enabling me to write this book.

I am astounded and touched by the generosity of wildlifers, conservationists, biologists, officials, journalists, foresters, photographers, naturalists, guides and 'ordinary' folks (who are really very extraordinary) who have thrown open the archives of their works, freely shared information and time, made me feel welcome in their homes—due to their innate hospitality, generosity and with the belief that it would help wildlife. I am touched by the faith.

I am fortunate to have as my mentors P.K. Sen, Ullas Karanth—who have been a source of strength, and offered every support. I would like to thank Brijendra Singh for his faith and affection, Bittu Sahgal for giving me my first 'wild' job and keeping me in the family thereafter, Ravi Singh (WWF-India) for his unfailing support, M.K. Ranjitsinh for his patient guidance.

My eternal gratitude to George Schaller for his incredible generosity and encouragement.

A salute to Jairam Ramesh, most unconventional of politicians, for speaking up for wildlife, encouraging diverse voices and his sense of humour—all increasingly endangered traits! Thanks for the faith—and for empowering a 'young' generation of conservationists.

I owe a debt of gratitude to the late Ashok Kumar who led me into this wild world and lent me support in the worst of times. And the late Billy Arjan Singh and Fatji (Fateh Singh Rathore) for their love and guidance—I so miss their wit and wisdom.

Prakriti Srivastava, a very special thanks for your encouragement. Your courageous battles for wildlife have been a source of inspiration. 'Pammi' Paramjit Singh, I owe you much. Thanks for sharing your love of the forest, and for all that you do for the wilds. Thanks to Amit Bhaduri, Pradip Krishen, Mahesh

Rangarajan, Tishyarakshit Chatterjee, Bonani and Pradeep Kakkar for their wise counsel. Dia Mirza, nature's child, and her gutsy champion. Thanks, Dia, for your faith, and for speaking up.

Thanks to Valmik Thapar, for his constant support given in his usual gruff manner, and Belinda Wright, for dishing out scoops and a wealth of information. Vivek Menon, for his encouragement. Bikram Grewal, I missed you so in doing this one—doing a book without your constant nagging (and considerable expertise) is simply no fun! Owe you.

I would also like to thank Rajesh Gopal, who in his years at National Tiger Conservation Authority was a tremendous support, as were his colleagues S.P. Yadav, H.S. Negi and Sanjay Pathak.

My fellow members of the standing committee of the National Board for Wildlife, it was a tremendous experience working with all of you, and so miss being part of the team.

Through the years I have been helped by a great number of forest officers, who have shared their knowledge, provided logistical support and with whom I have spent many happy hours in the forest. Many have fought courageous battles to protect the wilds—and have become friends. Thanks to P.J. Dilip Kumar, Vinod Rishi, P.R. Sinha, D.V.S. Khati, Samir Sinha, B.S. Bonal, Pradeep Vyas, Shree Bhagwan, S.S. Sharma, G.V. Reddy, R.P. Singh, Ajay Kumar Naik, Rakesh Kumar Dogra, Rangaiah Sreenivasa Murthy, Raghuvir Singh Shekhawat, Vikas Gupta, Jasbir Singh Chouhan, Surendra Singh Rajpoot, Hari Upadhyay, Imtienla Ao, Rupak De, Sanjeeva Pandey, Ramesh Pandey, Rahul Pandey, Sujoy Bannerjee, Santosh Tewari, Anil Naggar, Parag M. Dhakate, Tejaswini Dhakate Patil, Sonali Ghosh, Sumita Ghatak, Padma Mohanty, Saket Badola, Kahkashan Naseem, Neha Verma, Amit Verma, Tahir Shawl, Anil Patel, O.P. Tiwari, Pratibha Singh, Shyamal Tikadar, Shekhar Kumar Niraj, Ashok Mishra, Arun Mishra, Gopal Singh Karkee, Rajneesh Singh, Shiv Pal Singh.

Rashid Naqash, my friend, thanks for introducing me to Dachigam, and the wildlife of Kashmir. Nazir Malik, shukriya.

Gobind Sagar Bhardhwaj for opening my eyes, and heart, to the wildlife of the desert: We simply must save the great Indian bustard.

I am grateful to V.B. Mathur and his team at Wildlife Institute of India.

A number of people have shared their expertise, helped me correct many a mistake, negotiate stuff I didn't understand, and for that I would like to thank Asad Rahmani, Harsh Vardhan, Rom Whitaker, Himanshu Thakkar, Brij Gopal, Y.V. Jhala, Sutirtha Dutta, Ritwick Dutta, S.A. Hussain, Nitin Desai, Milind Pariwakam, Biswajit Mohanty, Neeraj Vagholikar, Sudarshan Rodriguez, Aarthi Sridhar, Nandikesh Sivalingam, Girish A. Punjabi, Ananda Kumar, Kishor Rithe, Pramod Patil, Nitin Desai, Kanchi Kohli, Nick Haddad, Neha Sinha, Rajeev Mehta, Bibhuti Lahkar, Meghna Banerjee, Tiasa Adhya, Riyaz Ahmed, Raza Kazmi, Shrenik Shah, Praveen Bhargav, Parikshit Gautam, Nachiket Kelkar, Divya Karnad, Rahul Chaudhary, Rohit Chaudhary, Shardul Bajikar, Tito Joseph, Koustabh Sharma, Sanjeev Kumar Yadav, Qamar Qureshi, Anish Andheria, S.P. Goyal, Mudit Gupta, Siddharth Chakravarty.

Working in wildlife can be a frustrating task. What makes it worthwhile—besides the magical moments you spend in the wilds—are the friendships that evolve in the field, a shared kinship with fellow conservationists, many of whom are now friends. Again, too many people here . . . but I must name a few.

Thanks, Aditya Chandra Panda, my dearest friend, and one among the 'elephant men' of Athgarh, for your immense help—and battles—for the Odisha landscape, for your patience in translating and thus helping me converse with the remarkable conflict-mitigation squad! D.V. Girish, I owe you much, for sharing your forests, for your endless battles to protect them, and feeding me the most delicious uttapams and vadais . . . ever! I am coming your way soon.

Thanks to India's 'Leopard Lady' Vidya Athreya for guiding me though the leopard article. A shout-out to Nikit Surve, Nayan Khanolkar (my eternal gratitude for sharing your spectacular photograph), Vidya Venkatesh, Snowy Baptista, Dipti Humraskar, Sonu Singh, Ranjeet Jadhav, Manish Gadia, Virat Singh, Krishna Tiwari—the 'leopard team' in Mumbai.

Poonam and Harshawardhan Dhanwatey, with what words do I thank thee, for your love and support, and the wonderful jungle days.

My salaams to Claude Alvares—and the other warriors of the Goa I know and love—Norma Alvares, Abhijit Prabhudesai, Alina Saldanha, Nitin Sawant, Denzil Sequeira, Diana Tavares, Puja Mitra, Nihar Gokhale, Nirmal Kulkarni, Atul S. Borker, Armando Gonsalves.

Sujoy Bannerjee, Rajeev Chauhan, Ram Pratap Singh, for your love for the Chambal, and ensuring I fell in the trap too. Thanks are also due to Jeffery Lang, Tarun Nair, Rajeev Tomar, Govardhan Singh Rathore, Dharamendra Khandal.

A special thanks to Bivash Pandav for helping me understand turtles (Turtle Rabbi, I owe you much too), and for his help in fact-checking.

I owe a debt of gratitude to photographers who have generously shared their incredible work with me: No questions asked, as long as their images were used to further the cause of conservation. There are many, but I must express my deepest gratitude to Aditya 'Dicky' Singh, Kalyan Varma, Dhritiman Mukherjee, Biju Boro, Karan Tejpal, Isshaan Ghosh, Rashid Naqash, Aditya Panda, Steve Winter, Gobind Sagar Bhardwaj, Roni Chowdhury, Mayank Ghedia, Udayan Rao Pawar, Samyak Kaninde, Abhishek Gulshan, Nanak Dhingra, Ramki Sreenivasan, Kedar Bhide, Indrajit Ghorpade, Manoj Dholakia, Nikhil Devasar, Shivang Mehta, Agam Singh Gokani, Anurag Sharma.

Thanks to all those who provided quotes, and photographs, for the book, and apologies if I have only been able to use excerpts or unable to use them at all due to space constraints.

Geetan Batra, you are so special. Thanks for your loving support and granting me sanctuary in Gethia and Birdsong.

Through this book, and my wildlife wanderings, I have enjoyed the warm hospitality of many kind hosts and friends—Mohit Aggarwal, Shreedev Hulikere, Aditya 'Dicky' Singh and Poonam Singh, Tom Alter, Minakshi Pandey and Ritish Suri, Vinnie Singh and Bhavna Kumari, R.P. Singh and Anu Singh, Dhanraj Malik at Desert Coursers, Rann Riders. Peter Smetacek (and Sheilaji) whose lovely homestay in Bhimtal helped me tide over my (all too frequent) writing blocks. I am indebted to the many people, especially in villages, I met in the course of my travels who welcomed me into their homes, and shared with me their stories and experiences.

Samir Sinha, when are we doing Valmiki again, along with litti-chokka?

Rohan Chakravorty, a warm hug for bringing in (green) humour in the bleakest of situations! Laughter is the *best* medicine. Arjun Srivathsa—salute from an ardent admirer of Pocket Science-India!

Thanks are also due to Ajith Kumar, Divyabhanusinh Chavda, Pradyut Bordoloi, Brinda Dubey, Priya Davidar, Shekar Dattatri, Keshav Varma, Keshav Kumar, Aravind Chaturvedi, Tarun Tejpal, Rajashree Khalap, Joanna van Gruisen, Sejal Worah, A.J.T. Johnsingh, Amit Sankhala, Joydip and Suchendra Kundu, Sulabha Chakravorty, Nadeem Qadri, Sree Nandy, Rakesh Agarwal, Suniti Bhushan Datta, Chandni Gurusrikar, Jose Louies, Shaleen Attre, Firoz Ahmed, Santanu Sarkar, Dipankar Ghose, Murli Dhar Parashar, Suvrajyoti Chatterjee, Rajesh Madan, Rajashree Bhuyan, Kartik Shukul.

My deepest gratitude to rangers, foresters, guards, trackers, mahouts, guides—our unsung green army. They are all brave warriors and had it not been for them, our precious wildlife could well have vanished much earlier. Many thanks to the staff of various forest rest houses I have stayed in and whose luxuriant hospitality matches none. In the book, I write about some of the good practices, and highlight a few 'earth heroes'—but there are many officers, researchers, foresters, communities, and many more such extraordinary folks who have greatly contributed to conserving wildlife. My salaams, shukriya.

Thank you, all of the 'wild people' with whom I have spent many precious hours discussing wildlife, and who now have their work cut out. More power to all of you.

I have greatly been inspired by the works of M. Krishnan, F.W. Champion, Amitav Ghosh, Arundhati Roy, George Monbiot, Ruth Padel, Bernie Krause, Elizabeth Kolbert, Douglas Adams, Paul Kingsnorth, John Vidal, Gerald Durrell, Ramachandra Guha, to name a few.

Vikram Seth, 'The Elephant and the Tragopan' says it all, so lyrically and beautifully and poignantly. Thanks for inspiring.

I have drawn from the reportage and works of Arati Kumar Rao, Janaki Lenin, Bahar Dutt, Nitin Sethi, Neha Sinha, M. Rajshekhar, Shoma Chaudhury, Ananda Banerjee, Nihar Gokhale, Nikhil Ghanekar, Mayank Aggarwal, Rohini Mohan Sambhav Shrivastava, Vijay Pinjarkar, Roopak Goswami, Krishnendu Mukherjee, Jay Mazoomdaar, Nityanand Jayaraman . . . again to name a few.

I, unfortunately, do not possess the memory of an elephant. Quite the contrary. I have undoubtedly left out a few *very* important people who have played a significant role in the making of this book. *Please* forgive me, even if I can't forgive myself.

A writer trying to finish her book is frankly a pain in those wrong, unprintable places. Especially if that writer is wont to share cheerful nuggets about impending doom while sitting down to enjoy a meal, like how cling film that the bread is wrapped in is choking turtles, or refuses a friendly outing to the mall that destroyed a wetland. Or doling out unwanted information on how the train we were chugging along in cuts through an elephant corridor . . .

Thanks, my long-suffering friends and family . . . Cheers! The crabby days are over. Really.

Joy Majumdar, my very dear friend, I owe you much for your endless patience in helping me negotiate this project. Thanks for cracking the whip, and your sharp eye.

Bijal Vachharajani, Sharon Guynup—soul sisters, cheerleaders, friends—for keeping my spirits up through this project, for your valuable inputs and helping structure the book by reading parts of the manuscript. Thanks, Maya Ramaswamy, Pranav Capila, Nayantara Patel for your adept advice and support. Rashmi Singh, for helping with the research. Cara Tejpal—friend and fellow-warrior—and Vaishali Rawat . . . in you I *hope*.

Kam, my forever friend, you taught me the power of words. Thank you. To my not-so-wild friends for being there, always: Geeta Kanupillai, Bhavna Ramrakhiani, Gayatri Jadeja, Meghna Bhaduri (who has gone, leaving wounds), Gauri Keskar, Sangeeta Vengsarkar Shah (and Nimish), Phagun Dhaka, Manjula Narayan, Rajee Sood, Neha Dara, Supriya Mehta Chawla, Premlata Choudhary, Kiran Bhatti, Anuradha Sehgal, Sonia Agnani, Margaret Mascarenhas, Shefali Juneja, Aniruddha Bahal. I am grateful to Aruna, Malati, Tejal, Amit for their affection, and making life easier. Sheila masi, for her wealth of love and caring, and my loving sister Renee didi. Thanks Bobby, Ginny. My nephews—Hargun, Harjaap, Mayank Dandriyal, Aryan, and the irrepressible Sarah Sood; you are the future.

Thanks to my father J.S. Bindra, who has always encouraged my unusual interest in the wilds, even if it meant keeping his counsel. I have the best brother in the world, and it is his support that has enabled me to follow the path I have chosen, and to do this book. Thanks Jaspreet, for *everything*! Frooti, Snoopi, Jimmy, Junglee, Aimee Sood, Hobbes, Sandy, Sad, Miss Grey and my numerous canine friends, who taught what love and loyalty is all about—you are so missed. A shout-out to Sofie Sood. And, of course, my best friend Doginder Singh, who occupies my heart, and most of my room. The Dog was a great source of energy and encouragement—mainly provided by peacefully snoring through the night (and day) as I burnt the midnight oil to write the book.

My life's greatest support was my mother, whose love and caring for me can never be repaid in several lifetimes. It's for you . . . Ma.

Endnotes

Prologue

1. Indian blackberry.
2. 'What Are Animals Thinking? (Hint: More than You Suspect)', Jeffrey Kluger, *Time*, 26 August 2014.
3. 'Risk and Resilience in a New Era', *Living Planet Report 2016*, WWF International, Gland, Switzerland, 2016.
4. 'Catastrophic Declines in Wilderness Areas Undermine Global Environment Targets', James E.M. Watson, et al., *Current Biology*, Volume 26, Issue 21, pp. 2,929–2,934, 2016.
5. An assessment by the Intergovernmental Science-Policy Platform on Biodiversity and Ecosystem Services, established under United Nations auspices in 2012 to assess the state of ecosystems and biodiversity; '"Decline of Bees Poses Potential Risks to Major Crops," says UN', AFP, 26 February 2016.
6. The Food and Agriculture Organization of the United Nations; Food and Water Programme.
7. 'India's Forest and Green Cover: Contribution as Carbon Sink', ministry of environment and forests, August 2009.
8. Data acquired through RTI (Right to Information) and analysed by Environmental Impact Assessment Resources and Response Centre. The actual land diverted would be much higher as this accounted for diversions of forest larger than 40 hectares.
9. Climate change.
10. 'Deforestation Causes Global Warming', Food and Agriculture Organization of the United Nations, 2006.

Fall of the Wild

1. Rediscovered in November 1997 by Pamela Rasmussen, David Abbot and Ben King at Shahada near Taloda in the Nandurbar district of Maharashtra,

http://www.kolkatabirds.com/forestowlet.htm; 'The Rediscovery of the Forest Owlet Athene (Heteroglaux) Blewitti', B.F. King and P.C. Rasmussen (1998), *Forktail* (14), pp. 53–55.

2. 'Big Cats in Our Backyards: Persistence of Large Carnivores in a Human Dominated Landscape in India', V. Athreya, M. Odden, J.D.C. Linnell, J. Krishnaswamy, U. Karanth, *PLoS ONE* 8(3), 2013.

3. 'National Board for Wildlife Clears BG Railway Line Project through Melghat', Vijay Pinjarkar, *Times of India*, 10 February 2017.

4. In conversation with the author; Interview with Bittu Sahgal, *Sanctuary Asia*, Volume XXXI No. 4, August 2011.

5. Shashi Tharoor's speech at the Oxford Union Debate 2015.

6. 'But What About the Railways . . .? The Myth of Britain's Gifts to India', Shashi Tharoor, *Guardian*, 8 March 2017.

7. *India's Wildlife History*, Mahesh Rangarajan, Permanent Black, 2001.

8. *India's Wildlife History*, Mahesh Rangarajan, Permanent Black, 2001.

9. *India's Wildlife History*, Mahesh Rangarajan, Permanent Black, 2001.

10. 'Animals of the Dwindling Forest', M. Krishnan, 1970, from *Nature's Spokesman, M. Krishnan and Indian Wildlife*, Ramachandra Guha (ed.), Oxford University Press, 2000.

11. 'Defending the Green Realm: The Forest Conservation Act 1980 of India in Theory and Practice', P.J. Dilip Kumar, Institute for Social and Economic Change, Bangalore, 2015.

12. 'Defending the Green Realm: The Forest Conservation Act 1980 of India in Theory and Practice', P.J. Dilip Kumar, Institute for Social and Economic Change, Bangalore, 2015.

13. In 2002, this became the National Board for Wildlife, also with a change in composition and functions.

14. *The Last Tiger: Struggling for Survival*, Valmik Thapar, Oxford University Press, 2006.

15. The ostensible reason for the denotification of the Great Himalayan National Park was the settlements of rights of two villages in the area. But environmentalists, and even locals, called this absurd, the actual motive being the hydroelectricity project, which had been stalled due to the national park. 'A Troubled Heritage: The Great Himalayan National Park', Ashish Kothari, *Sanctuary Asia*; 'Damning eco-reserves', Usha Rai, *The Hindu*, 9 January 2000; and conversations with local people and conservationists.

16. According to a Supreme Court Order in 2006, no project can be allowed within a 10-km boundary of national parks and sanctuaries without the approval of the standing committee of the NBWL, unless site-specific Eco Sensitive Zones have been notified by the state, after which activities will be regulated as defined by the notification.

17. 'Why Govindrajan Is Happy? The Collapse of Environmental Governance in India', Ritwick Dutta, *ERC Journal*, February 2009.

18. 'Why Govindrajan Is Happy? The Collapse of Environmental Governance in India', Ritwick Dutta, *ERC Journal*, Feb. 2009.

19. *Churning of the Earth*, Ashish Kothari and Aseem Shrivatsava, Penguin India, 2012; Aarthi Sridhar on email.

20. 'RTI Response from MoEF Obtained by ERC in 2008', *ERC Journal*, February 2009.

21. 'Raja's Environment Role under Scanner', Yatish Yadav, *Sunday Guardian,* 10 April 2011.

22. Information of 2,880-MW Dibang Hydel Multipurpose Project obtained from documents of government, including relevant minutes of Forest Advisory Committee; conversations with Neeraj Vagholikar, Kalpavriksh; 'Manipulating Environment and Forest Clearances for Dibang Project: Déjà Vu: History Repeated: Will It Be Tragedy or Comedy?', *SANDRP*, 6 October 2014; 'Dibang Project Rejected Forest Clearance for the Second Time', *SANDRP*, 17 May 2014; 'Nod to Dibang Project Shows Why Present Forest Clearance Process Needs to Be Scrapped', Chandra Bhushan, *Down to Earth*; *Green Wars: Dispatches from a Vanishing World*, Bahar Dutt, HarperCollins, 2014; Comments on the EIA of Dibang Multipurpose Project from Dr Anwaruddin Choudhury.

23. 'Nod to Dibang Project Shows Why Present Forest Clearance Process Needs to Be Scrapped', Chandra Bhushan, *Down to Earth*, 30 November 2014.

24. 'Truth vs Hype: Bypassing Green Checks by Nominating "Compliant" Members?', NDTV, 8 December 2014, anchored by Sreenivasan Jain.

25. '23,716 Industrial Projects Replace Forests over 30 Years', Himadri Ghosh, 3 June 2016, IndiaSpend.com.

26. 'The Forest Conservation Act Is Sacrosanct', Prerna Singh Bindra, *Tehelka*, 27 June 2009.

27. Manmohan Singh at the 11th Delhi Sustainable Development Summit on 3 February 2011, and which he was to repeat again in 2013 in a cabinet meeting as per a report in the *Times of India*, January 2013 ('Manmohan Calls Environmental Clearances New "Licence-Permit-Quota Raj"', Subodh Ghildiyal); 'We Need a Regulatory Framework that Does Not Become Licence Permit Raj', Manmohan Singh, *Indian Express,* 26 July 2011.

28. 'Green Terror', Devesh Kumar, Prachi Bhuchar, *India Today*, 5 October 2012.

29. 'What Jairam Did and Didn't Do as Green Minister', Himanshu Thakkar, http://www.rediff.com, 20 July 2011.

30. 'Green Challenges', Praful Bidwai, *Frontline*, Volume 28, Issue 16, 30 July– 12 August 2011.

31. 'Green Terror', Devesh Kumar, Prachi Bhuchar, *India Today*, 5 October 2012.

32. 'Green Terror', Devesh Kumar, Prachi Bhuchar, *India Today*, 5 October 2012.

33. '2.43 Lakh Hectares of Forests Cleared for Projects during UPA Regime', Nitin Sethi, *The Hindu*, 25 January 2014.

34. 'Green Challenges', Praful Bidwai, *Frontline*, Volume 28, Issue 16, 30 July– 12 August 2011.

35. Written statement by Prakriti Srivastava submitted to the Central Bureau of Investigation in the matter relating to grant of mining lease for iron ore and manganese ore to M/s JSW Steel Ltd on receipt of the summons (CBI/

EOU–VIEO–II/N as per letter No.1383 PE220/2014/E/0003); 'MoEF Subverts Its Own Conservation Mandate', Cara Tejpal, *Tehelka*, 2 June 2012.

36. With a combined capacity of 583 million tonnes per annum.

37. Letter by minister of state (independent charge) environment and forests, Jayanthi Natarajan, to Prime Minister Manmohan Singh, 9 October 2012, D.O. No.1–52/MoS(E&F)/2012; 'Environment Is Not Impeding Growth', Centre for Science and Environment (CSE) responds to industry leaders' open letter, 13 October 2011.

38. By Centre for Monitoring Indian Economy; 'Government Clearances Have Got Faster but Lack of Promoter Interest Stalls Projects', Sandeep Singh, Anil Sasi, *Indian Express*, 25 May 2016.

39. 'In 20 Days, I Cleared over 70 Projects: Moily', Sujay Mehdudia, *The Hindu*, 12 January 2014.

40. 'A Battle that Hasn't Been Won in Nine Years', Kanchi Kohli, *India Together*, 5 May 2014; 'POSCO Project Has Taken Away Rights of Communities', K. Venkateshwarlu, *The Hindu*, 29 June 2013.

41. After the NDA government came to power in May 2014, the nomenclature of the ministry of environment and forests (MoEF) was changed to the ministry of environment, forests and climate change (MoEFCC).

42. 'Proactive PMO Takes Control of Easing Green Clearances', Mayank Aggarwal, *DNA India,* 16 November 2014.

43. 'Proactive PMO Takes Control of Easing Green Clearances', Mayank Aggarwal, *DNA India,* 16 November 2014.

44. 'Environment Ministry Says Now Up to Industry to Perform', Mayank Aggarwal, *Live Mint*, 7 January 2015.

45. 'T.S.R. Subramanian Committee Report Undermines Democracy, Renders Projected-Affected People Voiceless, Is Blind to Climate Change', Ritwick Dutta, Debi Goenka, Manoj Mishra and Himanshu Thakkar, *Counterview*, 17 January 2015.

46. It did, however, allow for a lengthier comment by email; http://www.moef. nic.in/content/comments-invited-suggestionscomments-are-invited-high-level-committee-hlc-review-various-env.

47. Parliamentary standing committee on science and technology, environment and forests, headed by Ashwani Kumar.

48. 'Environment Ministry Asked to Form New Committee to Review Laws', Mayank Aggarwal, *Mint,* 22 July 2015.

49. Conversation with environmental lawyer Ritwick Dutta; also, 'Scrapping Green Clearances Is a Bad Way to Promote the Ease of Doing Business', Neha Sinha, 6 June 2016, https://thewire.in.

50. Populations of the Yangtze river dolphin dropped drastically after China undertook massive waterways development. Damming the river and indiscriminate, illegal fishing practices were the other main causes.

51. 'NDA Cleared More Projects in Wildlife Habitats in 2 Yrs than UPA Did in 5 Yrs', Kumar Sambhav Shrivastava, *Hindustan Times*, 15 June 2016.

52. 'Environmental Governance: Two years of NDA', CSE, 2016.
53. 'Towards Transparency and Good Governance', ministry of environment, forests and climate change, January 2015.

India's Notional Board for Wildlife

1. Minister of state (independent charge) for environment and forests.
2. The agenda, however, did not mention anything about the involvement of the sanctuary. In fact, it said 'just outside Shergarh Wildlife Sanctuary, Rajasthan'. But in a dissent note standing committee, NBWL member, M.K. Ranjitsinh was to point out that, 'The Parvan major irrigation project, Rajasthan, which will submerge 81.67 sq km of the Shergarh Wildlife Sanctuary.' The committee was to come under heavy criticism that the NBWL decided to clear the project even without knowing if the Shergarh Wildlife Sanctuary will be affected.
3. Summary records of the 22nd meeting of the standing committee of the NBWL held on 25 April 2011 in Paryavaran Bhavan, New Delhi, and various letters and emails written by me, other members (both individually and collectively) to the then chair of the standing committee and minister for environment and forests, Jairam Ramesh, and the subsequent minister Jayanthi Natarajan.
4. Which is not to say it was smooth sailing before. Conservation has always been a battle, and I recall M. Krishnan's piece of 1970 in which he laments the setting up of a hydroelectric project inside a sanctuary (Ramganga inside Corbett, which became a tiger reserve three years later), and the Moyar project bordering Bandipur and Mudumalai—both tiger reserves now.
5. Submitted by Bittu Sahgal, member of the IBWL on 11 July 1997.
6. According to a Supreme Court order in 2006, all projects granted environment clearances within a 10-km boundary of national parks and sanctuaries would have to be approved by the standing committee of the NBWL, unless a site-specific ESZ has been notified by the state, after which activities will be regulated as per the notification. This was in pursuance of a decision of the Indian Board of Wildlife in its 21st meeting.
7. Written statement by Prakriti Srivastava submitted to the CBI in the matter relating to the granting of mining lease for iron ore and manganese ore to M/s JSW Steel Ltd on receipt of the summons as per letter No.1383 PE220/2014/E/0003. The probe (preliminary inquiries) was for environment clearances given during Environment Minister Jayanthi Natarajan's regime.
8. M/S Jaiprakash Associates Limited.
9. Kaimur Information: 'Report on site visit for M/s Jaypee Super Cement Plant (Clinker 2.01 MTPA; Cement 2.50 MTPA) located at village Kota, District Sonebhadra, Uttar Pradesh (A unit of Jai Prakash Associates) Limited, 2.1 km from Kaimur Wildlife Sanctuary', Prerna Singh Bindra, member, standing committee, NBWL, 24 April 2011; letter to MoEF, File

No. II/1119/CEC/2009, regarding environmental clearance, Y.K. Singh Chauhan, conservator of forests (central), MoEF (Regional Office-Central Region) 1 April 2011; mail from A.K. Srivastava, inspector general of forests (wildlife) written on 25 April 2011 to the member secretary, standing committee, NBWL and additional director general of forests (wildlife), ministry of environment and forests, New Delhi.

10. Ramesh's reply? 'Your advice is well taken. The problem is that all ministers want me to be automatic!' From *Green Signals: Ecology, Growth, and Democracy in India*, Jairam Ramesh, Oxford University Press, 2015.

11. 'Manmohan Admits to Pressuring Jairam', Priscilla Jebaraj, *The Hindu*, 29 June 2011.

12. *Green Signals: Ecology, Growth, and Democracy in India*, Jairam Ramesh, Oxford University Press, 2015.

13. From the agenda and the minutes of the 20th meeting of the standing committee of the NBWL held on 13 October 2010. Letter to Jairam Ramesh, minister of environment and forests on 26 January 2010 by members of the NBWL: Prerna Singh Bindra, T.R. Shankar Raman, Biswajit Mohanty, A.J.T. Johnsingh and Bittu Sahgal.

14. Minutes of the 28th meeting of the standing committee of NBWL held on 20 March 2013.

15. Minutes of the 29th meeting of the standing committee of NBWL held on 6 June 2013.

16. Written statement to the CBI in the matter relating to the granting of a mining lease for iron ore and manganese ore to M/s JSW Steel Ltd on receipt of the summons CBI/EOU-VIEO-II/N as per letter No.1383 PE220/2014/E0003.

17. Our comments and corrections were incorporated later.

18. 'Betraying India's Wildlife', Praveen Bhargav, *Conservation India*, 18 July 2012; on email with Praveen Bhargav.

19. Vulture is called *gidh* in Urdu and Hindi.

20. Site visit report by Divyabhanusinh Chavda and Nita Shah on diversion of 7.2871 ha of forest land for construction of ropeway from Bhavnath Taleti to Ambaji Temple in Girnar Wildlife Sanctuary, Gujarat.

21. 'Scrapping Green Clearances Is a Bad Way to Promote the Ease of Doing Business', Neha Sinha, https://thewire.in/, 6 June 2016.

22. Gujarat Ecological Education and Research (GEER) Foundation is the nominated NGO member, and is represented by its director, a serving forest official. It is an autonomous body, set up in 1982 by the forest and environment department, Government of Gujarat, and is governed by a board of governors chaired by the state's chief minister.

23. 'NDA Cleared More Projects in Wildlife Habitats in 2 yrs than UPA Did in 5 yrs', Kumar Sambhav Shrivastava, *Hindustan Times*, 15 June 2016.

24. 'Cleared 650 Projects in 7 months, Environment Minister Prakash Javadekar tells NDTV', NDTV, Shweta Rajpal Kohli, 2 January 2015.

25. 'Cleared 650 Projects in 7 months, Environment Minister Prakash Javadekar tells NDTV', NDTV, Shweta Rajpal Kohli, 2 January 2015.
26. 'NDA Cleared More Projects in Wildlife Habitats in 2 yrs than UPA Did in 5 yrs', Kumar Sambhav Shrivastava, *Hindustan Times*, 15 June 2016.
27. The 520-MW hydroelectric power project, Teesta Stage-IV on the river Teesta in North Sikkim.
28. 'An Elephant Scientist Who Missed the Jumbo on the Track', Bahar Dutt, *Mint*, 18 September 2015.
29. In an email response Dr Sukumar maintained that the area in question is not an elephant corridor, and said, 'The land requested by the railways close to Sevoke station was about 1 hectare to construct a feeder line of about 200 metres length before tunnelling into the hillside. Even if a few elephants cross the (existing) railway line, they will encounter Sevoke settlement, a major highway at a tricky section (ghat section) and, most important, the steep cliffs along the Teesta river. Elephants cannot and do not cross the Teesta river at this point but several kilometres south that has no connection to the railway line.' He also said that what was important was the 'significance of this spot for the broader elephant movement in the region'.

  While I accept that elephants do not cross at the area in question due to steep cliffs, a major highway and other impediments, what has not been considered while granting that clearance is the havoc the construction of the line will cause—blasting a tunnel and the consequent, continuing disturbance in this habitat. Local conservationists opine that construction will affect the broader elephant movement in the region. The railway line, and therefore the expansion, goes through, or skirts, the forest blocks of the Golla–Chawa–Ruyen–Andhera–upper Gorumara blocks of Mahananda Wildlife Sanctuary. These areas have water and fodder to sustain elephants during the pinch period. This is where the elephants come during the lean season—largely January to May. With the disturbance caused in the landscape, this refuge will be lost to the elephants.

  The elephants here are surviving in small forest fragments due to which they have to make large-scale movement, bringing them into confrontation with people. Such displacement, and the search for food and water, will push them further into human habitation, greatly exacerbating the conflict. This is already a major issue in the landscape as detailed in the chapter, 'Failing Our Gods'.
30. *Right of Passage*, Wildlife Trust of India, 2004; 'An Elephant Scientist Who Missed the Jumbo on the Track', Bahar Dutt, *Mint*, 18 September 2015.
31. *ERC Journal*, Issue 2, Volume VIII, June 2015.
32. 'Undermining Its Own Mandate: A review of the Minutes of the 34th Meeting of the SC NBWL', Suman Jumani, *ERC Journal*, Issue 2, Volume VIII, June 2015.
33. 33rd meeting of the standing committee, NBWL.

Lines of Blood

1. The Brazilian Centre for the Study of Road Ecology.
2. 'An App to Save 400 Million Animals', Alex Rodriguez, *Mongabay*, 11 December 2014.
3. Conversation with Bivash Pandav; 'Over 15 Wild Animals' Death Reported on Haridwar Highway', Seema Sharma, *Times of India*, 8 September 2016.
4. 'At 7.64% Growth, India Fastest Growing Passenger Car Market', Amrit Raj, *Mint*, 13 January 2016.
5. *Road Transport Yearbook (2011–2012)*, transport research wing, ministry of road transport and highways, Government of India.
6. 'Deforestation in the Congo Rainforest', Rhett Butler, https://www.mongabay.com, 24 July 2013.
7. 'What Roads Have Wrought', Michelle Nijhuis', *New Yorker*, 20 March 2015.
8. All information of Mughal Road sourced from conversations with M.K. Ranjitsinh, Riyaz Ahmad and Bashir Ahmad Bhat (both with the Wildlife Trust of India [WTI]). *Endangered Markhor Capra Falconeri in India: Through War and Insurgency*, Y.V. Bhatnagar et al., Fauna and Flora International, Oryx, 2009; 'Assessing the Distribution of Markhor (Capra falconeri) and Other Important Fauna Along the Southern Slopes of Pir Panjal, with Special Emphasis on Resource Competition with Local Grazier Communities, in Hirpora Wildlife Sanctuary, Jammu and Kashmir', WTI and NCS, 2011; 'Goats on the Border: A Rapid Assessment of the Pir Panjal Markhor in Jammu and Kashmir: Distribution, Status and Threats', M.K. Ranjitsinh, C.M. Seth, Riyaz Ahmad, Yash Veer Bhatnagar and Sunil Subba Kyarong, WTI, 2005; 'Mughal Road: Revitalizing an Ancient Route in Kashmir', *HCC*, February 2013.
9. 'Mass Movement Events in the Himalaya: The Impact of Landslides on Ladakh, India', Sian Hodgkins, *Geology for Global Development* (http://www.gfgd.org/).
10. 'A Global Map of Roadless Areas and Their Conservation Status', Pierre L. Ibisch, Monika T. Hoffmann, Stefan Kreft, Guy Pe'er, Vassiliki Kati, Lisa Biber-Freudenberger, Dominick A. DellaSala, Mariana M. Vale, Peter R. Hobson, Nuria Selva, *Science*, 2016.
11. The Kanha–Pench–Achanakmar landscape holds 215 (185–246) as per the 2014 all-India tiger estimate. *Status of Tigers in India 2014*, Y.V. Jhala, Q. Qureshi and R. Gopal (eds), National Tiger Conservation Authority, New Delhi and the Wildlife Institute of India, Dehradun, 2015.
12. 'Report of Site Inspection of Diversion of 79.474 ha of Forest Land in Kutch Desert Wildlife Sanctuary for Construction of Gaduli to Hajipir–Khavda–Kunaria–Dholavira–Maovana–Gadakbet–Santalpur Road (S.H. Road) Gujarat', M.K. Ranjitsinh, Divyabhanusinh Chavda, Asad Rahmani.
13. 'Report of Site Inspection of Diversion of 79.474 ha of Forest Land in Kutch Desert Wildlife Sanctuary for Construction of Gaduli to Hajipir–Khavda–

Kunaria–Dholavira–Maovana–Gadakbet–Santalpur Road (S.H. Road) Gujarat', M.K. Ranjitsinh, Divyabhanusinh Chavda, Asad Rahmani.

14. 'Gaduli–Santalpur Road Faces Environmental Hurdle', *Times of India*, 15 March 2012.

15. 'A Global Strategy for Road Building', W.F. Laurance, G.R. Clements, S. Sloan, C.S. O'Connell, N.D. Mueller, M. Goosem, O. Venter, D.P. Edwards, B. Phalan, A. Balmford, R. Van Der Ree, I.B. Arrea, *Nature*, pp. 229–232, 2014.

Sinking a Tiger Forest

1. 'Uma Bharti Threatens Hunger Strike over Ken-Betwa Project Delay,' IANS, New Delhi, 7 June 2016.

2. 'Why Linking Rivers Won't Work', Asit Jolly, *India Today*, 14 April 2016.

3. Conversations with Parineeta Dandekar; 'National River Linking Project: Dream or Disaster?', Swati Bansal, India Water Portal, 14 September 2014.

4. As against a country average of 45–46 per cent, or 98 per cent in Punjab.

5. 'Marathwada Drought: Maha Has the Most Dams in the Country, but the Least Effective Irrigation Network, Leaving Lakhs in the Lurch', Tushar Dhara, *Firstpost*, 11 April 2016.

6. 'Why Linking Rivers Won't Work', Asit Jolly, *India Today*, 14 April 2016.

7. In terms of loss of livelihoods, agricultural lands and produce, fisheries and loss of ecosystem services rendered by destruction of forests.

8. 'Why Linking Rivers Won't Work', Asit Jolly, *India Today*, 14 April 2016.

9. 'Field Director, Panna Tiger Reserve's Disagreement Note to NTCA Committee's Report Dated 7 September 2014 to Find Out a New Area in Lieu of Proposed Ken–Betwa River Link (RL) Project', R. Sreenivasa Murthy.

10. 'Minister in Needless Hurry', Himanshu Thakkar, *Civil Society*, 2015.

11. 'Note for EAC MoEF&CC from H.S. Panwar on DPR and EIA of Ken-Betwa Link Project', H.S. Panwar, 26 October 2015.

12. 'Submission to Expert Appraisal Committee on Ken–Betwa Link Project; Environmental Clearance of NWDA's Ken–Betwa Link Project Phase-I (Agenda for meeting on 26 October 2015)', Dr Brij Gopal, 24 October 2015.

13. 'Submission to EAC on Ken–Betwa Link Project; Environmental Clearance of NWDA's Ken–Betwa Link Project', Dr Brij Gopal, 17 January 2016 https://sandrp.wordpress.com

14. EIAs are a legal requirement under India's environment laws, and a crucial decision-making tool which assesses the potential environmental damage a proposed project can cause.

15. 'Panna Tiger Reserve, Ken Gharial Sanctuary and the Ken–Betwa Link Project Written Statement of Members of the M.P. State Wildlife Board'; 13th meeting, M.K. Ranjitsinh, Belinda Wright, 22 September 2015.

16. 'Quality of EIA Reports a Major Concern', Sagnik Dutta, *Frontline*, 21 February 2014.

17. Letter from R. Sreenivasa Murthy, IFS, CCF and field director, Panna Tiger Reserve, Madhya Pradesh to the member secretary, National Tiger Conservation Authority, ministry of environment, forests and climate change dated 9 October 2014 (PTR/Steno/DM/2014/1765).

18. Intrinsic in its report, 'Feasibility Assessment on Compensatory Arrangement on Ken-Betwa River Link Project in Panna Tiger Reserve, Madhya Pradesh'.

19. 'Minutes of 39th Meeting of the Standing Committee of NBWL Held on 23 August 2016', F.N0.6-109/2016 WL(39th meeting).

20. 'Environment Ministry Is a Part of Team India', Lola Nayar interviews Anil Madhav Dave, *Outlook*, 19 September 2016.

The Real Tiger Story

1. IUCN Red List: http://www.iucnredlist.org/details/15955/0.

2. *India's Wildlife History*, Mahesh Rangarajan, Permanent Black, 2001.

3. *The Last Tiger*, Valmik Thapar, Oxford University Press, 2006.

4. The escalating demand for tiger bones could not be met by the rapidly dwindling tiger populations of East and South East Asia, so the traders turned their attention on India.

5. '"Massacre" Geoffrey Ward', *Saving Wild Tigers 1900–2000*, Valmik Thapar (ed.), Permanent Black, 2001.

6. This was in an interview with me for the *Asian Age*. The numbers are also quoted in *Saving Wild Tigers 1900–2000*, Valmik Thapar (ed.), Permanent Black, 2001. In conversation with P.K. Sen.

7. These are mean figures. For instance, 1,411 is the mean of an estimated population range of 1,165–1,657; 1,706 is a mean of 1,520–1,909; while the current estimate of 2,226 tigers is the mean of 1,945–2,491 tigers.

8. *Bihar: The Heart of India*, Sir John Houlton, Orient Longman, 1949.

9. 'Javadekar Vows to Make Kutku Dam Operational', Santosh Narayan, *Pioneer*, 21 August 2015.

10. 'Task Force to Expedite Work on Kutku Dam Project', *Times of India*, 9 May 2015.

11. 'Report of Site Visit to Ratapani Wildlife Sanctuary to Inspect Effects of Upgradation of NH69', Prerna Singh Bindra, member, standing committee, NBWL, and Rajeev Sharma, Assistant Inspector General NTCA.

12. 'Dams Threaten Manas WHS Status', Subir Ghosh, *Asian Correspondent*, 27 October 2011.

13. 'Sheikh Hasina Affirms Rampal Coal Power Plant Won't Harm Sundarbans World Heritage Site', ANI/IANS, Dhaka, 27–28 August 2016.

14. 'India PM Modi Endorses Controversial Sundarbans Coal Plant', Avik Roy, *Climate Home*, 8 June 2016.

15. Agenda (Annexure) for Standing Committee, NBWL meeting on 25 April 2011.

16. Summary records of the 22nd meeting of the standing committee of NBWL held on 25 April 2011.

17. 'Swap Okay but Haridwar Ashram, Rajaji also Locked in Land Dispute', Seema Sharma, *Times of India*, 21 April 2016.
18. Personal interviews with concerned officials and conservationists.
19. 'Connectivity of Tiger (*Panthera tigris*) Populations in the Human-Influenced Forest Mosaic of Central India', Aditya Joshi, et al., *PLoS ONE*, 2016.
20. 'Only 5 Out of 47 Reserves Can Sustain Tiger Population: Report', Chetan Chauhan, *Hindustan Times*, 8 March 2015.
21. A pastoral agricultural ethnic group, that used to be nomadic but many now live in settled colonies.
22. 'The Battle for Tiger Conservation Must Move to the Corridors that Link the Big Cats' Habitat', Nitin Sethi, *Business Standard*, 7 March 2015.
23. 'Proposed Mitigation Measures for Maintaining Habitat Contiguity and Reducing Wild Animal Mortality on NH 6 & 7 in the Central Indian Landscape', Bilal Habib, Akanksha Saxena, Indranil Mondal, Asha Rajvanshi, V.B. Mathur and H.S. Negi. Technical report, WII, Dehradun and NTCA, 2015.
24. 'Will Try (to Conserve) but Can't Allow Something Crazy', Interview by Jay Mazoomdaar, *Indian Express*, 3 August 2015.
25. 'Real Danger to Tigers Not from Road Traffic, but Poachers: SC', Dhananjay Mahapatra, *Economic Times*, 21 January 2016.
26. In 2010, as per a report by the PTI, the 2014 all-India estimate also indicated the presence of five tigers in the state.
27. Wildlife Protection Society of India; 'As Asian Luxury Market Grows, A Surge in Tiger killings in India', Sharon Guynup, *Yale Environment 360*, 10 January 2017.
28. The method to kill was the usual, where metal foot traps—jaw-like contraptions with an invincible grip—are placed on paths frequented by tigers. Once trapped, a spear is thrust into the tiger's mouth, to silence its roars of agony. The cat is then beaten to death. Corbett information from field sources and news reports.
29. All tigers have an individual stripe pattern. The skins were matched using a software called Extract Compare from the National Tiger Photo Database—which is a repository of photographs of individual tigers camera-trapped across India.
30. 'Emerging issues update: Illegal Trade in Wildlife', *UN Year Book 2014*.
31. 'Secretary of State Clinton Calls for End to Illegal Wildlife Trafficking', WWF, 8 November 2012.
32. 'CITES Welcomes Secretary Clinton's "Call for Action" on Illegal Wildlife Trade', Geneva, 11 November 2012.
33. 'A Gujarat Model that Works', Nitin Desai, *Indian Express*, 13 June 2014.

To Save a Tiger

1. Machali was awarded the 'Lifetime Achievement Award' by Travel Operators for Tigers for her contribution to conservation, and for being a tourist attraction. Bandavgarh's celebrity male tiger, known as B2 (or Sundar) was

her co-awardee! However, for unavoidable reasons and for being otherwise occupied, the tigers could not personally receive the award at the glittering ceremony held at the British High Commissioner's residence in Delhi.

2. 'Two Tigers Poisoned in Ranthambhore Tiger Reserve', Aditya Dicky Singh, www.dickysingh.com, 8 March 2010, and conversations with Singh.

3. *Dynamics of Tiger Management in Priority Landscapes*, Rajesh Gopal, Natraj Publishers, 2015.

4. *Mindless Mining*, a film by Shekar Dattatri; 'The Kudremukh Saga—A Triumph for Conservation', Shekar Dattatri, http://www.conservationindia.org/.

5. The CEC was constituted vide notification—Notification File No.1-1/CEC/SC/2002—by the ministry of environment and forests under subsection (3) of Section 3 of the Environment Protection Act, 1986. It was constituted primarily to deal with the large number of cases pending with the Supreme Court of India on matters related to the Wildlife (Protection) Act, forest and other environmental laws. Since 2007, the CEC is functioning as a Supreme Court appointed committee on matters related to forests and wildlife.

6. *Status of Tigers in India 2014*, Y.V. Jhala, Q. Qureshi and R. Gopal (eds), 2015, NTCA, New Delhi and the WII, Dehradun.

7. Bivash Pandav, WII.

8. 'NHRC Asks CS to Rehabilitate Satkosia Villagers', *Pioneer*, 20 April 2016, Bhubaneswar; 'NTCA Report on Satkosia Village Relocation Sought', Express News Service, 13 November 2016.

9. *The Fall of the Sparrow*, Sálim Ali, Oxford University Press, 1986.

10. Dr Shyama Prasad Mukherjee, Jan Van Vikas Yojana.

Failing Our Gods

1. One quintal equals 100 kg, an elephant may consume 200–250 kg of food a day.

2. 'Forest Elephants: Tree Planters of the Congo', S. Blake, S.L. Deem, E. Mossimbo, F. Maisels, P. Walsh, *Biotropica* 41, 459–468 (2009); 'Elephants: The Gardeners of Asia's and Africa's forests', Jeremy Hance, 25 April 2011, news.mongabay.com.

3. Tropical deciduous forests where sal (*Shorea robusta*), a valuable timber tree, is the dominant species. However, I hate to dismiss a tree as 'timber', and the most beautiful description I have come across of a sal forest is by Pradip Krishen in the foreword of *The Hidden Life of Trees: What They Feel, How They Communicate* by Peter Wohlleben. The sal is described as a gregarious tree—one that won't grow in isolation nor would you find it standing on its own in a park. Writes Krishen, 'foresters tell us that sal trees die of "loneliness" when they are planted singly. This epithet is used in right earnest completely without wry humour by British foresters because they could find no other apt word to describe why sal trees died when they became isolated.'

4. 'Six Elephants Run over by Speeding Train in Odisha', *Hindustan Times*, 30 December 2012.
5. 'Elephant Graveyard', *Sanctuary Asia*, Vol. XXXVI No. 2, February 2016.
6. 'Holi, the Elephant,' Brijendra Singh, *Sanctuary Asia*, June 2009.
7. 'The Science Is In: Elephants Are Even Smarter than We Realized', Ferris Jabr, *Scientific American*, 26 February 2014.
8. 'Eight Elephants Trapped in an Island in Baitarani River in Odisha', PTI, 5 September 2016.
9. By 2022, according to the United Nations, 'India will be world's most populous country by 2022', www.firstpost.com, 30 July 2015.
10. '*Gajah*. Securing the Future for Elephants in India', The report of the Elephant Task Force, ministry of environment and forests, 31 August 2010.
11. 'Baby Elephant Killed with Spears, Sticks on Camera', NDTV, 27 October 2010.
12. 'Painful Death of an Elephant through Rumour and Gunshots, North-West India', Ritesh Joshi, *Journal of American Science*, 4(4), 2008.
13. The elephant photograph and related information is courtesy Wildlife Trust of India.
14. For Sonitpur, Assam issues I have drawn information from: 'Assessment of Habitat Loss in Kameng and Sonitpur Elephant Reserves', S.P.S. Kushwaha and Rubul Hazarika, *Current Science*, Vol. 87, No. 10, 25 November 2004; 'Ganesha to Bin Laden: Human–Elephant Conflict in Sonitpur District of Assam', Nidhi Gureja et al., Wildlife Trust of India, New Delhi, 2002; 'Human–Elephant Conflicts in Northeast India', Anwaruddin Choudhury, *Human Dimensions of Wildlife*, 2004, Taylor & Francis Inc.
15. 'Concepts: Elephant Breakdown', G.A. Bradshaw, Allan N. Schore, Janine L. Brown, Joyce H. Poole and Cynthia J. Moss, *Nature* 433, 807, 24 February 2005.
16. Dating back to about 200 BCE.
17. Written reply by Odisha Forest Minister Bikram Keshari Arukh in the State Assembly on 17 March 2015 as reported in *The Hindu* on 18 March, 'Man–Elephant Conflict in Odisha: 685 Jumbos, 660 People Killed in a Decade'.
18. An ancient Indian treatise often attributed to Kautilya, also known as Chanakya, (c. 350–275 BCE) an Indian statesman and philosopher, chief adviser and prime minister of the Indian Emperor Chandragupta, the first ruler of the Mauryan Empire.
19. Jairam Ramesh, at the E8 ministerial meet on 24 May, New Delhi, 'Mining a Threat to Elephant Habitats, Need a Way Out: Jairam', NDTV/Odisha TV, 26 May 2011.
20. Biswajit Mohanty on email; conversations with Aditya Chandra Panda; personal interviews with forest officers in Odisha, off the record; 'Orissa Government Withdraws Elephant Reserve Plan', *Down to Earth*, 15 September 2007.

21. 'Elephant in the Room—A Case Study on Human–Elephant Conflict within Hasdeo-Arand and Mandraigarh coalfields in Chhattisgarh', Nandikesh Sivalingam, Greenpeace, October 2014.

22. 'Impact of Mining on Elephants of Chhotanagpur Plateau, Central India', Kisor Chaudhuri, *Gajah* 42, 2015.

23. An association of Indian businesses which works to create an environment conducive to the growth of industry in the country.

24. 'Elephant in the Room—A Case Study on Human–Elephant Conflict within Hasdeo–Arand and Mandraigarh Coalfields in Chhattisgarh', Nandikesh Sivalingam, Greenpeace, October 2014.

25. 'Chhattisgarh Govt Scraps Elephant Reserve Plan for Coal Mining', Supriya Sharma, *Times of India*, 16 January 2011.

26. *Green Signals: Ecology, Growth, and Democracy in India*, Jairam Ramesh, Oxford University Press, 2015.

27. 'Your No-Go Areas for Coal Mining Hurts, So Review: PMO to Jairam', Priyadarshi Siddhanta, *Indian Express*, New Delhi, 27 May 2010.

28. 'Elephant in the Room—A Case Study on Human–Elephant Conflict within Hasdeo-Arand and Mandraigarh Coalfields in Chhattisgarh', Nandikesh Sivalingam, Greenpeace, October 2014; 'Jairam Loses "No-Go" Battle, Allows Coal Mining in Forested Hasdeo Arand', *The Hindu*, 24 June 2011.

29. 'PMO Says No to National Body to Save Elephants', Nitin Sethi, *Times of India*, 6 May 2011.

30. The title of a popular yesteryear Bollywood film translating to 'the elephant is my friend'.

31. Writ petition filed in the high court of Kerala on 3 October 2012 by Raghavan K., aged thirty-seven years, S/o Kannachetty, Kurichiyad Tribal Settlement, Chethalayam, P.O., Wayanad and others against the Union of India and others.

The Shadow Cat

1. The Asiatic cheetah is extinct in India with the last authentic record in 1947. A small population of about forty survive in Iran, but the situation is critical with only two female cheetahs known to survive in the wild.

2. 'Cheetahs on the Prowl near Hosur', *New Indian Express*, 18 January 2011.

3. 'Human Attacks by Leopards in Uttarakhand, India: An Assessment Based on Perceptions of Affected People and Stakeholders', S. Sondhi, V. Athreya, A. Sondhi, A. Prasad, A. Verma and N. Verma, a technical report submitted to the Uttarakhand Forest Department, 2016.

4. 'Brutality in Purulia: Forest Officials Hunt for Villagers Who Chopped Off Claws, Tail of Leopard', *Indian Express*, 23 June 2015.

5. 'Angry Villagers Burn Alive Captured Leopard', IANS, 24 March 2011; conversations with forest staff and officials.

6. 'Washington State Begins Killing Wolf Pack for Preying on Livestock', Steve Gorman, Reuters, 29 August 2016.

7. 'Predator Control Should Not Be a Shot in the Dark', A. Treves et al., *Frontiers in Ecology and the Environment*, September 2016.

8. 'Colorado Embarks on Experimental "Predator Control" Killing of More Lions and Bears to Try and Save Dwindling Deer', Bruce Finley, *Denver Post*, 15 December 2016.

9. A cursory search on the Internet reveals the varied outfits offering bear hunting packages, though Canada is by no means the only country, in fact one among many that counts hunting as a sport.

10. This confided in hushed whispers and with a laugh, given that hunting of wildlife is illegal.

11. 'First Ever Leopard Census: India Should Not Feel Too Smug Too Soon', Jay Mazoomdaar, *Indian Express*, 7 October 2016.

12. 'Illuminating the Blind Spot: A Study on Illegal Trade in Leopard Parts in India (2001–2010)', R.H. Raza, D.S. Chauhan, M.K.S. Pasha and S. Sinha, TRAFFIC India/WWF-India, New Delhi, 2012.

13. 'Leopard (*Panthera pardus*) Status, Distribution, and the Research Efforts Across Its Range', A.P. Jacobson, P. Gerngross, J.R. Lemeris Jr., R.F. Schoonover, C. Anco, C. Breitenmoser-Würsten, S.M. Durant, M.S. Farhadinia, P. Henschel, J.F. Kamler, A. Laguardia, S. Rostro-García, A.B. Stein, L. Dollar, *PeerJ* 4:e1974, 4 May 2016; 'Leopards Have Lost 75% of Their Historical Habitat', Adam Vaughan, *Guardian*, 4 May 2016.

14. Information from Junnar, Akole, Nashik is largely sourced through the following articles (besides conversations/emails with Vidya Athreya): 'Human–Leopard Conflict: Lessons from Junnar, Maharashtra', Vidya Athreya, http://www.conservationindia.org; 'Translocation as a Tool for Mitigating Conflict with Leopards in Human-Dominated Landscapes of India', Vidya Athreya, Morten Odden, John D.C. Linnell and K. Ullas Karanth, *Conservation Biology*, 2010; 'Sugarcane Leopards', Janaki Lenin, *Current Conservation* 4.4.; 'Living with Leopards Outside Protected Areas in India', Vidya Athreya, *Pioneer*, 11 August 2012; 'Leopards in Our Alley', Vidya Athreya, *Down To Earth*, 16–28 February 2011; 'Waghoba Tales: Adventures in Leopard Land', A. Ghule, V. Athreya, J. Linnell, M. Odden and J. Lenin, *NINA Special Report* 58. 58 s., Trondheim, September 2014.

15. 'Delhi Tries to Catch Its Leopard Even as the Law and Best Practice Forbid', Neha Sinha, https://thewire.in, 29 November 2016.

16. 'Human–Leopard Conflict: Lessons from Junnar, Maharashtra', Vidya Athreya, http://www.conservationindia.org.

17. 'A Preliminary Study on the Ecology of the Leopard, *Panthera pardus fusca* in Sanjay Gandhi National Park, Maharashtra', Advait Edgaonkar and Ravi Chellam, Wildlife Institute of India, Dehradun, 1998.

18. IndiaSpend analysis of data from Government Railway Police (GRP), Maharashtra, http://www.indiaspend.com.

19. 'Leopards in Human-Dominated Areas: A Spillover from Sustained Translocations into Nearby Forests?', Vidya Athreya, Sanjay S. Thakur, Sujoy Chaudhuri, Aniruddha V. Belsare, www.projectwaghoba.in.
20. 'Supreme Court Cleared Freight Corridor's Sanjay Gandhi National Park Sojourn in 2013', Binoo Nair, *DNA,* 3 March 2016.

The River Guardian's Last Vigil

1. The Queen of Chambal; Chambal's Promise; The Bandits of Chambal.
2. 'Forest Guard Dies While Trying to Stop Sand Smuggling in Gwalior', Press Trust of India, 6 March 2016; and conversations with concerned officers of the region.
3. 'Truck Carrying Illegally Mined Sand Crushes Constable in MP', Milind Ghatwai, *Indian Express,* 6 April 2015.
4. Letter from Tarun Nair dated 7 April 2016 to the additional director general of wildlife, ministry of environment, forests and climate change.
5. 'Flourishing Illegal Mining in Madhya Pradesh: Are Politicians Involved?', NDTV, 24 March 2012; 'Badal Family Has Stake in Illegal Sand Mining, Alleges Chotepur', Rachna Khaira, *Tribune,* 11 April 2017; 'Politicians Aren't Only Messing with Tamil Nadu's Water–They're Making Rs 20,000 Crore From Sand', M. Rajshekhar, http://scroll.in/, 19 September 2016; 'Think Sand Mining Damages the Ecology? It Ruins Politics as Well', M. Rajshekhar, http://scroll.in/, 20 September 2016; 'Sand Mining in Tamil Nadu Is Incredibly Destructive—But It's also Unstoppable', M. Rajshekhar, http://scroll.in/, 21 September 2016; 'Illegal Sand Mining in Tamil Nadu Worth Rs 15,000 Crore?', Jayaraj Sivani, *Times of India,* 21 August 2013.
6. 'Parching the Chambal River Basin: Unrelenting Irrigation Schemes Wring the Unique Chambal Dry', Tarun Nair, 2009; 'Basking Site and Water Depth Selection by Gharial Gavialis Gangeticus Gmelin 1789 (Crocodylia, Reptilia) in National Chambal Sanctuary, India and Its Implication for River Conservation', S.A. Hussain, *Aquatic Conservation-Marine and Freshwater Ecosystems* 19:127–133, 2009.
7. Of Chambal river for its aquatic wildlife, 'Assessment of Minimum Water Flow Requirements of Chambal River in the Context of Gharial (Gavialis gangeticus) and Gangetic Dolphin (Platanista gangetica) Conservation', Syed Ainul Hussain, R.H. Sharma, Niladri Dasgupta, Angshuman Raha, April 2011.
8. WWF-India; conversation with Parikshit Gautam, Sanjeev Kumar Yadav.
9. *WWF Living Planet Report,* 2016.

Bird on a Free Fall

1. *The Vanishing Bustard: 'Nature's Spokesman' M. Krishnan and Indian Wildlife,* Ramachandra Guha (ed.), Oxford University Press, 2000.

2. Dharmakumarsinhji 1971; Dharmakumarsinhji 1978; and email correspondence with Harsh Vardhan, Tourism and Wildlife Society of India, Jaipur.

3. Later to become India's prime minister.

4. 'Bustards: A Conservation Dateline', Harsh Vardhan, special issue of *Cheetal* magazine; WWF Newsletter *Panda* Special Issue, 2012; conversation with Asad R. Rahmani, former director, BNHS; Harsh Vardhan, Tourism and Wildlife Society of India, Jaipur.

5. Guidelines for the Great Indian Bustard Recovery Programme, ministry of environment and forests, Government of India.

6. 'The Great Indian Bustard', Asad R. Rahmani; *In Danger: Habitats, Species and People*, Paola Manfredi (ed.), Local Colour Private Limited in association with Ranthambhore Foundation, 1997; conversation with Asad Rahmani.

7. 'Status, Threats and Conservation of Great Indian Bustard (*Ardeotis nigriceps*) in Pakistan', Aleem Ahmed Khan, Imran Khaliq, Muhammad Jamshed Iqbal Choudhry, Amjad Farooq and Nazim Hussain, *Current Science* 95(8), pp. 1079–1082, October 2008.

8. 'The Great Indian Bustard', Asad R. Rahmani; *In Danger: Habitats, Species and People*, Paola Manfredi (ed.), Local Colour Private Limited in association with Ranthambhore Foundation, 1997.

9. The Gujarat government maintains that the state supports about forty birds, though reports from the ground indicate no more than twenty birds in the state. A report in *Times of India* in November 2016, was even more alarming saying only six bustards survived in the region.

10. 'Bijli, Sadak, Paani and Bustard', Sutirtha Dutta, Indian Express, 10 September 2016.

11. 'The Time to Act Was Yesterday: Mourning Alpha, the GIB', Vaijayanti Vijayaraghavan, 16 September 2015.

12. It's called the Platform Terminal Transmitter.

13. 'Despite National Green Tribunal Ban, Work on Windmills Continues Near Desert National Park', *Times of India*, 30 December 2016.

The Last Voyage . . .

1. *Snakeman: The Story of a Naturalist*, Penguin, 1989.

2. 'Massacre at Digha', Dilip Bobb, *India Today*, March 1982; 'Viji, the Turtle Girl', Janaki Lenin, http://janakilenin.blogspot.in, 10 August 2006.

3. 'The Trap of the Empty Net', Rohini Mohan, *Tehelka*, 10 December 2011.

4. Conversations with Biswajit Mohanty, on email, phone and meetings.

5. 'Efficacy of Turtle Excluder Devices on Incidental Captures of Olive Ridley Sea Turtles (*Lepidochelys Olivacea*) in the Trawl Fisheries of Orissa, India', G.V. Gopi, B. Pandav, B.C. Choudhury, *Testudo*, Vol. 6, No. 4, 2007.

6. 'Incidental Capture and Mortality of Olive Ridley Turtles (Lepidochelys olivacea) in Commercial Trawl Fisheries in Coastal Waters of Orissa, India',

G.V. Gopi, B. Pandav, B.C. Choudhury, *Chelonian Conservation and Biology*, Volume 5, No. 2, 2006.

7. Sea surface temperatures are rising along the entire Indian coast. The average annual sea surface temperature ranged between 27.7°C–28°C, which from 1997–2005 had risen to 28.7°C–29°C. From 'Why Tamil Nadu's Fisherfolk Can No Longer Find Fish', M. Rajshekhar, Scroll.in 8 July 2016 (2010); 'Impact of Climate Change in the Indian Marine Fisheries and the Potential Adaptation Options', E. Vivekanandan, *Coastal Fishery Resources of India: Conservation and Sustainable Utilisation*, Society of Fisheries Technologists, pp. 169–185.

8. 'An Account of the East Indies', being the observations and remarks of Captain Alexander Hamilton who spent his time there between year 1688 to 1773.

9. 'Nesting Habitat Suitability for Olive Ridley Turtles (*Lepidochelys olivacea*) at the Gahirmatha Rookery, Odisha Coast of India', S. Behera et al., *International Journal of Conservation Science*, 2013; 'Nowhere to Nest', Sayantan Bera, *Down to Earth*, 15 April 2011.

10. 'India: Lightmare on Olive Ridley Street', Divya Karnad, Indian Ocean–South-East Asian Marine Turtles, 19 October 2009.

11. 'The Deep Water Blues', Cara Tejpal, *Sanctuary Asia*, Vol. XXXV No. 8, August 2015.

12. International Sea Ports was the original proponent, but subsequently the proponents were to change, as was the scale of the project.

13. Information on Dhamra is credited to and sourced from Ashish Fernandes, Greenpeace and Biswajit Mohanty, Wildlife Protection Society of Orissa; 'Dhamra Port: How Environmental Regulatory Failure Fuels Corporate Irreverence', Sudarshan Rodriguez and Aarthi Sridhar, *Marine Turtle Newsletter*, 2008; 'Chronology of Events Related to the Dhamra Port', Greenpeace, 2005; 'Bhitarkanika: Port Threatens Olive Ridley Turtle Nesting Grounds', *Sanctuary Asia*, February 2001; 'The Dhamra Port in Orissa', Pankaj Sekhsaria, *Indian Ocean Turtle Newsletter No. 1*, January 2005; 'Biodiversity Assessment of Dhamra Port Site and Surrounding Areas, Orissa', Greenpeace India, 2007; government letter no. 11693 dated 20th June 1997; letter written by the principle chief conservator of forests (wildlife) on 22 July 1997, in response to government letter no. 31 Wl/4/97/13670(F&E) on 21 July 1997 to commissioner cum secretary, forest and environment department, Government of Orissa; 'The IUCN'S New Clothes: An Update on the Dhamra-Turtle Saga', Janaki Lenin, Ashish Fernandes, Aarthi Sridhar, B.C. Choudhury, Jack Frazier, Sanjiv Gopal, Areeba Hamid, Sandra Kloff, Biswajit Mohanty, Bivash Pandav, Sudarshan Rodriguez, Basudev Tripathy, Romulus Whitaker, Sejal Worah, Belinda Wright and Kartik Shanker, *Marine Turtle Newsletter*, 16 December 2009; 'Vanishing Point', Prerna Singh Bindra, *Tehelka*, 14 March 2009, Issue 10, Volume 6; 'Government Bowing to TATA Pressure Is Now in the Open', Greenpeace India, 16 December 2010; 'Double Standards in Environment Ministry', Greenpeace India, 18 October 2010; letter to additional director general of forests (FC division),

MoEF, from chief conservator of forests, (central), Eastern Regional Office of the MoEF in Bhubaneswar dated 1 April 2010; 'MPs Ask Jairam Ramesh to Act on Dhamra Port Forest Violation', http://www.greenpeace.in, 17 May 2010; 'Environment Ministry's Affidavit on Dhamra Contrary to Own Findings: Greenpeace', Sreejiraj Eluvangal, 24 February 2010.

14. 'Port of Disaster', Prerna Singh Bindra, *Tehelka*, Vol. 5, Issue 28, 19 July 2008. The quote was vehemently denied by an official from Dhamra Pvt. Ltd. The gist of the correspondence can be viewed here: http://prernabindra. com/2008/07/27/some-correspondence-ref-the-turtle-article/

15. Earlier a joint venture between Tata Steel and L&T Infrastructure Development Projects, it was acquired by Adani Ports and Special Economic Zone in 2014.

16. 'Casuarina Forests Ruin Turtle Nesting Beaches in Orissa', Biswajit Mohanty, Wildlife Society of Orissa, *Kachhapa 7*, September 2002.

17. 'Nesting Habitat Suitability for Olive Ridley Turtles (*Lepidochelys olivacea*) at the Gahirmatha Rookery, Odisha Coast of India', S. Behera et al., *International Journal of Conservation Science*, 2013.

18. 'PM's Inaugural Address at the Maritime India Summit, 2016', *PMIndia*, 14 April 2016.

19. 'Harbouring Trouble: The Social and Environmental Upshot of Port Growth in India', S. Rodriguez and A. Sridhar, Dakshin Foundation, Bangalore, 2010; 'The Challenged Coast of India', Ahana Lakshmi, Aurofilio Schiavina, Probir Banerjee, Ajit Reddy, Sunaina Mandeen, Sudarshan Rodriguez and Deepak Apte, a report prepared by PondyCAN in collaboration with Bombay Natural History Society and Tata Institute of Social Sciences, October 2012.

20. '45% of India's Coastline Facing Erosion', Manupriya, *IndiaSpend*, 11 August 2015.

21. Coastal zone management authorities and district-level coastal committees.

22. On email with Aarthi Sridhar; 'Coastal Law Got a Skewed Review—and Now, an Opaque Revamp', Meenakshi Kapoor, *The Wire*, 3 August 2016.

The Sounds of Silence

1. 'A Great Silence Is Spreading over the Natural World', John Vidal, *Guardian*, 3 September 2012.

2. *The Great Animal Orchestra: Origins of Music in the World's Wild Places*, Bernie Krause, Little, Brown and Company, 2012.

3. Now called the jacobin cuckoo.

4. *Nature Watch*, Khushwant Singh, Lustre Press, 1990.

5. 'Nature Studies by Michael McCarthy: The End of Abundance', *Independent*, 25 November 2010; 'Nature Studies: Our Generation Has Seen a Great Thinning that We Can't Quite Name', Michael McCarthy, *Independent*, 19 December 2012.

6. '3 Billion to Zero: What Happened to the Passenger Pigeon?', David Biello, *Scientific American*, 27 June 2014.

7. 'Human Anthrax in India May Be Linked to Vulture Decline', Ganapati Mudur, National Centre for Biotechnology Information, 10 February 2010.

8. On the 'cost' of vulture declines: 'Counting the Cost of Vulture Declines— Economic Appraisal of the Benefits of the Gyps Vulture in India', A. Markandya, T. Taylor, A. Longo, University of Bath, and M.N. Murty, S. Murty and K.K. Dhavala, Institute of Economic Growth, India; *What Has Nature Ever Done for Us: How Money Really Does Grow on Trees*, Tony Juniper, Profile Books, 2013.

9. 'How India's Concretising Cities Are Becoming Heat Islands', Max Martin, *IndiaSpend*, 12 July 2016.

10. An urban renewal and retrofitting programme by the Government of India with a mission to develop 100 cities.

11. http://iamgurgaon.org/aravalli-bio-diversity-park/

12. *Restoration of the Kaikondrahalli Lake in Bangalore: Forging a New Urban Commons*, H. Nagendra, Kalpavriksh, Pune, Maharashtra, 2016.

13. 'Kaikondrahalli Lake: The Uncommon Story of an Urban Commons', which can be viewed at https://www.youtube.com/ watch?v=RAN4IGZi3pI.

Deceptions of Development

1. Decisions are taken considering how they would impact, and whether they would benefit their children seven generations into the future. It is frequently associated with the concept of environmental stewardship.

2. NBWL is India's apex statutory body on matters pertaining to wildlife conservation, particularly within Protected Areas.

3. According to a Supreme Court order in 2006, no project can be allowed within a 10-km boundary of national parks and sanctuaries unless approved by the standing committee of the NBWL, and/or unless a site-specific ESZ has been notified by the state, after which activities will be regulated as per the notification.

4. 'Study: Forests Absorb Much More Greenhouse Gas than Previously Known', Mark Clayton, *Christian Science Monitor*, 5 July 2011.

5. 'Concerted Efforts by Select Foreign Funded NGOs to "Take Down" Indian Development Projects', IR/IS No. 002, Intelligence Bureau, 3 June 2014; 'Foreign-aided NGOs Are Actively Stalling Development, IB tells PMO in a Report', Amitav Ranjan, *Indian Express*, 7 June 2014.

6. 'PM Indicates Foreign NGOs Behind Nuclear Protests', Jacob P. Koshy, *Live Mint*, 23 February 2012; Q&A: Manmohan Singh: 'India's Scholar–Prime Minister Aims for Inclusive Development', Pallava Bagla, Richard Stone, *Science*, Vol. 335 no. 6,071 pp. 907–908, 24 February 2012.

7. 'Concerted Efforts by Select Foreign Funded NGOs to "Take Down" Indian Development Projects', IR/IS No. 002, Intelligence Bureau, 3 June 2014.

8. 'How Coal Mining Is Trashing Tigerland', Ashish Fernandes, Greenpeace, August 2012.

9. All Party Parliamentary Group (APPG) on Indo-British relations.

10. As per information given by the ministry in response to a RTI by Greenpeace in March 2015; 'Mahan Coal Block Not to Be Auctioned: Coal Ministry', http://www.firstpost.com, 20 March 2015.

11. 'Dissent Will Be Brushed Aside If It Impedes Growth', *The Hindu Business Line*, 10 December 2006.

12. 'Human Rights Groups Face Global Crackdown "Not Seen in a Generation",' Harriet Sherwood, *Guardian*, 26 August 2015. The NGOs/ groups range from those working on human rights issues to environment.

13. 'At Least 185 Environmental Activists Were Murdered Last Year', Alexander Sammon, http://www.motherjones.com, 23 June 2016; 'On Dangerous Ground', *Global Witness*, June 2016.

14. Reporters Without Borders, 26 November 2015.

15. '15.2% of Indians Are Undernourished: Global Hunger Index', Sayantan Bera, *Live Mint*, 12 October 2016.

16. 'One in Three Children Have Stunted Growth in India: Why Malnutrition Is Such a Big Challenge', Anuradha Mascarenhas, *Indian Express,* 14 October 2016.

17. '37% of All the Illiterate Adults in the World Are Indian', Nilanjana Bhowmick, *Time*, 29 January 2014.

18. 'Yes, India Has Massive Income Inequality–But It Isn't the Second-Most Unequal Country in the World', Mayank Jain, https://scroll.in, 6 September 2016; 'The Richest 1% of Indians Now Own 58.4% of Wealth', Manas Chakravarty, *Mint*, 24 November 2016.

19. 'The Problem of Jobless Growth', Anil Padmanabhan, *Mint*, 24 May 2016.

20. 'Six Indicators of India's Looming Demographic Disaster', Abhishek Waghmare, *Scroll,* 3 May 2016.

21. 'Economic Growth: A Meaningless Obsession?', Amit Bhaduri, *India-Seminar*, based on the author's B.N. Ganguly Memorial Lecture, Centre for the Study of Developing Societies, Delhi, November 2006; and on email with Amit Bhaduri.

22. 'Displacement and Rehabilitation of People Due to Developmental Projects', Reference note, No.30/RN/Ref/December/2013, Lok Sabha Secretariat.

23. Robert F. Kennedy speaks of the Gross National Product (GNP). Both GNP and GDP reflect the national output and income of an economy. The main difference is that GNP takes into account net income receipts from abroad, while the GDP is a measure of national income/national output and national expenditure produced in a particular country.

24. Robert F. Kennedy Speeches: Remarks at the University of Kansas, 18 March 1968, John F. Kennedy Presidential Library and Museum, read the entire speech at www.jfklibrary.org.

25. *Churning the Earth: The Making of Global India*, Aseem Shrivastava and Ashish Kothari, Penguin Books India, 2012.

26. 'Inside China's "Cancer Villages"', Jonathan Kaiman, *Guardian*, 4 June 2013.

27. 'Report: One-fifth of China's Soil Contaminated', BBC, 18 April 2014; 'Is China's New plan to Tackle Soil Pollution Too Little, Too Late?', Ada Kong and Wang Jing, Greenpeace, 3 June 2016.

28. 'Air Pollution in China: Mapping of Concentrations and Sources', Robert A. Rohde, Richard A. Muller, *Berkeley Earth*, 2015; 'Study Links Polluted Air in China to 1.6 Million Deaths a Year', Dan Levin, *New York Times*, 13 August 2015; 'Air Pollution Causes 4,400 Deaths in China Every Single Day: Study', Dominique Mosbergen, *Huffington Post*, 14 August 2015.

29. '30% of Yellow River Fish Species Extinct', Jonathan Watts, *Guardian*, 18 January 2007.

30. 'China's Environment: An Economic Death Sentence', Minxin Pei, *Fortune*, 28 January 2013.

31. 'China Wakes Up to Its Environmental Catastrophe', Elizabeth Economy, *Bloomberg*, 14 March 2014.

32. 2017 Global Burden of Disease (GBD) report, US-based Health Effect Institute, Centre for Science and Environment, New Delhi, press release, 14 February 2017; '2 Indians Die Every Minute Due to Air Pollution: Study', Press Trust of India, 19 February 2017.

33. 'India—Diagnostic Assessment of Select Environmental Challenges: An Analysis of Physical and Monetary Losses of Environmental Health and Natural Resources', World Bank, 5 June 2013.

34. Facts from *The Story of Stuff*, Annie Leonard.

35. 'India's Demand on Nature Approaching Critical Limits, Report Finds', Footprint Network News.

36. 'India Will Become the World's Most Populous Country by 2022, the U.N. Says', Sania Farooqui, *Time*, 30 July 2015.

37. http://www.oecdbetterlifeindex.org/

38. 'The Way to a Green GDP', Jairam Ramesh, minister of state (independent charge), environment and forests, Government of India, delivered at the 10th India Today Conclave on 18 March 2011.

39. Inaugural address of the 3rd Asia Ministerial Conference on Tiger Conservation in Delhi on 12 April 2016, http://www.narendramodi.in/pm-modi-inaugurates-3rd-asia-ministerial-conference-on-tiger-conservation-440277

40. 'National Bird and State Animal—A Nuisance in Goa?', Rajeshwari Ganesan, *Down to Earth*, 15 February 2016.

41. As per Land Acquisition Act, 1894. (This was before the Land Acquisition Act, 2013, came into force.)

42. Association of Farmers Aggrieved by the Mopa Airport.

43. 'Environmental Impact Assessment Study for the Proposed Greenfield International Airport at Mopa, Goa', Government of Goa, October 2014; 'Disaster Airport: Goa's New Runway in Mopa Will Run the Ecology Over', Nihar Gokhale, *Catch News*, 8 March 2016.

44. 'Environmental Impact Assessment Study for the Proposed Greenfield International Airport at Mopa, Goa', Government of Goa, October 2014.

45. 'Report on Two Days Survey Conducted to Find Evidences of Plant and Bird Species Presence at Mopa Plateau', Aparna Watve, Sanjay Thakur, 15 September 2015.

46. 'Hydrogeological Studies on and around Barazan Plateau, North Goa District, Goa State', Jairaj Rajguru, Rakesh Gupta, Himanshu Kulkarni, Technical Report: ACWA/Hydro/2014/H39, Advanced Centre for Water Resources Development and Management; 'Disaster Airport: Goa's New Runway in Mopa Will Run the Ecology Over', Nihar Gokhale, *Catch News*, 8 March 2016.

47. 'The *Goan* Exposes Mopa's Irregularities', *Goan*, 11 October 2014.

48. 'Mopa Is an Unsafe and Inadequate Airport Site: Ex AAI Director', Ajay Thakur, *Goan*, 9 February 2013.

49. 'PM Narendra Modi to Lay Foundation Stone of Mopa Airport on November 13', Press Trust of India, 3 November 2016; 'PM Modi Lays Foundation Stone of Mopa Greenfield Airport in Goa', Zee News, 13 November 2016.

50. Information on Mopa also from conversation with Vithal and Sandeep Kambli at Mopa on 9 July 2016, and also meetings with Abhijit Prabhudesai and Claude Alvares in Goa on 9 July 2016.

51. Maximum Retail Price.

52. Along the Andhra Pradesh–Tamil Nadu coast.

53. 'Coal India Has Planned Output of 1 Billion Tonnes by 2020: Goyal', IANS, 4 December 2014.

54. 'India Plans Nearly 60% of Electricity Capacity from Non-Fossil Fuels by 2027', Michael Safi, *Guardian*, 22 December 2016.

55. 'Green Norms for Wind Power', Chandra Bhushan, Jonas Hamberg and Kanchan Kumar Agrawal, Centre for Science and Environment, New Delhi, 2013; 'A Renewable Energy Future for India', Chandra Bhushan, *Down to Earth*, 22 August 2016; 'Green Norms for Wind Power (presentation)', Chandra Bhushan, Centre for Science and Environment; comments on Indian Wind Turbine Manufacturers Association report 'Advocacy of EIA for Wind Power: Untimely and Unjust' (also drawn on some of these reports for the renewable energy information and the way forward).

56. 'India Loses 23% of Power during T&D, Reveals Piyush Goyal', Rama Mohan, *International Business Times*, 15 July 2014.

57. 'Maharashtra Switches over to LED Bulbs, Saves 93MW Daily', Chittaranjan Tembhekar, *Times of India*, 5 November 2015.

Afterword

1. 'At Least Five People Die of Heat Stroke in Maharashtra As Mercury Rises', https://scroll.in/, 30 March 2017; '5 Die of Heat Stroke in Maharashtra, Record Temperatures in North India', *Deccan Chronicle*, 30 March 2017.

2. 'Water Crisis Looms in Tamil Nadu, with Just 7–8% Storage in Reservoirs', Gireesh Babu and T.E. Narasimhan, *Business Standard*, 1 April 2017.

3. 'Drought in Nilgiris Spells Doom for Jumbos', Rohan Premkumar, *The Hindu*, 7 March 2017.

4. 'Man–Animal Conflict Increases as Kerala Faces Severe Drought', Ramesh Babu K.C., *Hindustan Times*, 19 February 2017; reports from the field.

5. 'India Is Facing Its Worst Water Crisis in Generations', Asit K. Biswas, Cecilia Tortajada and Udisha Saklan, https://qz.com/, 15 March 2017.

6. 'Forest Guard Killed Near Corbett By Mining Mafia', Vineet Upadhyay, *Times of India*, 26 March 2017.

7. 'Uranium Survey Proposal in Amrabad Tiger Reserve Gets Nod', V. Nilesh, *New Indian Express*, April 2017.

8. Lamas (Buddhist monks) and villagers came together to form the 'Save Mon Region Federation', which approached the green tribunal to challenge the environmental clearance given to the 780 MW Naymjang Chhu project. 'Arunachal Hydropower Project Halted to Save Black-necked Cranes', Nivedita Khandekar, 9 May 2016, https://www.thethirdpole.net/.

9. 'Arunachal Monastery Declares Forest Near Bhutan as Protected Zone for Red Pandas', Rahul Karmakar, *Hindustan Times*, 28 April 2017.

10. 'Nine-Year-Old Sues Indian Government over Climate Change Inaction', Reuters, 7 April 2017.

11. 'No Data to Link Deaths Exclusively with Air Pollution: Govt', Press Trust of India, 6 February 2017.

12. 'Thinking about Climate Change Is Like Thinking about Death: Amitav Ghosh', Kaushani Banerjee, *Hindustan Times*, 11 December 2016.

13. *Protected Planet Report 2014*, D. Juffe-Bignoli, N.D. Burgess, H. Bingham, E.M.S. Belle, M.G. de Lima, M. Deguignet, B. Bertzky, A.N. Milam, J. Martinez-Lopez, E. Lewis, A. Eassom, S. Wicander, J. Geldmann, A. van Soesbergen, A.P. Arnell, B. O'Connor, S. Park, Y.N. Shi, F.S. Danks, B. MacSharry, N. Kingston, UNEP-WCMC: Cambridge, UK, 2014.

14. *Half-Earth: Our Planet's Fight for Life*, E.O. Wilson, Liveright, 2016.

Index